PREFACE

Our aim in writing this book has been to provide an accessible and modern understanding of European Union (EU) law, based upon an analysis of the principles which have underpinned EU integration. EU law has evolved since 1957 when economic cooperation was the primary objective of the original six Member States. In 2004 twenty-five European States signed a Constitutional Treaty confirming the EU as an omni-competent organisation that dominates the political and legislative agenda not only of its Member States but of States which have relations with the EU. EU law has, through its adherence to fundamental principles that promote integration, changed the legal landscape of Europe. Today, in addition to economic regulation, the EU, in varying degrees, regulates environmental, industrial, social and employment policy, cooperates formally in police and judicial matters and is pursuing a single foreign policy.

Central to the process of EU integration today is the role of the citizen. The EU's commitment to fundamental rights and the development of citizenship has refocused integration recognising that it is the individual, through his or her exercise of rights within the constitutional order which is the tangible expression of integration. The book emphasises throughout that the rights and freedoms contained within the Treaty distinguish EU integration from all other forms of international cooperation. EU law, through the principle of supremacy, has ensured that the individual can enforce primary and secondary rights in their national courts. The European Court of Justice described this as the defining feature of integration in the 1962 *Van Gend en Loos* judgment, where it referred to European law as being the creation of a "new legal order".

The structure of European integration has developed radically from the 1957 EEC Treaty. Today the EC Treaty remains the primary source of law and is the legal framework for the regulation of the Internal Market. Since 1992 the Treaty structure has included the Treaty on European Union (TEU). This Treaty contains the provisions for intergovernmental cooperation and through which the common foreign and security policy and judicial and police cooperation are pursued. These Treaties create the European Union and, more precisely, provide the framework for EU law.

In October 2004 the Member States signed the Constitutional Treaty. This Treaty merges the EC Treaty and the TEU in to one comprehensive document. Significantly, if ratified, this will bring to an end the distinction between EC and EU law and all legislation will be referred to as EU law. Throughout the book we have adopted this new norm of the Constitutional Treaty when referring to legislation but where relevant have highlighted that competence for an activity arises from the EC Treaty. The book uses the post-Amsterdam Treaty numbers, but where appropriate has referred to the old numbers.

We thank our students over the years at the Universities of London, Nottingham and Leicester. We have also benefited from seminars and conference papers presented in the UK, Poland and Slovenia and at the ERA, Trier. Through the many years of teaching and discussing EU law with these students we have refined our own understanding of EU law and the processes of European integration. We would like to express our thanks to Tania Rowlett for her assistance in compiling the case list and Bibliography. Adam Cygan would like to acknowledge the Study Leave he was granted by the University of Leicester to write this book and the advice and encouragement received from Basia Bogusz.

Leicester, May 1, 2005.

INSTITUTIONAL, ECONOMIC AND POLITICAL INTEGRATION IN THE EUROPEAN UNION

INTRODUCTION

European Union (EU) law cannot be understood without considering the geopolitical relationships that prevail within the European continent, and examining the EU's interaction with the wider world. The EU dominates the geopolitical area of the continent of Europe and following the 2004 enlargement consists of twenty-five Member States and a population of over 450M citizens. This makes the EU the world's largest supranational trading bloc in terms of population. The geographic land mass of the EU spans from the Arctic Circle in Finland to the Azores in the Atlantic Ocean. Yet following the 2004 enlargement, many European countries remain outside the process of EU integration. One consequence of the 2004 enlargement is that the centre of gravity of the EU has shifted eastwards and its surface area has increased by a quarter. In particular, this means that for the first time the EU shares a border with countries of the former Soviet Union.

The continent of Europe can be divided in to those countries inside the EU and those situated on its periphery. For some, such as Norway and Switzerland referenda have confirmed their intention to remain outside. Others, for example, Romania and Bulgaria are referred to as "second wave applicants" and are engaged in a process of accession leading to EU membership in 2009. Turkey, the only non-Christian country to seek EU membership, is unlikely to complete accession negotiations before 2015 and can be categorised as a "third wave applicant". Yet countries such as the Ukraine, which shares the EU's eastern border, remain outside the formal accession process. Political developments in 2004 may alter the EU's relations with the Ukraine, though in the medium to long term membership of the EU remains an aspiration. Despite being outside the governance structures of the EU, accession states, and even countries such as the Ukraine, cannot ignore the consequences of having the world's most populous single economic and political zone as their neighbour. The day-to-day decision-making of the EU's neighbours is influenced by the spill over of the EU's policy objectives. In addition to economic policies, EU norms also influence environmental policies and increasingly immigration and human rights strategies.

EU integration and the creation of what Harding refers to as a "European legal space" (2000:130), is embodied in the Constitutional Treaty signed by the Member States in 2004. This Treaty consolidates nearly 50 years of economic, social, political and human rights integration. Furthermore, the Constitutional Treaty confirms that EU integration is a multi-faceted and multi-level process. At one level is the internal integration process which includes the economic cooperation of the Internal Market, the process of political integration initiated by the Maastricht Treaty in 1992 and the recent adoption by the EU of the Charter of Fundamental Rights. Secondly, and inextricably linked to this internal integration, is the relationship which the EU enjoys with the wider world. The objective of an EU common foreign and security policy (CFSP) is the defining characteristic of EU political integration and complements the EU's economic relations with third countries.

The primary objective of the Internal Market was the removal of internal barriers to trade and the creation of a corresponding common policy towards third countries. Article 133 EC regulates the import of products from third countries and is the Treaty base for the EU's Common Commercial Policy (CCP). To protect the integrity of the Internal Market in goods it has been necessary to employ controls, both physical and fiscal, which regulate access in to the Internal Market from third countries. Today the trading relationship which the EU enjoys with third countries is influenced by an external set of rules arising form the World Trade Organisation (WTO) in which the Member States are, in certain circumstances, represented as a single trading bloc. This will occur where the Member States have granted exclusive competence to the EU through the Treaty. The European Court of Justice (ECJ) confirmed this in *Opinion 1/94*,[1] but also held that in the absence of exclusive EU competence, Member States retain the right to regulate certain aspects of the WTO.

Following the Maastricht Treaty, the focus of Internal Market regulation has shifted away from goods and has become more orientated towards the free movement of persons and EU citizenship.[2] Additionally, the influx of economic migrants in to the EU, following the collapse of the Berlin Wall, required a coherent policy towards third country nationals entering the EU. The strategic policy has been part of a broader package of measures which have sought to ease internal movement for EU nationals while simultaneously improving security and tackling illegal immigration and organised crime. The incorporation of the Schengen *acquis* in to the EU has been a central part of this strategy. Within the enlarged EU wide discrepancies exist in the pace of economic development between the 25 Member States, and these discrepancies are even greater when compared with the EU's neighbours. The challenge for the EU is to facilitate economic migration and individual mobility for EU nationals, while maintaining effective barriers towards third country nationals (Cygan, 2004:251).

The process of internal integration influences the development of the EU's external policies. Post enlargement the EU's relationship with its neighbours is a paramount consideration and includes a degree of quasi-integration which did not exist between the EU and its neighbours throughout the cold war period. While pressing for its neighbours to improve their economic and social polices, and providing financial assistance for this, the EU has correspondingly restricted access to its territory for nationals from the neighbouring states. The EU is attempting to control migration and labour markets within its own borders and seeks to influence the migration policies and practice of its neighbours. Free movement of persons in the EU requires a common policy with regard to the removal of internal borders and close cooperation with its neighbours to manage movement across the EU's external borders. EU polices such at the Neighbourhood Strategy[3] have recognised that the external aspect of the Schengen *acquis* can only be achieved with the cooperation of its neighbours. The incentive offered to, amongst others, North African countries and the Ukraine is nearly one billion Euro between 2004–2006 in technical assistance for improved border controls and economic regeneration.[4]

Despite nearly 50 years of integration and the signing of the Constitutional Treaty in 2004, which includes the Charter of Fundamental Rights, the EU lacks homogeneity with regard to many of the political aspirations it seeks to achieve. The Laeken Declaration[5] identified that EU citizens are feeling disconnected with the integration project. Furthermore, the *acquis communautaire*, the whole breadth of laws and policies which make up the EU, has not guaranteed uniformity of action. For example,

co-operation in the area of foreign and security policy, first introduced at Maastricht, and broadened at Amsterdam, has not led to
uniform responses to political crises which have concerned the
EU since 1992. The lack of a coherent policy towards the break up
of Yugoslavia and the fragmented approach to the Iraq War in
2003, demonstrates that full political integration remains an
objective.

The process of EU integration, whether economic or political,
cannot be understood without considering both the internal
aspects of integration, and the EU's external relations policy. EU
integration is a multifaceted package of legislation and policies
which binds the Member States together, yet the reach and impact
of this law and policy goes beyond the borders of the EU. The
standpoint of this book is that in order to understand EU law it is
necessary to understand *how* EU integration has developed inter-
nally, how it is positioned within the geopolitical context of the
continent of Europe, and finally what integration brings to the
EU's relations with the wider world.

THE HISTORICAL CONTEXT OF EUROPEAN INTEGRATION

European integration is not a post-war twentieth-century concept.
European history up to the mid twentieth century is categorised
by military expansionists from the Romans to Napoleon and
Hitler, who have pursued aggressive campaigns through which
they sought to unify the continent (Chalmers, 1998:2). These
attempts were based on the assumption that military superiority
would create and maintain an empire. As the history books illustrate, this forced integration has, sooner or later, ended in failure.
Consequently, post World War II European integration has been
pursued through creating a political consensus amongst political
elites and citizens, with the objective of creating a shared
European identity.

The roots of the EU lie in the Second World War. Since 1945
European cooperation and integration has taken place at various
levels and is characterised by a desire to avoid conflict. Jean
Monnet, described as the architect of European integration,
argued that only a federal Europe could avoid future military
conflict (Monnet Memoirs, 1978). The Council of Europe in 1948,
was the first formal cooperation in post war Europe. The genesis
of the Council of Europe can be traced back to Winston
Churchill's Zurich University speech in 1946. Here he spoke of a

"common European home" and "united states of Europe" which required Franco-German reconciliation. The most notable and enduring achievement of the Council of Europe has been the European Convention on the Protection of Human Rights and Fundamental Freedoms (ECHR). The jurisprudence of the European Court of Human Rights, which has interpreted the principles of the ECHR, has provided uniform minimum standards of human rights norms for all signatories.

The process of reconciliation began with the French Foreign Minister Robert Schuman advocating the eponymous Schuman Plan on May 9, 1950. In this post-war period, Europe was still reliant upon the Marshall Aid programme which the United States had provided since 1945 to assist European regeneration. Schuman was advocating that Marshall Aid be replaced with a distinct European renaissance. At the core was a belief that economic integration would deliver prosperity for individuals. The plan would require nation states to work within a formal supranational institutional framework. Schuman viewed his plan as a blueprint for economic, political and military co-operation in Europe. But from 1950 to the early 1990s the Cold War would dominate European politics and provide a diversion and barrier to wider European integration.

A feature of European cooperation in the early 1950's is that it lacked trust and commitment from those involved. France, still wary of recent events, remained cautious of Germany and was unenthusiastic about military cooperation. The French Parliament refused to ratify the European Defence Community Treaty in 1952. Although some military cooperation existed in form of the Western European Union, the North Atlantic Treaty Organisation (NATO) signed in 1949 overshadowed this informal cooperation. Ironically, despite the desire for an independent European identity, NATO has remained dominated by the USA and suggests that military cooperation requires a strong transatlantic relationship. The Western European Union did evolve in the 1980's and was formally absorbed in to the EU under the CFSP.

The UK was a reluctant participant in the early years of European integration, primarily because it remained distrustful of political cooperation with France. The UK participated in NATO and was closer to the USA in its strategic aims. This tense relationship with its European neighbours would see the UK outside the formal framework of European integration until 1973.

The European Coal and Steel Community

At the heart of the Schuman Plan was the proposal to place Franco-German coal and steel production under the control of supra-national institutions. The reasons for this were twofold. Firstly, it recognised that coal and steel had been used as the raw materials of war. If production of these basic commodities was placed beyond the exclusive control of nation states, this could prevent their use for aggressive military purposes. Secondly, Schuman recognised that to be independent of United States' economic assistance, there would need to be economies of scale in the production of coal and steel. This required that production of these raw materials would be managed centrally by supranational institutions. The result was the European Coal and Steel Community (ECSC), which came in to force in 1952 and expired in 2002. This Treaty is significant because it transferred competence in decision-making, albeit in the limited sphere of coal and steel, to supra national institutions. Italy and the Benelux countries joined France and Germany in the ECSC while the UK watched suspiciously from the sidelines.

The formal economic cooperation of the ECSC was a marked progress in European integration from the Council of Europe (Craig and De Búrca, 2003:9). The cooperation was founded on economic collaboration and free trade in coal and steel. In addition to the decision-making institutions, the Treaty established a Court of Justice that would guarantee implementation of the Treaty and secondary legislation and arbitrate between Member States. These distinct features of the European integration, which seemed radical at the time, are now the accepted norms of European integration.

The ECSC had spill over effects that went beyond economic integration. It undoubtedly contained elements of political integration through transfer of decision-making power to the supranational institutions. These were a High Authority under the control of a President, which was the most powerful body, a Council of Ministers, and an Assembly composed of representatives from national parliaments. While the Council of Europe remained a forum for discussion, the ECSC created a formal decision-making structure, which unlike other international agreements required the surrender of sovereign policy-making and legal powers. Crucially, the ECSC required solidarity between the Member States. The prevailing objective was that by acting together the benefits derived by the Member States would be greater than if they acted individually. Accordingly, if a Member State did not abide by the rules of the ECSC Treaty, the Court of Justice would ensure that the objectives of the Treaty were enforced. In this lies the beginning of the principle of supremacy which is the foundation of European Community (EC) law and through which the sophisticated economic integration of the Internal Market has been achieved.

The EEC and Euratom Treaties

The failure of a European defence policy and limited progress on political integration suggested that in the early 1950s European integration lacked clear and tangible objectives. The relative success of the ECSC provided those six Member States with a structure within which to operate. The 1955 Messina Conference culminated in the production of the *Spaak Report*.[6] The conclusions of the Spaak inquiry were presented to an intergovernmental meeting of the Six and led to the establishment of the European Economic Community (EEC) and the European Atomic Energy Community (Euratom). The Treaties of Rome signed in 1957 established both Communities and came in to force in 1958. The EEC and Euratom followed the institutional structure of the ECSC. Two new institutions were established for the EEC and Euratom, namely a Commission and Council of Ministers, with the Court of Justice and Assembly serving all three Communities. The economic integration process which began with these Treaties is often described as being functionalist, because it focussed on delivering tangible economic benefits through sectoral management of economic activity by a technocratic elite (Craig, 1999:2).

For those countries outside the Treaties the European Free Trade Association (EFTA) was established in 1960 as an alternative means for economic cooperation. The UK took the lead in EFTA demonstrating its reluctance to join a Franco-German dominated EEC. Most of the EFTA countries have now joined the EU, with the exception of Switzerland and Norway. Both countries enjoy strong economic links with the EU Member States and have adopted many Internal Market principles with respect to their own external trade policies. This reinforces the proposition that EU law and policy has spill over effects and that even prosperous European countries cannot ignore the norms of the Internal Market.

The creation of three separate Treaties was inefficient in terms of administration. In 1965 the Merger Treaty was signed and this came in to force in 1967. The effect of this was to merge the High Authority of the ECSC, with the two Commissions, in to one body which is still known as the European Commission. Furthermore, the Merger Treaty provided that there would only be one Council of Ministers, which is the primary decision making body. Other institutional changes included the creation of a European Assembly which elected its MEPs for the first time in 1979. The Single European Act (SEA) 1987 officially changed the name to the European Parliament. The change of name prompted the European Parliament to seek an increased role as co-legislator with the Council of Ministers. The question of how to increase the powers of the European Parliament has been a central issue in Treaty changes that have taken place since 1986. One reason for this was that the EEC was described as undemocratic and lacking a system of checks and balances. According to Westlake (1998:433) and Shackleton (2000:334), the phased increase of legislative powers for the European Parliament has proved the most effective way in which to remedy this so called "democratic deficit" in the political process.

The Single European Act (SEA) 1987

Since the 1950s economic integration has passed through many phases. The 1960s and 1970s were categorised by "Eurosclerosis" when integration was slow primarily because of national self-interest (Nichol, 1984:36). During this period the ECJ ensured that the foundations for an economic constitution were laid. Following the 1985 White Paper on the Completion of the Internal Market[7] which was accepted by the 1984 Intergovernmental Conference (IGC), economic integration achieved a new impetus. Pescatore, sceptical about this development, argued that significant progress towards economic integration had already been achieved by 1985 and the SEA did no more than reaffirm existing provisions of the EEC Treaty (Pescatore, 1987:11).

The SEA is characterised by its single market objective. In a procedural context it restricted the national veto, the primary reason for Eurosclerosis and replaced it with qualified majority voting (QMV). This created a *communautaire* method of economic integration, based upon majoritarian principles. The SEA also included a fixed deadline of December 31, 1992 for completion of the Internal Market. Taken together these developments were important for several reasons. Firstly, they focussed the Member States to achieve the objectives of the White Paper within a given timescale. Secondly, this task was made easier through the White Paper utilising the principle of mutual recognition, which came from the Court's 1979 *Cassis de Dijon* judgment,[8] as the guiding principle for economic integration. In practice this meant a move away from highly technical, complex and maximum standard sectoral legislation, to the introduction of legislation based upon minimum standard harmonisation. Thirdly, the completion of economic integration was identified as a necessary precursor to more ambitious political integration initiated by the Maastricht Treaty. This latter point represents a neofunctionalist interpretation of integration which suggests that economic integration will have spill over effects that lead to integration in other, more sensitive, policy areas (Craig, 1999:3).

The objectives of the White Paper were broadly successful and in 1989 the European Council held two intergovernmental conferences which were intended to examine the next steps for European integration. In the first IGC the Member States considered how to move forward with Economic and Monetary Union (EMU). The adoption of a single European currency was viewed as the next logical step to follow the completion of the Internal Market. In 1999 the Euro became the single European currency for all transactions involving financial institutions in 12 out of 15 Member States, with notes and coins entering circulation in 2002.

The second IGC considered the controversial issue of political integration. For some Member States, most notably the UK, closer political integration has presented problems. The primary effect of closer integration is the transfer of sovereignty and the power of political decision-making to the European level. Policies such as immigration, defence and foreign affairs, which were considered to be the exclusive domain of Member States, were brought within the competence of the EU. The outcome of the two IGCs was brought together in the Maastricht Treaty.

The Treaty of Maastricht 1993

The Maastricht Treaty introduced intergovernmental cooperation between the Member States in two new pillars of foreign policy and justice and home affairs. These intergovernmental pillars, based on political cooperation were distinct from the economic cooperation of the Internal Market and did not utilise the same decision-making procedures. Furthermore, decisions taken under the pillars were not subject to automatic review by the ECJ. Consequently the development of political cooperation at the

European level created the European Union (EU), the umbrella term for all EU activity. The change of name to the EU was intended to reflect more accurately the depth of cooperation and the desire expressed in the Maastricht Treaty for "ever closer integration". The two new pillars were in addition to the central pillar of economic cooperation, the European Community (EC) pillar. The central pillar itself had changed its name from the EEC to the EC with the word "Economic" having been dropped. This reflected the new competence of the EC in social policy and environmental matters which, while flanking economic integration, also have broader social objectives. The United Kingdom was sceptical of this "social Europe" and secured an opt-out from the Social Chapter of the Maastricht Treaty which led to criticism that an *à la carte* Europe undermined integration (Szyszczak 1994:313).

In the early 1990s European politics was dominated by the effects of the collapse of the Soviet Union and the democratisation of Eastern Europe. One immediate impact of this was the determination of the new democracies (such as Poland and Hungary) to become integrated in to the EU. The Maastricht Treaty came too early for any significant development towards this proposed enlargement. Several Member States questioned whether such an enlargement was prudent while the EU was pursuing deeper political integration and monetary union. The post-Maastricht debate was dominated by discussions of whether widening membership, or deepening integration of the existing Member States, should be the priority. The result was to try and do both and the 1996 IGC was established to consider how eastward enlargement and deeper integration could be assimilated.

The Treaty of Amsterdam 1997

The 1996 IGC resulted in the Amsterdam Treaty which proved a mixed success with regard to preparing for enlargement (Langrish, 1998:18). The crucial questions of the institutional structure and decision-making post enlargement were deferred to a further IGC in 2000, but a commitment to enlargement, sooner rather than later, was given. The Member States agreed March 1998 as the date for the formal opening of talks with those countries selected for enlargement, though no final commitment to a completion date for accession negotiations was given.

With regard to the objective of deeper integration the Amsterdam Treaty consolidated many of the Maastricht developments and the United Kingdom, with a new Labour government signed the Social Chapter. One significant development came in the area of immigration policy. The Schengen Agreement, hitherto outside the scope of the EU was incorporated in to the EC pillar and this integration reflects the "communitarisation" of immigration policy. The Schengen Agreement had allowed for free movement of nationals from Schengen countries across all Schengen borders, and for third country nationals to move freely once they have entered the Schengen area. The UK, which had always remained outside the Schengen Agreement, secured an opt-out from the Schengen *acquis*, which was incorporated in to the EC pillar. Additionally, some aspects of immigration policy moved from pillar three to the EC pillar with the United Kingdom again securing an opt-out, but reserving the right to participate when it was in the national interest. This move of immigration policy in to the EC pillar is significant. The primary effect is that these aspects of border control and immigration policy are now subject to different decision-making procedures where the veto is less prominent. Furthermore, such legislation is subject to judicial review by the Court of Justice.

The Treaty of Nice 2000

It was the lack of progress towards institutional reform in preparation for enlargement that defines the Amsterdam Treaty. The prospect of enlargement posed several challenges for the EU. The Nice Treaty was intended to reform the Institutions in preparation for enlargement but was agreed against a backdrop of popular disenchantment with the EU and a feeling of disconnection between the citizens and the EU integration project. Criticisms of over intrusive and prescriptive legislation, an absence of relevance in the daily lives of citizens and disagreement between Member States on the scope of integration required a change of direction for the integration process.

The rejection of the Nice Treaty by Irish citizens in the 2001 referendum embodied the feeling of mistrust which many citizens felt towards the EU. The Irish gave their consent to the Treaty in a second referendum and the Nice Treaty entered in to force on February 1, 2003. Within the Nice Treaty a Declaration was attached expressing the need to "re-connect" the citizen with the political process of integration. Consequently, in July 2001, the Commission published a White Paper on the Future Governance of the EU setting out various options for Institutional reform.[9] The issue of citizen disengagement with the EU has dominated the EU since before the Nice Treaty, despite the citizen being the recipient of EU rights in areas such as social and employment policy. The strategy post Nice of the EU has been to place the individual at the heart of the integration process and can be considered as recognition of the role which the citizen has contributed to achieving economic prosperity.

The Charter of Fundamental Rights

At the Cologne Summit in 1999 the European Council decided to establish a Convention to study the drafting of a European Charter of Human Rights.[10] This Convention, which was broadly composed, was intended to devise a distinct human rights document for EU citizens and which is tailored towards the specific powers of the EU and its Institutions. The Charter, known as the Fundamental Charter of Rights of the European Union, was not included in the Nice Treaty, despite the wishes of several Member States. The UK argued that the Charter was unnecessary and failed to advance human rights protection in the EU and threatened to veto if the Charter was included in the Treaty. Accordingly, the Charter was merely "proclaimed" at the Nice Council and has no binding legal effect, though Advocates General and the Court of First Instance have referred to the Charter.[11] The ECJ, because of the absence of a clear legal status, has not acknowledged the Charter in its judgments, continuing to cite the ECHR as a benchmark of human rights norms within EU Member States.

The Convention on the Future of Europe and the Constitutional Treaty

In December 2001 the Laeken European Council issued the Laeken Declaration which created a process known as the European Convention in which all Member States and the proposed Accession States openly discussed the future direction of the EU. The Convention on the Future of Europe, modelled broadly on the Convention established to consider the content of the Charter of Fundamental Rights, opened in March 2002 under the Chairmanship of former French President Giscard d'Estaing. The Convention was based on broad participation and discussion between governmental actors and civil society. The Convention concluded in March 2003 and presented a draft Treaty to the Thessaloniki European Council in June 2003. The draft Treaty was considered by an IGC but failed to reach a final agreement before the 2004 Accession. This was primarily because

of a failure by Spain and Poland to accept reforms to the allocation of weighted votes in the Council of Ministers. In June 2004,
following negotiations under the Irish Presidency the Member
States agreed the Constitutional Treaty for the EU. The document
was formally signed in Rome on October 29, 2004. The ratification
process is to be completed by December 2006 and requires all 25
Member States to ratify.

The Constitutional Treaty has been variously described as the
Constitution of an EU superstate, or merely a tidying up and
consolidation exercise of the existing Treaties. Significantly the
Constitutional Treaty includes the Charter of Fundamental Rights
and this will make the Charter enforceable before the ECJ. The
Constitutional Treaty is different from previous Treaties because
of the comprehensive nature of its content. Some provisions are
new, for example the Treaty explicitly refers to the primacy of EU
law over national law in Art.I–6 which was absent in the previous
Treaties. Another innovation of this Treaty is that includes, in
Art.I–5,6 the formal procedure which Member States are required
to follow if they wish to leave the EU.

Since 1957 supremacy has developed through the ECJ constitutionalising the Treaty through judgments such as *Van Gend en
Loos*.[12] In this context, the Constitutional Treaty can be viewed
partly as a codification of previously unwritten principles. A comprehensive document such as the Constitutional Treaty has the
capacity to, not only alter the decision-making structure of the
EU, but also to define more closely what are the fundamental
objectives and values in an enlarged EU. Provisions relating to a
clear delineation between EU and Member State competence are
therefore broadly welcomed. The outstanding question, which
may be answered in the course of the ratification process,
is whether the Constitutional Treaty includes the values and
objectives of EU citizens.

Modernising the Integration Process

In parallel with the requirement to address constitutional issues,
the Member States recognised that enlargement must be accom-
panied with reforms to the EU's decision-making procedures and
the regulatory framework within which the Internal Market operates (Weatherill, 2000:596). To achieve the EU's objectives, of economic and social integration, new mechanisms and practices
which went beyond the traditional Community method of law
making have been introduced. The Community method is the

common name for the legislative process which begins with a Commission proposal and culminates in the Council and European Parliament agreeing a piece of "hard" law such as a regulation or directive. This method has remained unaltered since 1957 and provides a one size fits all approach to the creation and implementation EC legislation.

The Lisbon European Council of 2000 endorsed a process which can be characterised as the modernisation of Community action, particularly in the areas of social and commercial policy. The Lisbon Council concluded that the objective is for the EU to become the "most dynamic knowledge based economy in the world" by 2010.[13] At the centre of the Lisbon process is the open method of co-ordination (OMC) which operates through development of soft law mechanisms, such as exchange of information by Member States, to develop principles of best practice and a shift away from heavy handed top-down regulation and enforcement which characterises the Community method (Szyszczak, 2001:1129). The OMC is now an integral part of policy formulation in a diverse range of areas such as immigration policy, the European Employment Strategy and the combating of social exclusion. In 2005 the EU acknowledged that, at the halfway stage of the Lisbon process, many of its objectives remain distant.[14]

The key facet of the OMC is that it allows Member States to cooperate on strategic policies, which are of particular concern to them without necessarily involving all Member States. The OMC involves non-governmental actors and civil society in the policy formulation process and it can be most appropriately described as a process of interactive learning through which Member States with shared problems seek common solutions. The enforcement of policy objectives devised under the OMC has distinctive and new features, which complement judicial enforcement. These include the use of scoreboards, peer group pressure and a "name and shame" practice of those Member States who do not meet the goals set.

EU TREATIES OR AN EU CONSTITUTION?

The shared characteristic of all Treaty developments has been the incremental extension of individual rights whether economic or social, for example Art.13 EC, which provides for non-discrimination on grounds of race, gender, sexual orientation and religious belief. The inclusion of Art.13 EC in the Amsterdam

Treaty was based upon forty years of jurisprudence and policy that have gradually extended the scope of non-discrimination beyond the traditional notion of nationality seen in Art.12 EC. In this context, what factors can be identified that have enabled EU law to provide individuals with a diverse and comprehensive set of rights enforceable before national courts? This increased protection has occurred *despite* the absence of a Constitutional Treaty such as that agreed in 2004.

Agreement between the Member States to create the Treaties has its roots in supra-national cooperation using classical diplomatic techniques between sovereign nation states (Hartley, 2001:238). The Treaties, being a form of international law, have required a commitment by the Member States to a principle of solidarity, contained in Art.10 EC, that they will uphold the objectives of the Treaties. In the absence of a supremacy provision in the Treaties, it has been left to the ECJ to ensure, through techniques such as direct effect and state liability,[15] that individuals can enforce their Treaty rights.

The role of the ECJ is to ensure compliance with the Treaties and the secondary legislation, the latter expanding upon the basic Treaty principle. The Treaties, written by the Member States, are a statement of EU competence and provide the legal base for further action. Questions relating to EU competence to introduce secondary legislation have regularly been considered by the Court. Where competence exists the Court has sought to maximise the protection individuals receive under the legislation. In the absence of specific Treaty provisions granting competence, for example, in areas such as health or education, the Court has refrained from re-writing the Treaties and bringing such policies within EU competence. The only exception to this is where the activity is incidental to the exercise of the specific rights granted by the Treaty, for example in relation to rights of free movement.[16] In these situations, the objective of the Court has been to maximise the circumstances where Community rights are available, rather than rewrite the Treaty to extend competence. Similarly, in circumstances where the Member States have introduced secondary legislation which is beyond the competence of the Treaty, the Court of Justice has declared that this is *ultra vires*,[17] thereby confirming that the Treaties define the parameters of EU action.

The absence of one single constitutional document should not necessarily be considered as a weakness or a restriction to integration. The Court has ensured that, where the EU has competence the rights contained within the Treaty are guaranteed. The

Treaty structure can be explained as an expression of what sovereign nation states have wanted to achieve at a given moment. Integration has been incremental which is characteristic of the supra-national structure of the EU. It remains for the Court to act as both guarantor of Treaty rights and guardian of legal competence. Consequently, the success or otherwise of European integration should be judged upon the basis of achieving the expressly stated Treaty objectives.

Wyatt *et al* contend that European integration has been achieved incrementally through several Treaty amendments with further competencies being added on each occasion (Wyatt and Dashwood, 2000:155). This observation has been challenged by other commentators who have contended that the Court of Justice is an activist judicial institution (Rasmussen, 1988:29). Through judgments such as *Defrenne*[18] has the Court pushed forward the process of integration beyond the intentions of the Member States? Have the Court's judgments interpreted Community rights further than the Member States intended? If so, has the Court acted as an integrationist and quasi-constitutional court which has invented new rights, or extended existing ones? Alternatively, has the Court of Justice merely fulfilled its remit under Art.220 EC? The answer to these issues lies partly within the Treaty itself and partly through the case law of the Court.

Since 1957 the objective of the Treaty has been the creation of an "ever closer union". The construction of an Internal Market was likewise a clear Treaty objective. The Court has used judgments such as *Cassis de Dijon* and *Bosman*[19] to move forward the process of economic integration and create an "economic constitution" (Maduro, 1998:98). The Court, mindful of the ambivalence of Member States to pursue economic integration in the 1960s and 70s, took it upon itself to keep momentum in the integration process when the political will was absent.

The Court's teleological, or purposive, interpretation of the Treaties can be identified as the central element through which an economic constitution has been created (Weiler, 1999:42). The legal integration promulgated by the Court is part of the wider objective of integration and governance which is the responsibility of all Institutions. Though the EU does not have a government, it possesses clear governance structures and legislative procedures which are based on institutional interaction and the use of clearly defined powers. The Court has regularly acted as arbiter of the relationship between the political institutions, and its primary role has been to ensure that the legislative powers given to the Institutions by the Treaties can be fully exercised. It is these legislative procedures and institutional structure which will now be considered in more detail.

THE ISSUE OF LEGAL BASE

EU competence arises from the Treaty which provides a legal foundation for all EU action. As the EU has a multi-level governance structure this requires that competencies are allocated between the various levels. In some instances the EU has exclusive competence to act, whereas in others it shares competence with the Member States. In such circumstances, according to the principle of subsidiarity in Art.5 EC, the Community should only act if the Member States acting independently could not achieve the result. Though the presumption for action would, under Art.5 EC, appear to lie with the Member States, it can be argued that the principle of subsidiarity conflicts with the objective an "ever closer union" which presupposes action at the EU level to achieve integration. The Amsterdam Protocol on Subsidiarity contains rules relating to the application of subsidiarity against which the Commission benchmarks legislative proposals. According to Chalmers (1998:223) the Commission should only act if a failure to do so would conflict with the Treaty requirements. The Court, perceived as an integrationist institution, has through its judgments, applied a narrow interpretation of subsidiarity and viewed it as a restriction to further integration.[20]

Subsidiarity is a political concept because it concerns the choice of legislative actor and, in part, explains why the Court is reluctant to review legislation. Article 5 EC also contains the closely related principle of proportionality, which is a legal concept. This principle, developed by the Court in judgments such as *Cassis de Dijon*, requires legislative action to not go beyond that which is absolutely necessary to achieve the desired objective. It reflects a criticism which many citizens share about EU legislation, that it is too prescriptive and detailed. The Amsterdam Protocol on Subsidiarity also extends to the principle of proportionality and requires Institutional justification for the contents of the legislative proposal.

The choice of legal base for legislation is crucial, as this will determine which legislative process is used, and in turn defines the extent of institutional participation. Treaty amendments have introduced new legislative procedures and it remains in the hands of the Commission to decide which Treaty base is the most appropriate. The choice of Treaty base has proved controversial on occasion because this has led to the exclusion of the European Parliament from the decision-making process. In the *Commission v Council (Titanium Dioxide)*[21] the legislative measure concerned the setting of titanium dioxide levels. The purpose of the Directive was twofold. Firstly, it promoted a high level of environmental protection, and secondly, it sought to increase competition in the titanium dioxide market. Environmental matters are covered by Art.175 EC and require unanimity by the Council but under this legal base only require consultation with the European Parliament. By contrast, the issue of competition being an Internal Market measure required the use of qualified majority voting in Council and application of the co-operation procedure under Art.95 EC. This Treaty base gives Parliament the power to propose amendments to the legislation which is not possible under the Consultation process. The Commission selected Art.95 EC as the base but the Council substituted it for Art.175 EC.

The Court considered the objective of the measure and held the primary purpose was to promote the Internal Market and that environmental considerations were of secondary concern, making Art.95 EC the appropriate Treaty base. The Court was mindful of the need to guarantee Parliament's rights under the Treaty to participate in the legislative process and this is part of the Court's strategy to review choice of Treaty base and promote institutional balance within the EU.[22]

Treaty base is central to the concept of *vires* and the objective of the Court is to ensure the legality of decision-making. Without this, EU law would be devoid of its democratic legitimacy. Any system of public law requires a rule of law, which includes governance according to the law. In the absence of a specific Treaty base Art.308 EC permits Community action if this is necessary to promote the operation of the Internal Market. Article 308 EC requires the Council to act unanimously and merely to consult the Parliament. The Court is unenthusiastic about Art.308 EC as a Treaty base primarily because of the limited role which it affords to the European Parliament and has in certain circumstances, annulled the legislation.[23] The Court has in specific circumstances accepted Art.308 EC a Treaty base, for example in relation to a Directive which was intended to prohibit discrimination in access to vocational training. The Court stated the primary purpose of the measure was to prohibit discrimination on grounds of nationality and held that this was an implied power of the Council and accordingly it could use Art.308 EC to ensure effective remedial action was taken.[24]

The EU has no inherent powers and the Treaties define the scope of action. In *Germany v Parliament and Council* (*Tobacco Advertising Directive*) the Court acknowledged the boundary of EC competence and rejected the argument that economic integration *per se* is a justification for legislative action. In this case the Member States introduced a Directive which banned all forms of tobacco advertising, except for minimal promotion of tobacco products at the point of sale. The Commission used Arts 47 (2), 55 and 95 EC as the legal base and argued this was an Internal Market measure which sought to create a uniform market in tobacco products by prohibiting all forms of advertising. The Court agreed with the German government that the measure went beyond the scope of the Treaty base. The measure, banning all forms of tobacco advertising, had broader impact than the Internal Market and in particular had a public health objective which was beyond the scope of the Treaty and this included Art.308 EC.

Enhanced Cooperation

The Amsterdam Treaty included a Chapter that provided the framework for closer cooperation between Member States. This flexibility recognises that EU integration had developed a heterogeneous nature. Flexibility allows Member States to pursue an array of policies with different procedural and Institutional arrangements and several reasons may be identified for the inclusion of the closer cooperation provisions. Firstly, enlargement would create a more diverse EU and flexibility would be an essential tool to maintain the dynamic integration of an EU consisting of 25 Member States. Secondly, both the Maastricht and Amsterdam Treaties were characterised by dissidence and intransigence by Member States, for example the UK and Denmark. Flexibility would avoid blockage by one Member State where the majority wished to pursue integration. Thirdly, flexibility would avoid the creation of an *à la carte* Europe outside the Institutional framework, for example as seen with the creation of the Schengen Convention in 1985 which the Amsterdam Treaty incorporated in to the EC Treaty.

Article 11 EC sets out the conditions under which closer cooperation between Member States may be pursued. To avoid disintegration within the Internal Market it is only possible in areas that are not subject to exclusive EU competence. Furthermore, it cannot concern citizenship, distort competition or discriminate between nationals of Member States. Article 40 TEU also provides for closer cooperation in third pillar activity if it "would enable the EU to develop more rapidly an area of freedom security and justice". Under Art.17 TEU, there is some scope for flexibility in the operation of the CFSP, but this is on a case-by-case basis. This recognises the lack of foreign policy consensus that exists, and reflects the lack of political agreement that existed within the EU to the disintegration of Yugoslavia in the 1990s.

The Treaty also provides for what is referred to as pre-determined flexibility and through which the UK and Ireland have secured the right to remain outside integration in the area of Asylum and Immigration. Both countries have secured the right to opt-in to those provisions of Title IV where it would be beneficial. This 'opt-in' is, in practice, a more positive response to EU integration than the opt-out of the Social Chapter secured by the UK at Maastricht and both the UK and Ireland have regularly participated in initiatives introduced under Title IV.

The Nice Treaty amended and clarified the conditions under which closer cooperation operates. Article 43 TEU states the conditions under which such cooperation may be pursued and specifically provides that it can only operate as a last resort. Article 43 TEU has also reduced the number of Member States required for enhanced cooperation from a majority, to only eight Member States. Article 11 EC has removed the right of veto for a Member State and requires that they appeal to the European Council if they have concerns relating to the enhanced cooperation. The European Council can still approve the proposal by a qualified majority and the European Parliament must also assent if the measure would normally be subject to co-decision.

Article I–44 of the Constitutional Treaty contains the basic provisions for enhanced co-operation and brings together the complicated provisions governing enhanced co-operation which occur throughout the current Treaties; Arts 43 to 45 TEU for enhanced co-operation generally, Arts 11 and 11a EC for Community matters, Arts 27a to 27e TEU for the CFSP and Arts 40 to 40b TEU for police and judicial co-operation in criminal matters. The detailed provisions for the implementation of Art.I–44 are set out in Arts III–416 to III–427.

Paragraph 1 of Art.I–44 draws on the introductory phrase of Art.43 TEU and states that those Member States which wish to establish enhanced cooperation between themselves may make use of its Institutions and exercise those competences by applying the relevant provisions of the Constitutional Treaty. This is subject to the limits, and in accordance with, the procedures laid down in this Article and in Arts III–416 to III–423. The purpose of enhanced cooperation must be to further the objectives of the EU, protect its interests and reinforce the integration process. Such co-operation shall be open at any time to all Member States, in accordance with Art.III–418 and may only operate within the framework of the EU's non-exclusive competences.

Paragraph 2 is in substance the same as Art.43 TEU but revises the number of Member States required under that provision to form a quorum for an enhanced co-operation initiative. This has altered from a minimum of eight Member States to a minimum of "at least one third of the Member States". Under Art.III–419 the procedure for enhanced cooperation is in substance the same as that in Art.11 EC, except that the Constitutional Treaty requires the decision authorising enhanced cooperation to have the consent of the European Parliament, whereas Art.11 EC requires only consultation of the European Parliament.

THE STATUS OF PRIMARY AND SECONDARY LEGISLATION

The Treaties, which are the primary legislation of the EU, provide for the introduction of secondary legislation to achieve the objectives of integration. Article 249 EC provides that EC secondary legislation comes in the form of Regulations, Directives, Decisions, Recommendations and Opinions. Regulations and Directives have general legal application and are aimed at the Member States. By contrast, decisions are binding only upon the party to which they are addressed. Consequently, individuals can ordinarily only challenge a decision through the judicial review process under Art.230 EC. Recommendations and Opinions are not legally binding but are important because the Court has stated that national courts must consider them when interpreting EC law.[25]

Regulations are defined by Art.249 EC as being of general application and are directly applicable. Direct applicability means that the provision will apply directly in the legal order of the Member States without the need for incorporation in to national legislation. The Court has stated in *Commission v Italy* that subjecting Regulations to domestic implementation will endanger the uniform application of EC law.[26] By contrast Directives, which Art.249 EC defines as binding as to their effect, do require domestic implementation. Member States can choose the form of implementation, but cannot alter the content of the Directive itself. Crucially, Member States must implement the Directive by the final date stated within it. Questions relating to Member States' implementation have given rise to numerous cases before the Court. Firstly, there are instances of incorrect implementation, as in *Factortame*[27] where the UK's incorporation of Common Fisheries Policy Directives via the Merchant Shipping Act 1988 did not give effect to the EC measure. Alternatively, Member States may fail to implement the legislation altogether as occurred in *Francovich*[28] In this case, the Italian government failed to implement a Directive which provided for minimum state compensation for employees in the case of employer insolvency.

One issue relating to both primary and secondary legislation is whether the provision has direct effect. Direct effect is a constitutional principle of EC law, developed by the Court of Justice, that the legislation and the rights contained within it, can be used by an individual before the national courts. In *Van Gend en Loos* the Court stated that Treaty Articles will have direct effect if they satisfy the following criteria:

- They must be clear and precise;

- Unconditional; and

- Not subject to further implementation.

Not all Treaty provisions will fulfil these criteria but crucially the Court has extended the principle to the fundamental provisions of the Internal Market such as Arts 12, 28, 39, 43 and 49 EC. The Court has also acknowledged the direct effect of Arts.81 and 82 EC which regulate competition law. The effect of these judgments has been to facilitate integration by providing Communitarian interpretations of fundamental objectives, thereby making Treaty rights accessible to individuals.

With regard to secondary legislation, Regulations do not have automatic direct effect. The Court has applied the same conditions for regulations as for Treaty provisions to determine whether they have direct effect. With regard to Directives the question of direct effect is more complicated. Member States under Art.249 EC must implement the measure by the date contained within the directive. The Court in *Van Duyn v Home Office*[29] confirmed the direct effect of Directives. It stated:

"[i]t would be incompatible with the binding effect attributed to a directive by Art.[249] to exclude, in principle, the possibility that the obligation which it imposes may be invoked by those concerned.

... [t]he useful effect of such an act would be weakened if individuals were prevented from relying on it before their national courts and if the latter were prevented from taking it into consideration as an element of Community law."

In this case Directive 64/221/EEC, which was adopted under the old Art.49 EC, allows Member States to derogate form the free movement of workers on grounds of public policy, public security or public health. It is not subject to any condition nor does it require any further action by the Member State.

Directives cannot fulfil the same criteria for direct effect, as can Treaty provisions, because the third condition of no further implementation cannot, by its very nature, be fulfilled. In *Van Duyn* the Court held that for Directives the following criteria would need to be satisfied to establish direct effect. The measure must be:

* Clear and precise;

* Unconditional; and

* The time limit for implementation has expired.

In *Ministero del Publico v Ratti*[30] the Court reaffirmed *van Duyn* and stated further that a Member State which had not implemented a Directive within the prescribed period:

"[c]annot rely, as against individuals, on its own failure to perform the obligations of the directive. . ."

Direct effect is therefore an important constitutionalising technique developed by the Court, to ensure the uniform application of EC law, and guarantee individual rights granted by the EC Treaty (Pescatore, 1983:158). The application of direct effect by ECJ the as a tool of integration will be examined in more detail in Ch.2.

THE LEGISLATIVE PROCEDURES

The complicated legislative procedures and their incremental development reflect the supra-national structure of the EU. The Member States participate in the decision-making process through the Council together with the other political institutions. Each actor is acutely aware of the others presence and each Institution seeks to play its full part in the legislative process. The EU's desire to reconnect with the citizen has led to other non-governmental actors and civil society being brought within the consultation stage of the legislative process. This is part of a broader attempt, going back to the SEA 1986, to democratise decision-making and to make legislation more acceptable to the citizen. There are several decision-making procedures and their use depends upon the Treaty base for the legislative measure as seen in the *Titanium Dioxide* case. The most important and widely used procedure is the co-decision procedure. The defining features of co-decision is that it brings together the Council and European Parliament in a process of joint decision-making.

One other, though rarely used procedure is the consultation procedure, the original decision-making procedure within the Treaty of Rome. This process, utilised under Art.308 EC, only involves the Council and Commission. The Parliament will be consulted, but its opinions have no binding qualities, except that Consultation is an "essential procedural requirement". The Court has acknowledged that though Parliament's views are not binding it does have the procedural right to give an Opinion and will annul an act where this does not occur.[31] Even where the input of the Parliament is peripheral, the Court has protected its interests and promoted institutional balance and procedural propriety in the decision-making process.

The Co-decision Procedure: Article 251 EC

The Maastricht Treaty introduced the co-decision procedure. This was a development from the co-operation procedure introduced in the SEA. The purpose of the co-operation procedure was twofold. Firstly, it introduced the process of qualified majority voting (QMV), which replaced unanimity and limited the national veto, thereby making decision-making in Council easier. Secondly, the co-operation procedure brought the European Parliament within the decision-making process and gave it the power to propose amendments. The objective of this was to enhance the democratic quality of legislation. The power of amendment was limited because the Council retained the right to reject amendments and adopt the legislative proposal in its original form.

The Maastricht co-decision procedure remedied some of the defects of the co-operation procedure by protecting the power to propose amendments. The co-decision procedure introduced a new stage, a so-called "third reading", whereby a new joint body called a Conciliation Committee would be convened if the Parliament and Council failed to agree an amended proposal. This Conciliation Committee seeks to agree, within six weeks of being convened, an amended legislative proposal which both Institutions can support. Though an improvement over the co-operation procedure, co-decision was still subject to drawbacks, not least that the Council could still adopt the original proposal by unanimity if the Conciliation Committee could not agree a joint text.

The co-decision procedure finally became *real* joint decision-making through changes introduced by the Amsterdam Treaty (Shackleton, 2000:326). In 1997, the crucial development introduced at Amsterdam comes at the stage when the Conciliation Committee is convened (see diagram below). Under the Maastricht Treaty, Art.251 EC stated that if the Council and Parliament failed to agree on the content of a measure in the Conciliation Committee then the Council could, using unanimity, agree its original common position. Significantly, under the post Amsterdam version of Art.251 EC such unilateral Council action is prohibited. The effect of the Amsterdam amendments was to shift the centre of gravity, within the co-decision procedure, in favour of the European Parliament and this was a definitive attempt by the Member States to address the democratic deficit. Co-decision is now the common legislative procedure for Internal Market measures introduced under Art.95 EC. The Nice Treaty extended the scope of Art.251 EC scope to cover additional policy areas and the Constitutional Treaty will move 15 Articles from a unanimous voting mechanism to QMV. The Constitutional Treaty introduces qualified majority voting as the norm for JHA issues, which is a consequence of the abolition of the pillar structure. This has brought decision-making on issues such as cross-border crime, drug trafficking, illegal immigration and terrorism within the scope of the co-decision process.

The Co-decision procedure post Amsterdam – Article 251 EC

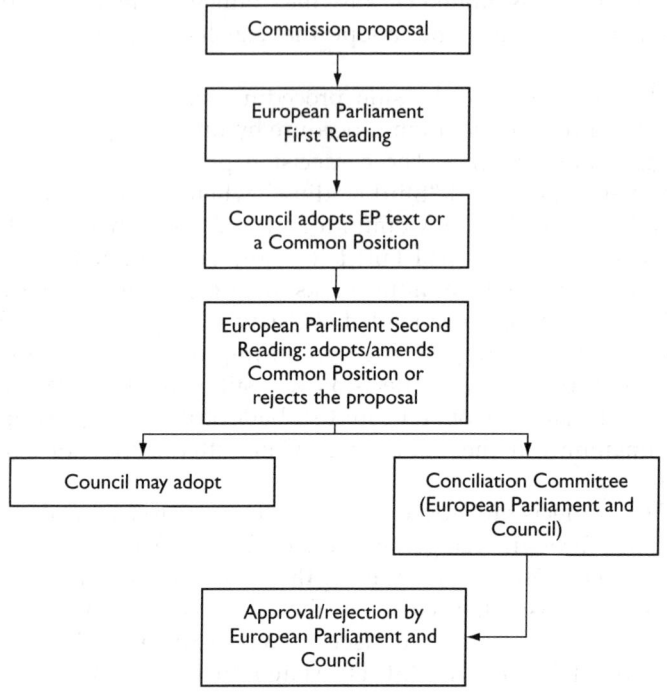

The Assent Procedure – Article 250 EC

The assent procedure was used by the SEA and extended by the Maastricht Treaty. It is used in a limited number of cases such as when voting on the decision to admit new Member States under Art.49 TEU or to sign Association Agreements. In this procedure, the proposal can only be adopted following a positive vote by both the Parliament and the Council.

The Assent Procedure – Article 250 EC

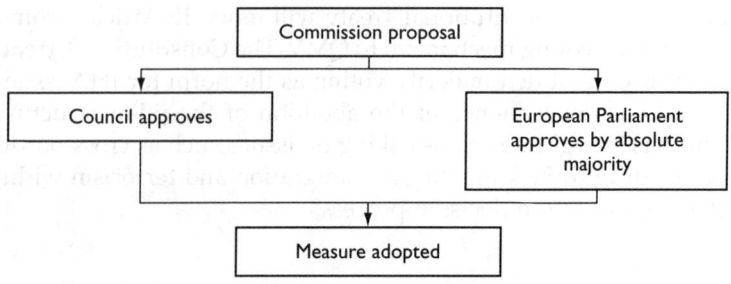

THE INSTITUTIONAL STRUCTURE OF THE EU

Institutional dynamics

Any system of governance requires an institutional structure and capacity to fulfil the tasks of administration and the EU is no different in this respect. For example, in the legislative process the political institutions have clearly defined roles and the ECJ ensures that there is no concentration of legislative power in the hands of one institution. Article 7 EC states that the tasks entrusted to the Community shall be carried out by the following Institutions:

- A European Parliament;
- A Council;
- A Commission;
- A Court of Justice; and
- A Court of Auditors.

Two advisory Committees in the form of the Economic and Social Committee and Committee of the Regions advise the Commission and Council in relation to policy development, but they are not formal Institutions and their opinions are not binding. With the exception of the Court of Justice and the Court of Auditors, which conducts a financial review of the EU budget, the remaining institutions are all political.

Article 7 EC states that the each Institution shall act within the limits of the powers conferred upon it. The Treaty defines the scope of institutional activity and, as within all systems of democratic governance, requires the Institutions to act *inter vires*. Treaty base is the determinant of institutional action. The requirement to act within the limit of powers conferred by the Treaty is intended to ensure that each political institution participates fully in the governance process and that power is not concentrated in the hands of one body.

The maintenance of institutional balance is a task which is entrusted to the Court of Justice and requires the Court to review the choice of Treaty base for secondary legislation.[32] Accordingly, the Treaty base will determine the scope of participation in legislative decision-making by the institutions, and in particular the European Parliament. For example, Art.95 EC, the provision through which Internal Market measures are introduced, requires legislation to be introduced through the co-decision procedure of Art.251 EC.

The Court has consistently taken the view that where a legislative procedure grants the Parliament a right of participation, then Parliament should be able to enforce this right. In the *Chernobyl* judgment,[33] the Court stated that by allowing Parliament to protect these rights it was upholding the institutional balance of the Community. The Court applied teleological reasoning with regard to two Treaty provisions. Firstly, the Court gave a purposive meaning to Art.7 EC. Each Institution having to act within the limits of its powers implies that each Institution can utilise *fully* the powers, which it has been given by the Treaty.

Secondly, the Court examined the operation of Art.230 EC which permits judicial review of EC legislation by Institutions and individuals. Post Nice all Institutions and the Member States are categorised as privileged applicants who can bring an action as of right. Individuals are classified as non-privileged applicants, who must first fulfil the narrow criteria of Art.230 EC[34] which require an applicant to demonstrate that a measure has "direct and individual concern". Prior to Maastricht the European Parliament was categorised as a non-privileged applicant and so could not bring an action as of right. In *Chernobyl*, the Council had introduced legislation using Art.175 EC as the Treaty base, which resulted in the Parliament only having a limited consultative role. The Parliament argued that the legislation should have been introduced through Art.95 EC, which, pre-Maastricht, would have triggered the co-operation procedure, resulting in an increased role for the Parliament to propose amendments.

The Court agreed with the Parliament and stated that, despite the absence of automatic *locus standi* under Art.230 EC, the judicial review action would be permitted in the interests of the "institutional balance" of the Community. The Court reasoned that Parliament was given a right of participation in the legislative process and the measure should have been introduced under Art.95 EC. Accordingly, a corollary of this right to involvement was a right to protect and enforce the guaranteed Treaty rights before the Court. In this case, as Parliament was challenging the Commission and Council it could not rely upon either Institution to bring an action upon its behalf. To avoid a democratic deficit, the Court held that the Parliament must be able to challenge the measure itself. The Court therefore stands as arbiter and protector not only of individual rights, but also as guarantor of institutional participation in the political decision-making process.

The decision-making procedures of the EU are complex and contribute to the institutional dynamics and tension that exist in the relationship between the Institutions. The complexity arises from the fact that decision-making is supra-national and not based upon a traditional parliamentary procedure that exists in nation states. To fully understand the role of each Institution within the structures of EU governance it is necessary to consider the participation by each in the decision-making process and the political relationship that exists between them.

The Commission

The Commission consists of 25 Commissioners, one each from the Member States. The Commissioners, though appointed by their national governments, do not represent their Member State and operate under a principle of collective responsibility. The Constitutional Treaty provides in Art.I–26 that the current composition of the Commission, with one Commissioner per Member State, will remain in place until 2014. From then on, the Commission will comprise a number of Commissioners corresponding to two thirds of the number of Member States. The members of the Commission will be chosen according to a system based on equal rotation among the Member States decided by the Nice Treaty.

In recent years the Commission has been criticised for its failure to ensure internal propriety. Under Art.201 EC the European Parliament has the power to approve the appointment of Commissioners and dismiss the entire Commission. In 1999, following allegations of fraud and mismanagement against the Santer Commission, a committee of the European Parliament and the Court of Auditors inquired in to the alleged fraud. The Report led to the resignation of the entire Commission, which would have been dismissed by the Parliament had it not resigned. The Report stated that "it is difficult to find anyone who has even the slightest sense of responsibility".[35] This review of Commission activity demonstrates the presence of institutional checks and balances within the Treaty which provide a degree of democratic accountability of the un-elected Commission. The aftermath of this affair led to the appointment of a new Commission under Romano Prodi and precipitated a more general discussion on EU constitutional reform (Tomkins 1999:758). The subsequent developments originating in the Commission's White Paper on EU Governance, the Laeken Declaration and the Convention on the Future of Europe have their roots in the Commission's resignation and shared the objective of reconnecting with sceptical EU citizens who distrust *all* EU Institutions. In 2004 the Commission was again subject to review by the European Parliament, when it objected to the proposed appointment of the Italian nominee Rocco Buttiglione for the Freedom, Security and Justice portfolio in the Barosso Commission. The Parliament considered Buttiglione's personal opinions conflicted with his function as Commissioner with prime responsibility for fundamental rights. Following Parliament's rejection of the entire Commission, Buttiglione was replaced and his nomination withdrawn by Italian government.

The European Commission is often described as the Executive of the EU, but its role is more than that of a civil service. Article 211 EC requires the Commission to ensure the proper functioning of the Internal Market by ensuring application of the Treaty and secondary legislation. It will initiate infringement actions before the ECJ under Art.226 EC against any Member State which breaches the Treaty. The Commission's enforcement role also extends to issuing fines against Member States for non-compliance with an ECJ judgment under Art.228 EC.[36] Until May 2004 the Commission also had sole responsibility for enforcement of competition law under Arts.81 and 82 EC, though Regulation 1/2003 has transferred primary competence for this to National Competition Authorities in the Member States.

To ensure the proper functioning of the Internal Market the Treaty has also given the Commission a legislative role. The Commission is the primary initiator of legislation and is arguably the political driving force behind the integration process. The Commission also possesses its own legislative powers under the comitology process through which legislative acts are agreed in specialist committees composed of technocrat representatives from Member States and chaired by a Commission official. This power conferred upon it by Art.202 EC involves the creation of highly technical and complex legislative measures. These expert committees are a technocratic form of government, and though concerned with technical measures, the process is often criticised for lacking transparency and accountability (Craig, 1999:47).

Comitology has been challenged by individuals and other institutional actors under Art.230 EC. In *Köster*[37] the Court confirmed that the Council had legitimately delegated powers to the Commission under Art.202 EC. The most criticised aspect of the comitology process is the absence of participation by the European Parliament. Since the SEA 1986 the European Parliament has through successive Treaty developments gained additional decision-making powers, except in the area of comitology where it remains, by comparison, a bystander. The Parliament challenged this in *European Parliament v Council (Comitology)*.[38] The Parliament sought standing under Art.230 EC to challenge a legislative measure which was introduced through comitology, arguing that the co-operation procedure was more appropriate. Parliament's argument focussed on the need to maintain institutional balance within the EU. The Court's judgment in *Comitology*, delivered one year before the *Chernobyl* judgment, rejected this argument by stating that Art.202 EC specifically excludes the Parliament from comitology and places it within the domain of the Commission and Council. Accordingly, the Court held that the Parliament had no automatic right to participate when Art.202 EC was the Treaty base. This distinguishes the judgment from *Chernobyl* where the Court accepted that an alternative Treaty base of Art.95 EC was appropriate because the measure had an Internal Market objective and as such required Parliament's input.

Douglas-Scott (2002:135) defines comitology as one of the "necessary evils of EU governance". The breadth of competence and the need for swift action in certain circumstances, for example, as with the BSE crisis, requires executive action and the Commission is the most appropriate Institution for this. The preoccupation with transparency and greater accountability of EU activity suggests that the opaque comitology process should be restricted to merely technical measures. Delegated legislation is part of all systems of governance, for example UK ministers are awarded powers of delegated legislation under the Statutory Instrument procedure and its use in the EU should not be criticised *per se*.

The Commission plays a central role in the integration process but is still dogged by questions of democratic accountability, despite the check provided by the European Parliament. It has both pre and post legislative function and provides a degree of political continuity while the composition of the Council and Parliament may change. The workload of the Commission has increased dramatically as the EU has acquired increased competence and through the reforms required for the 2004 enlargement. Commission personnel and resources have lagged behind these developments with the result that EU political governance has adopted the practice of outsourcing the monitoring of certain policies to specific agencies such as the European Environment

Agency (EEA) and European Food Standards Agency (EFSA). These agencies provide expert evidence to the Commission, for example EFSA has taken a lead role in advising the Commission in relation to the access of Genetically Modified Organisms (GMOs) in to the Internal Market. They also provide expert advice when the Commission formulates policy, are part of the comitology process and advise on best practice for implementing policy under the OMC. The use of such agencies is part of a strategy to modernise EU governance and improve the delivery of policy objectives.

The Council

The Council is the legislative arm of the EU, though the legislative function is now shared with the Parliament when the co-decision procedure is being used. Under Art.203 EC the Council is composed of ministers who are authorised to commit the government of their Member State. The composition of the Council is not fixed and varies according to the policy area under discussion. On some occasions this will include politicians from regional, devolved or federal institutions. The Council has a Presidency which rotates every six months to a different Member State. A degree of continuity in Council activities is maintained through the so-called "Troika" of the immediately preceding, the present and the future Council President co-ordinating policy priorities. The Council also has its own civil service in the Committee of Permanent Representatives (COREPER) which is composed of the Ambassadors of each Member State. COREPER provides information on technical aspects of legislative proposals and keeps the minister informed of any political problems which may arise in the course of the decision-making process.

The task of the Council is to take the final decision on proposals submitted to it by the Commission under the EC Treaty and to act on an intergovernmental basis when considering matters under pillars two and three. The primary difference between decision-making under the TEU and the EC Treaty is that unanimity is the norm for intergovernmental decisions, whereas QMV is used under the EC pillar. This was first introduced in the SEA 1986 and has been extended to cover all measures introduced under Art.95 EC. The effect of QMV has been to rationalise decision-making by restricting the national veto. Under the QMV process Member States are allotted votes according to population with currently a total of 321 votes allotted to the 25 Member

States. For a qualified majority to be agreed, and a measure passed, it must receive 232 votes. The allocated votes are important and reflect the fact that the Council is dominated by political relationships. All Member States seek to maximise their influence in decision-making and use their votes to form alliances, where necessary, and create blocking minorities.

If ratified, the Constitutional Treaty will introduce a new system of qualified majority voting which is set out in Art.I–24 and will operate from November 2009. It is a "dual majority" system which means that a minimum number of Member States representing a minimum percentage of the EU's population is required to pass legislation. Under the formula set out in Art.I–25, 55 per cent of Member States (*i.e.* 15 of the EU's then likely membership of 27) representing 65 per cent of the EU's population will need to support a proposed law in order for it to pass. That is 45 per cent of the Member States, or Member States representing 35 per cent of the EU's population can block. There is, in addition, a mechanism which will operate if Member States representing at least three quarters of either of those figures indicate their opposition to a proposal. In such circumstances, the Council must delay a decision and do all in its power to reach a satisfactory solution. This mechanism is set out in the Declaration expanding upon Art.I–25. This Declaration lasts until 2014 and thereafter can be removed from the Constitutional Treaty by QMV. The Treaty maintains unanimity for those areas which Member States consider to be of vital national interest, such as Treaty change, tax, social security, defence, key areas of criminal procedural law and the system of own resources (the EU's revenue-raising mechanism). Unanimity will also remain the general rule for CFSP.

The relationship the Council shares with the European Parliament differs depending upon whether decision-making is under the EC pillar or intergovernmental. Under pillars two and three the European Parliament is only consulted on broader questions of policy rather than specific legislative decisions. By Contrast, the Commission is integrated in to decision-making in all three pillars, raising questions relating to a democratic deficit that the un-elected institution has pre-eminence over the elected Parliament.

The political accountability of the Council is an important issue. Though there exists a degree of Council responsibility to the European Parliament arising out of the co-decision procedure, no corresponding accountability exists with regard to pillars two and three. Council members are politically accountable to their national parliaments, the Council is not accountable as a single body in the same way that the Commission is to the European Parliament. Council meetings are characterised as lacking transparency, with deliberations conducted in private and this contributes to the perception of a democratic deficit. Some changes have been made to the Council's Rules of Procedure to address these criticisms. For example, in 1993 the Council agreed to publish voting records under the co-decision and co-operation procedures. The Treaty of Amsterdam added Art.255 EC which is a commitment to institutional transparency and access to documentation for the EU citizen. The right to documents is not absolute and subject to grounds of public policy and public security, but the Court has stated that the Council must establish clear reasons for non-disclosure.[39]

The European Parliament has no corresponding powers to seek the removal of the Council as it can with the Commission under Art.201 EC. The Council, like the Parliament is composed of elected representatives from the Member States, and the relationship between them is one based on political dialogue. The two Institutions serve different constituencies, the Council represents the national government and the Parliament the citizens of the EU who have elected it. This relationship, perhaps more than any other, defines the supranational structure of the EU.

The European Council

The practice of heads of government summit meetings has taken place since 1969 but was only given legal recognition by the SEA. The heads of government meet at least twice during each Presidency and also provide the guidance for EU policy under the CFSP. Article 4 TEU provides for a more formal structure and states that the:

"European Council shall provide the Union with the necessary impetus for development and shall define the general policy guidelines thereof".

Though not a formal Institution the European Council does provide a political focus and direction for the EU (Craig and de Búrca, 2003:64). The European Council operates without any formal rules, rarely publishes agendas or minutes of meetings and though it is the highest legislative body in the EU it lacks a formal Treaty base. Arguably the European Council fills the political vacuum left by the absence of any form of EU government, but the existence of the European Council without a formal Treaty base, would seem to conflict with the objective of constitutionalising the Treaty through institutional balance.

The Constitutional Treaty has addressed this issue and arguably the most significant change to the EU's institutional arrangements arising out of the Constitutional Treaty is the creation of a full time President of the European Council under Art.I–21. This will replace the President under the rotating Presidency system. This new President will be elected by the members of the European Council for a mandate of two and a half years which will be renewable once. The President will chair the European Council, drive forward its work and ensure its preparation and continuity on the basis of the work of the General Affairs Council, and facilitate cohesion and consensus. The President will also have a role in the most high-level aspects of the Union's external relations.

The Constitutional Treaty also provides for the replacement of the existing six-monthly rotating Presidency by a "Team Presidency" system. Consequently, all Councils, apart from the Foreign Affairs Council, will be chaired by a team of three Member States holding the Presidency for 18 months. In principle, one Member State will preside over all the Councils for six months, supported by others in the Team, though the Member States concerned may agree alternative arrangements amongst themselves. The new post of EU Foreign Minister will chair the Foreign Affairs Council.

The European Parliament

The European Parliament has been elected by universal suffrage since 1979, but is not a parliament in the traditional sense. The Parliament shares legislative competence with the Council, but unlike the Council cannot pass legislation independently of the other. In the context of pillars two and three, the Parliament only has a consultative role. Nonetheless, the European Parliament is an important political institution. Through representative democracy it provides the EU with a degree of democratic legitimacy and together with national parliaments has contributed to the "parliamentarisation" of the EU. This parliamentarisation occurs through scrutiny of Council activities by national parliaments, and through the European Parliament drawing on principles of parliamentary practice and procedure when it participates in the legislative process. The purpose, which both national parliaments and the European Parliament share, is the accountability of decision-makers.

The European Parliament contributes to a more democratic EU by fulfilling a broad supervisory role. In addition to providing a check upon Council action in the legislative process, the Parliament reviews the activities of other Institutions. For example, under Art.193 EC it can establish temporary committees of inquiry. The 1999 Committee of Independent Experts in to Fraud and Mismanagement in the Commission is one such Committee. This was part of a broader scrutiny of Commission activity which allows for a censure motion censure against the Commission under Art.201 EC. Article 197 EC permits the Parliament to submit oral questions to the Commission and the Council. As part of its supervisory role, the European Parliament has one key power under Art.272 EC, namely the ability to veto Commission proposals for non-compulsory expenditure. It can also under Art.272 (8) EC veto the entire budget for "important reasons". In the 1999 Commission crisis the Parliament used the threat of this power as leverage over the Commission to force its resignation.

The relationship of the Parliament with the EU citizen is central, as it remains the primary contact point with the EU Institutions. Under Art.195 EC the European Parliament can appoint an Ombudsman who provides citizens with a direct opportunity of informing about institutional maladministration which he/she may have suffered. The creation of an EU Ombudsman reflects administrative practice in many Member States where they form a part of the process of ensuring good government. The establishment of the Ombudsman is yet another way in which the EU has tried to bridge the democracy gap to the citizen.

The above procedures have created a perception of a democratic EU accountable to its citizens but in practice the impact is minimal. For example, the Ombudsman while providing for a cheap and quick form of review lacks any corresponding power of enforcement (Douglass-Scott, 2002:107). The Laeken Declaration and Convention suggest that EU citizens remain distant from the EU. While the Parliament provides an internal institutional balance, it remains questionable whether on its own it can overcome the wider problem of citizen disconnection. The European Parliament has only had minimal success in bridging the democracy gap with the citizen. For example, though Art.255 EC extends the transparency principle to Parliamentary documents, this has not made a significant impact upon EU democratisation.

Though a political institution the Parliament has also been an effective litigator. The Parliament has regularly intervened in cases, for example, *Roquette Frères* and has also utilised Art.230 EC to initiate actions in its own name. The Court has through judgments such as *Chernobyl*, recognised Parliament's rights to protect its own prerogatives by granting *locus standi* under Art.230 EC. The Court's judgment reinforced the concept of institutional balance. Furthermore, the Maastricht Treaty added the language of the ECJ to Art.230 EC, which in its revised form, stated that Parliament could initiate judicial review proceedings of a measure where it was seeking to "protect its own prerogatives". This judgment is part of an incremental development in Parliament's status as a political institution which the Treaty amendments have also acknowledged through the extension of its role in the decision-making process. These gradual developments can be considered as a movement towards a constitutional structure based upon institutional balance and the separation of powers (Westlake, 1998:434). The Nice Treaty reinforced the argument of gradual constitutionality based upon increasing democratic legitimacy by awarding the European Parliament the status of privileged applicant for the purposes of Art.230 EC. This has placed it on a par with the other Institutions and Member States and it is now open to the Parliament to challenge the validity of any legislative proposal and not just one which affects its prerogatives.

Despite the Treaty developments the impact upon the citizen of Parliament's increased role remains unclear. The Constitutional Treaty recognises the central role of the European Parliament to provide democratic legitimacy in the EU but this has yet to be appreciated by EU citizens who are less enthusiastic at election time. Politically it vies for power with the other Institutions, yet any extension to its powers can only come at the expense of the other Institutions, and with their consent. Despite the aspirations for the Parliament, it is unlikely to assume the role of sole legislator or gain a legislative function beyond that which currently exists. In these circumstances, the assessment of Dehousse (1998:595) may be the most appropriate analysis of the institutional arrangements. Dehousse argues that the EU's Institutional development resembles a federal structure in which the legislative function will be shared between two branches, which represent the EU's population and the States. The Constitutional Treaty would seem to confirm that this is the future of EU decision-making.

The Constitutional Treaty strengthens the role of the European Parliament, primarily by increasing the number of policy areas subject to co-decision. The new Treaty applies co-decision to all areas where European laws and framework laws are adopted under the ordinary legislative procedure, unless an explicit provision to the contrary is made. This means that a number of areas will be transferred to co-decision by the Constitution, including laws on intellectual property, structural funds, the Common Agricultural Policy (CAP), asylum and immigration.

Under Art.I–19 of the Constitutional Treaty the European Parliament's size will increase and be capped at 750 MEPs. The number of MEPs each country have will depend on population size, but each country will be allowed a minimum of 6, and a maximum of 96, MEPs. The actual number of MEPs each country has will be decided by a European Council decision, on the initiative of the European Parliament and with its consent.

The House of Lords EU Select Committee stated that the balance of power in the European Union is going to shift from the Commission in favour of the Member States if the Convention's proposals were adopted (HL 106, 2002–3:7). Though this is correct in part, the Constitutional Treaty is perhaps more significant for its clarification of the respective roles of the Institutions rather than returning powers to the Member States. In particular, it recognises the different missions of the Commission, including its near monopoly of legislative initiative, its executive function and its function of representing the Union externally through the newly created position of EU Minister of Foreign Affairs. The Constitutional Treaty devotes the principle of inter-institutional programming to the Commission's initiative and crucially extends the scope of the co-decision procedure, which, significantly, will be referred to as "the legislative procedure". In this context it might be more appropriate to argue that the Constitutional Treaty is a document, while not creating an EU Constitution, will create a system of constitutional governance in the EU based on a strict allocation of powers that grant increased EU competence. This will result in EU action which is benchmarked against a legally enforceable Charter of Fundamental Rights before the ECJ.

The European Court of Justice and the Court of First Instance

The efficacy and uniformity of EC law cannot be guaranteed without a comprehensive system of enforcement. Under Art.220 EC the European Court of Justice and Court of First Instance are entrusted with the task to ensure that the Treaty is observed. This involves supervision of the decision-making procedures and application of EC law within the Institutions and in the Member States. The ECJ consists of 25 judges, one from each Member State and is assisted by eight Advocates General. Since the 2004 enlargement the ECJ sits in a Grand Chamber of eleven judges and in Chambers of three or five judges. The CFI also consists of 25 judges but does not have any Advocates General, but can appoint one of its own judges to fulfil this task if necessary.

It is the responsibility of the ECJ and CFI to ensure that the law is observed in the interpretation and application of the Treaties establishing the European Communities and of the secondary legislation laid down by the Community Institutions. To enable it to carry out that task, the Court has wide jurisdiction to hear various types of action, for example, enforcement actions under Art.226 EC, actions for annulment under Art.230 EC (with the CFI) and preliminary references from national courts under Art.234 EC. The ECJ also has competence to hear appeals against decisions of the CFI.

Since 1957 the objective of the European integration process has been the creation of an "ever closer union". The construction of an Internal Market was likewise a clear Treaty objective and the Court has used judgments such as *Cassis de Dijon* to move forward the process of economic integration and create an "economic constitution" (Craig, 2002:3). The Court, mindful of the ambivalence of Member States to pursue economic integration took it upon itself to keep the process alive when the political will was absent.

This raises the question of whether the Court has taken integration beyond that which the Member States intended? To answer this question it is necessary to consider more closely the methods the Court has used to enforce Community rights within the Member States. Article 220 EC states that it is the function of the Court of Justice to "ensure that in the interpretation and application of this Treaty the law is observed". The key Treaty provision, which explains the approach of the Court in its application of Community law, is Art.10 EC.

Articles 230 EC and 234 EC are central to the protection of individual rights in Community law. Access by individuals to judicial protection, whether at the national level through Art.234 EC or, directly to the ECJ under Art.230 EC has provided for incremental development of individual rights and consequently furthered integration. In the process of protecting individual rights and promoting integration the Court has been accused of being a judicially activist institution (Arnull, 1999:67; Tridimas, 1996:200). Through judgments such as *Van Gend en Loos*, *Costa v ENEL* and even *Chernobyl* the Court has upheld principles which are not explicitly mentioned in the Treaty. For example, the principle of supremacy though not expressly stated in the Treaty is a fundamental requirement if, in the words of the Court in *Van Gend en Loos*, European Union law is to be a "new legal order".

These early judgments, which provided a purposive interpretation of rights within the Treaty, have set the tone for the Court's subsequent expansive interpretation of Community law rights. Rather than being labelled an activist court, it may be more appropriate to describe the ECJ as exercising its inherent jurisdiction under Art.220 EC. Furthermore, through its judgments the ECJ has placed protection of Treaty rights at the core of its activities. The fundamental principles of EU law, such as non-discrimination, supremacy and human rights, and the techniques which the Court has employed to protect them, have arisen primarily from a judicial dialogue with national courts through Art.234 EC. It is this contribution by the ECJ to EU integration which is considered in Ch.2.

THE COURT OF JUSTICE AND THE FUNDAMENTAL PRINCIPLES OF COMMUNITY LAW

INTRODUCTION

Article 220 EC requires the ECJ to ensure that the Treaty objectives are fulfilled. According to O'Neill (1994), the Court has taken a broad interpretation of this provision. Most importantly the Court guarantees the supremacy of Community law in the Member States in the absence of a written Treaty provision. The emphasis upon integration by the Court's has been to maximise individual rights but this has lead to criticisms of judicial activism (Shapiro, 1999:321). ECJ judgments provide communitarian interpretations of fundamental Treaty principles, for example, the concept "worker" under Art.39 EC,[1] or abuse of a dominant position under Art.82 EC.[2] The judgments have guaranteed the uniform application of EC law and promoted the cause of economic integration.

Weiler (1999) has suggested that the ECJ displays the characteristics of a constitutional court. Though the EU agreed a Constitutional Treaty in 2004, judgments such as *Konstantinidis*[3] and *Johnson*,[4] have constitutionalised certain Treaty provisions because the Court has referred to them as "fundamental rights or principles". In *Konstantinidis* the applicant challenged the manner in which his Greek surname had been transliterated in to German, arguing that the incorrect spelling amounted to discrimination under Art.12 EC. Consequently, this infringed his rights under Art.43 EC. Advocate General Jacobs argued that his right to free movement under the Treaty, which was a "fundamental right", had been infringed because he suffered discrimination arising from an incorrect spelling of his name which could not be objectively justified. The Advocate General further stated that his fundamental right to human dignity had also been infringed and this violation would interfere with the exercise of his Community law rights. The right to human dignity was a higher legal norm that is protected by domestic human rights provisions and the ECHR.

The Court, while coming to the same conclusion, did not share the human rights reasoning of the Advocate General. The Court held that the discrimination suffered infringed a fundamental economic right of free movement under Art.43 EC because the incorrect spelling of a name could lead to confusion for potential clients. The Court described Art.43 EC as "one of the fundamental legal provisions of the Community". The reasoning of the Court's judgment was intended to promote economic integration while circumventing relevant, but difficult, questions of human rights protection in Community law (Coppell and O'Neill, 1992:671). In *Johnson* the Court considered fundamental rights in Community law within the context of the protection afforded by the ECHR. The case concerned the application of Directive 76/207/EEC, the Equal Treatment Directive, in circumstances where a female police officer in Northern Ireland was prevented, by ministerial action, from performing armed duties. The Court held that the applicant was entitled to "effective judicial protection", which would include review of the ministers" decision by a judicial body and whether the decision was compatible with the aims of the Directive. The ECJ's judgment referred to Arts 6 and 13 ECHR that provide for the right to effective judicial protection. Article 6 of the Directive, which provides for access to judicial procedures for employees in the event of a dispute, should, according to the Court, be read within the context of Arts 6 and 13 of the ECHR.

To guarantee both institutional participation and individual rights the Treaty provides several procedures through which the fundamental rights and principles of Community law can be protected. The common feature of these procedures is that they seek to ensure compliance with EC law, and two Treaty provisions stand out. Firstly, under Art.230 EC the Institutions and individuals can seek judicial review of a Community act with a view to obtaining its annulment. Access by individuals to Art.230 EC has, for many years, raised questions of whether fundamental rights are being adequately protected, in the light of the restrictive criteria for *locus standi* under Art.230 EC. Secondly, through Art.234 EC national courts are given a pivotal role to protect individual rights, reinforcing the concept that Community law has become an integral part of the domestic legal order. The Court's statement in *Van Gend en Loos* that Community law is a "new legal order" defines the integrationist stance taken by the Court. Direct effect and state liability developed by the ECJ have become the techniques through which the fundamental principles of Community law, such as the principle of non-discrimination, are enforced within the domestic courts. Before examining these in more detail it is first necessary to consider the procedures through which the Court guarantees Treaty rights.

THE JURISDICTION OF THE COURT OF JUSTICE

Article 226 EC and 228 EC: Enforcement actions

In fulfilling its task of enforcing Community law the Commission can seek recourse to the judicial procedure under Art.226 EC which permits the Commission to bring infringement proceedings against a Member State for breaching its obligations under EC law. This enforcement is a crucial task for the Commission and the impact of Art.226 EC cannot be understated. It is triggered by a Member State's failure to comply with a Treaty obligation. The procedure involves giving the State an opportunity to submit observations before the Commission delivers a reasoned opinion. If the State fails to comply with the opinion, proceedings are commenced before the Court.

A significant proportion of proceedings are settled before reaching the Court and Art.226 EC works effectively when Member States cooperate with the Commission. One problem is the question of enforcement of a judgment against the Member State. Until the Maastricht Treaty there was an absence of sanctions should the Court's ruling be ignored. Under Art.228(2) EC the Commission can impose a financial sanction on further application to the Court in the event of a failure by a State to comply with the ruling.[5] In *Commission v France* Advocate General Geelhoed emphasised that the purpose of Art.228 EC is to ensure Member State compliance with Community law.[6] In this respect the sanctions provided for in that Article serve a twofold purpose. Firstly, they should have a dissuasive preventive effect by making it economically unattractive for a Member State to infringe Community law. Secondly, the sanction has a specific persuasive effect by allowing sufficient pressure to be brought to bear on a Member State to ensure compliance with Community law after an infringement has been determined by the Court. Moreover the Advocate General stressed that these sanctions are particular to the Community legal order and cannot be compared to existing sanction mechanisms at the national level.

The Advocate General stated that the Court should be permitted to impose a lump sum fine in addition to a periodic payment for breach of Community law. The Advocate General's reasoning is that when determining whether the Court can impose both a lump sum and a periodic penalty payment, the objective and rationale of Art.228 EC is decisive. Advocate General Geelhoed considered the purpose of this Article is to ensure that Member States fulfill their obligations under Community law. By their nature the lump sum and the periodic penalty payment serve different purposes, the first being dissuasive and the latter persuasive. Accordingly, in the Opinion of the Advocate General, it must be open for the Court to impose both sanctions simultaneously.

Article 230 EC: Actions for annulment

Under Art.230 EC, an applicant seeks the annulment of a measure adopted by an Institution. An action for annulment may be commenced by a privileged applicant which under Art.230 EC are the Member States or Community Institutions. Individuals, whether legal or natural, are categorised as non-privileged applicants and can challenge a measure if it can be shown to be of "direct and individual concern". Accordingly, individuals are generally restricted to challenging decisions as they are addressed to specific parties. The Court, has in specific circumstances, permitted challenges to regulations but this has occurred where the measure exhibits the characteristic of a decision, for example, if it identifies particular undertakings. The Court has stated in *Calpak v Commission*[7] that, judicial review will be permitted on such occasions because of the substance and nature of the measure. Judicial review will not be denied merely by virtue of the nomenclature which the Commission has applied to a measure.

The granting of *locus standi* by the Court to individuals has since the judgment in *Plaumann v Commission*[8] only been permitted within very narrow criteria. Occasionally, the Court has relaxed the conditions, for example in *Cordoniu*[9] and *Extramet*,[10] where the Court demonstrated a broader willingness to protect specific commercial interests as part of a wider policy of promoting economic integration (Maduro, 1998:25; Arnull, 2001:7). Since *Plaumann*, the Court has consistently stated that *locus standi* to individuals will only be granted if the measure being challenged is of direct and individual concern. In *Plaumann* the Court stated this requires the applicant to demonstrate that:

"[b]y reason of certain attributes which are peculiar to them or by reason of circumstances in which they are differentiated from all other persons."

Individual applicants have tended to be successful in cases involving Decisions rather than general legislative measures. In *Nold v Commission*[11] the Commission introduced new trading procedures in the coal industry which resulted in the applicant losing its status as a direct wholesaler, and consequently, a direct supplier of coal. Nold argued that the new rules jeopardised profitability to the extent of undermining the entire business. This infringed the right to property and freedom to trade which are guaranteed by the German constitution. Nold satisfied the criteria of direct and individual concern because the measure was addressed directly at coal producers and did not require intervening action by a Member State. The decision was of individual concern because Nold, as an individual, constituted a finite group of potential applicants that are more commonly referred to as a "closed class".[12] This identification through the Commission Decision individualised the party from other applicants.

For an individual applicant to be successful then he/she must differentiate themselves from all other potential applicants. In competition cases, or other cases where an economic right is involved, it has proved factually easier for an applicant to demonstrate the impact which the decision has. For example, an applicant can demonstrate that a legitimate expectation has been infringed and that this has led to the applicant suffering a financial loss. This was the position in both *Nold* and *Cordoniu*. In cases involving general legislative measures such as a regulation or directive, or if the measure affects all applicants uniformly a challenge under Art.230 EC is less likely to succeed. Such cases, which tend to involve non-economic rights have broader impact, and the irony of the Art.230 EC requirement of individual concern is that the greater the number of individuals that are affected by a measure, the less likely that the Court will grant *locus standi* (Cygan, 2003:1004).

The restricted application of Art.230 EC by the Court has had the effect of preventing proxy or group actions by individuals who collectively are affected by a measure in the same way.[13] Harlow (2002) criticises this approach as restricting the development of popular justice in the EU and reinforcing the notion of a democratic deficit by preventing judicial review of a legislative act when a large group of citizens share the same concerns. In *Greenpeace* the applicants sought judicial review of Commission funding for two power stations which were to be built on the Canary Islands. The building work commenced without an Environmental Impact Assessment (EIA) under Directive 85/337/EEC being carried out. The Island's residents initiated proceedings in the national court and sought a reference under Art.234 EC. This domestic action for judicial review of the Commission's Decision was rejected by the Spanish Administrative Court which stated that it did not have jurisdiction to grant a remedy against the Commission. Greenpeace subsequently commenced a proxy action on behalf of the residents under Art.230 EC where it sought compliance with the EIA Directive.

The ECJ, rejecting the claim stated that Greenpeace could not be individually concerned because the EIA Directive was aimed at Member States and was a general legislative measure. In such circumstances any challenge relating to the application of the EIA Directive should be commenced before the national court.

The effect of the ECJ's judgment was to exclude *any* challenge to the Commission's funding of the project. The Court argued that Greenpeace was not in any special position *vis-à-vis* the Commission's decision, even if it represented a significant proportion of the Islanders. The Directive was a general legislative measure and consequently Greenpeace could not under the *Plaumann* formula be individualised. The Court's reasoning recognises that Greenpeace was not part of the decision-making process, and as such, was not contemplated by the Commission when it made the decision.

Cygan (2003:1006) criticises this decision and contrasts the Court's approach in *Greenpeace* with that of judicial review in the Member States, where national courts have viewed group actions as efficient mechanisms for the protection of the individual. Furthermore, he cites an inconsistent approach to protecting effective remedies under Community law, with actions against Community Institutions being less successful than those which involve Member States. The ECJ has based its objections to widening the grounds of *locus standi* on a floodgates policy, whereby any relaxation of the rules would lead to opportunistic litigants initiating challenges which may undermine the decision-making process. In the Opinion of Advocate General Jacobs in *Unión de Pequeños Agricultores (UPA)*[14] the floodgates argument was rejected as a justification for not extending *locus standi*. The Advocate General argues that the problem is not insurmountable and could be addressed through adequate procedural measures

The Court's judgment in *UPA* rejected this view and stated that any reform of Art.230 EC is a matter exclusively for the Treaty makers and added that the narrow criteria for *locus standi* should not be mitigated through use of the Court's Rules of Procedure.

The Opinion of Advocate General Jacobs is largely based on a fundamental rights argument. The Advocate General contends that access to an effective remedy through Art.230 EC is a fundamental right and one which *all* courts have a duty to protect. This view was shared by the CFI in the *Jégo-Quéré* judgment. In addition to referring to Arts 6 and 13 ECHR in support of his views, the Advocate General refers to Art.47 of the Charter of Fundamental Rights which protects the right to an effective remedy. Advocate General Jacobs stated:[15]

"That principle [of an effective remedy] is, as the Court has repeatedly stated, grounded in the constitutional traditions common to the Member States and in Articles 6 and 13 of the European Convention on Human Rights. Moreover, the Charter of fundamental rights of the European Union, while itself not legally binding, proclaims a generally recognised principle in stating in Article 47 that 'everyone whose rights and freedoms guaranteed by the law of the Union are violated has the right to an effective remedy before a tribunal."

For both the Advocate General and the CFI there is no compelling reason to read in to the notion of individual concern, a requirement that an individual applicant seeking to challenge a measure must be differentiated from all others affected by it. The overriding question should be the protection of fundamental rights, in this case the right to an effective remedy, which the Court has acknowledged in *Johnson*. In *UPA*, as in *Konstantinidis*, Advocate General Jacobs adopts a higher legal norms argument with regard to access to an effective remedy, the denial of which cannot be justified, even in the application of Community law.

The ECJ rejected the arguments advanced by the Advocate General. Furthermore the ECJ subsequently overturned on appeal the CFI's judgment in *Jégo-Quéré*.[16] In neither of these judgments did the Court apply Art.47 of the Charter, instead relying on the principles of Arts 6 and 13 of ECHR which it acknowledged in judgments such as *Johnson*. The Court argued that in cases such as *UPA*, the applicant could seek an effective remedy in the domestic courts, and apply Arts 6 and 13 ECHR. It will be remembered that in *Johnson* the right to judicial review of the ministerial decision was a right to be exercised in the national court and not before the ECJ. Cygan, (2003) and Usher (2003) criticise the judgment in *UPA* as being inconsistent with the Court's general approach to protecting individual rights. It will be recalled that in the *Chernobyl* case, the pre-Maastricht version of Art.230 EC did not permit the European Parliament to protect its prerogatives, yet through teleological reasoning the Court afforded Parliament this right. The Court's justification was the need to maintain institutional balance within the legislative procedure, but it is equally important that individuals have access to effective judicial protection when their rights are infringed. In *UPA* the Court stated it would not re-draft Art.230 EC to extend *locus standi* for individual applicants suggesting this was a task for the Treaty makers. The ECJ argued that it is for individuals to seek effective remedies in their domestic courts but *Greenpeace* demonstrates that this will not always be possible.

The Constitutional Treaty proposes several, albeit limited changes to Art.230 EC. Article III–270 of the Constitutional Treaty amends the wording of Art.230 EC. Private individuals' access to the ECJ will be facilitated by the provision that any natural or legal person may institute proceedings against "a regulatory act which is of direct concern to him or her and does not entail implementing measures". Arnull has described this reformulation of the criteria for individual access to the Court as a "small step in the right direction" (Arnull, 2004:1). The Constitutional Treaty seeks to make it easier for citizens to challenge the Union's regulatory acts under which penalties are imposed, even if these acts do not affect them individually. It remains unclear whether applicants such as those in *Greenpeace* or *UPA* would benefit from this change. The floodgates argument may prevail and cause the Court to continue to interpret standing in a narrow way. According to Arnull, *UPA* and *Jégo-Quéré* were a missed opportunity to provide some clarity to the law and an opportunity to re-connect with the EU citizen on the question of effective judicial protection.

Article 232 EC: Actions for failure to act

Under Art.232 EC the ECJ and the CFI may review the legality of a failure to act on the part of a Community Institution. The Court in *European Parliament v Council (Transport)*[17] held that such an action might be brought only after the Institution concerned has been called on to act. Furthermore, the complainant must specify the measures which the erring Institution has failed to take, and the necessary remedial action. Where the failure to act is held to be unlawful, it is for the Institution to put an end to the failure by appropriate measures.

Article 234 EC: References for a preliminary ruling

References for a preliminary ruling are specific to Community law. The ECJ is the supreme guardian of Community legality, but is not the only judicial body empowered to apply Community law. National courts have a key role to play inasmuch as they retain jurisdiction to review the administrative implementation of Community law by the Member State. Treaty provisions and secondary legislation directly confer rights upon EU citizens, which national courts must uphold. To ensure the effective and uniform application of Community legislation and to prevent divergent interpretations, Art.234 EC provides for a preliminary ruling procedure. Under Art.234 EC, where a national court seeks a preliminary ruling on the application of a legislative act, the ECJ will clarify the interpretation of Community law in order to ascertain whether the national legislation or administrative action comply with Community law.

The national court and not the parties to the action decides if a preliminary reference is required and the preliminary reference must ask clear, unambiguous and relevant questions to the ECJ. These should relate to the Community measure at issue and its application in national law.[18] The ECJ's reply is not merely an opinion, but takes the form of a judgment. The ECJ does not decide the domestic action, which is left to the national court, but the ECJ's preliminary ruling will provide a clear explanation of the Community law issue. In *Arsenal Football Club v Reed*[19] the English High Court made a reference to the ECJ seeking clarification on the application of Directive 89/104/EEC on the Community Trademark. When the preliminary ruling was received, Laddie J. rejected the judgment stating that the ECJ had decided the factual issues of the case and therefore exceeded its jurisdiction. Laddie J. did not consider himself bound by the preliminary ruling, but this action is outside of the spirit, let alone the requirement, of Art.234 EC. The Court of Appeal subsequently overturned the High Court judgment and applied the preliminary ruling, finding in favour of the applicant that the trademark had been infringed.

The fundamental question relating to preliminary rulings is in what circumstances should they be made? Article 234 EC states that when a matter is before a national court against which there is no further judicial remedy, then the national court is under an obligation to make a reference. Where the case is before any other court against whose judgment an appeal is possible then a discretion is retained. Even in these circumstances national courts are encouraged to make a reference to ensure that Community law rights are available and consistently applied.

Courts from which an appeal is possible may apply the doctrine of *acte clair*. This principle arises from French administrative law and as applied in Community law does not require national courts to make a reference if the legal issue in question has been decided by a previous court ruling. In *CILFIT*[20] the ECJ stated that *acte clair* could be used in circumstances where there was "no scope for reasonable doubt as to the manner in which the question raised is to be resolved." *Acte clair* is therefore a useful principle as it helps prevent the ECJ from being overwhelmed by references on established points of law. National courts must apply Community law correctly and should not use *acte clair* unless, according to Court of Appeal in *R v Stock Exchange ex parte Else*,[21] the national court is "completely confident" that it can resolve the issue itself. If any doubt exists then a reference should ordinarily be made.

The statement of the Court of Appeal in *ex parte Else* is a workable application of *acte clair* for all lower courts. It preserves their discretion to refer, but encourages them to do so if there is any doubt. For those courts from which there is no appeal, the doctrine of *acte clair* would seem to be of minimal assistance, though the ECJ has acknowledged that such courts do not need to make a reference if a matter has been clearly decided.[22] On a literal interpretation Art.234 EC places a positive obligation upon courts of last instance to refer, and this requirement has been reinforced through the Court's judgment in *Köbler*.[23] In this judgment the Court appears to reject the view that *acte clair* can be applied by courts of last instance and takes a pragmatic approach to Art.234 EC. The Court stated:

"Moreover, it is, in particular, in order to prevent rights conferred on individuals by Community law from being infringed that under the third paragraph of Article 234 EC a court against whose decisions there is no judicial remedy under national law is required to make a reference to the Court of Justice." (Para 34)

"The [Austrian] court was not entitled to take the view that resolution of the point of law at issue was clear from the settled case-law of the Court or left no room for any reasonable doubt (Case

283/81 *CILFIT and Others* [1982] ECR 3415, paragraphs 14 and 16). It was therefore obliged under the third paragraph of Article 234 of the Treaty to maintain its request for a preliminary ruling." (Para 118)

In *Köbler* the applicant was a university professor, who applied for a length-of-service increment provided for by Austrian law. He was refused on the ground that he had not completed 15 years' service as a professor at Austrian universities. Köbler claimed that service at universities elsewhere in the EU should be included. The Austrian Supreme Administrative Court made a reference to the ECJ seeking clarification whether the Austrian law infringed Art.39 EC. But after the Court's judgment the Austrian Court withdrew the reference and dismissed the applicant's claim arguing that the increment was a loyalty bonus and not part of his salary. This Austrian court based its decision on the *acte clair* doctrine stating that the question of loyalty bonuses in such circumstances had been decided by the ECJ in *Schöning-Kougebetopoulou*.[24] Köbler, through this action, sought compensation from the Austrian government under the state liability principle. His primary argument was that through the national court's judgment, which failed to account in to account the preliminary ruling, he had suffered a financial loss.

The ECJ stated that it had not expressed a view in *Schöning-Kougebetopoulou* on whether, and if so under what conditions, the obstacle to freedom of movement for workers constituted by a loyalty bonus could be justified. The inferences drawn by the Austrian court were incorrect and it was not entitled to take the view that the matter was *acte claire*. While the ECJ held that the Austrian court had failed to follow the requirements of Art.234 EC it concluded that Community law did not expressly cover the point at issue in relation to the loyalty bonus. Consequently, having regard to all the circumstances, the infringement could not be regarded as being sufficiently serious to give rise to State liability.

The ECJ's judgment was explicit on the point that as a court of last instance, the Austrian Administrative Court *must* make a reference and accept the preliminary ruling once provided. *Köbler* is an interesting judgment because it was delivered at a time when the future of the preliminary rulings procedure is the subject of much debate both judicially and academically (Tridimas, 2003:9). In 2004 the average waiting time for a preliminary ruling, even before the impact of enlargement is fully felt, is eighteen months.

While it is crucial to maintain the uniformity of Community law, this must be balanced against the need to ensure that the judicial process remains efficient. Significant delay can undermine the principle of an effective remedy[25] which the Court places so much emphasis upon. The *Köbler* judgment may be interpreted as the Court sending out a message to the Member States, and particularly the 2004 Accession States, reminding them of their obligations when applying Community law. The ECJ stated that incorrect application of Community law by national courts can give rise to State liability and this may be interpreted as a warning of the consequences of the failure to adequately protect individual rights. *Köbler* may be considered as the ECJ making a value judgment in which it is prepared to sacrifice a degree of expediency for uniform application and effective protection of individual rights in an enlarged EU.

The relationship between Article 230 EC and Article 234 EC

Actions under Art.230 EC are commenced directly before the ECJ, whereas to employ Art.234 EC an action must first be commenced before the national court. The two Treaty provisions have different objectives and use different procedures. The restricted *locus standi* for applicants under Art.230 EC has led litigants to commence actions before national courts with the expectation that the court will make a reference to clarify the issue of Community law. There are limitations to this, most notably the limited remedies which a national court may offer by comparison to those under Art.230 EC where an applicant will be seeking annulment of the offending measure. The *Greenpeace* case illustrates how applicants may be denied access to an effective remedy both before their national court and before the ECJ.

It will be recalled that the Spanish court dismissed the domestic action and this was supported by the Opinion of Advocate General Cosmas.[26] The Advocate General stated that such a challenge would not be permitted in national courts on the grounds that an indirect challenge to a Commission decision cannot be sought through Art.234 EC. The Spanish court could control domestic administrative action and whether an EIA had been carried out. However, it lacked the competence to provide a remedy on the substantive issue of the challenge in relation to the Commission decision to finance the project in the absence of an EIA.

In *UPA* Advocate General Jacobs examined the relationship between Arts 230 and 234 EC and in particular whether through

Art.234 EC an individual could obtain an effective remedy. Advocate General Jacobs argued[27] that proceedings brought directly before the ECJ are more appropriate for determining issues of validity than proceedings pursuant to Art.234 EC and they are less liable to cause legal uncertainty for individuals and the Community Institutions. In addition to those points, the Advocate General was of the view that the Court's restrictive attitude towards individual applicants is anomalous in the light of its case-law on other aspects of judicial review and recent developments in the administrative laws of the Member States.

Focussing on the principle of an effective remedy the Advocate General was sceptical as to the suitability of Art.234 EC. The principle of effective judicial protection requires that applicants have access to a court which is competent to grant remedies capable of protecting them against the effects of unlawful measures. Access to the ECJ via Art.234 EC is not a remedy available to individual applicants as a matter of right. National courts may refuse to refer questions, and although courts of last instance are obliged to refer under Art.234 EC, appeals within the national judicial systems are liable to entail long delays. Such delays may themselves be incompatible with the principle of effective judicial protection and the need for legal certainty. The Advocate General concluded that proceedings before the ECJ under Art.230 EC are generally more appropriate for determining issues of validity than reference proceedings under Art.234 EC. This is because the Institution which adopted the measure is challenged directly and is a party to the proceedings from the beginning.

The Court rejected the reasoning of the Advocate General, though it accepted that the right to an effective remedy for individuals is part of Community law and protected by Arts.6 and 13 of the ECHR. The Court referred to the judgment in *Johnson* and stated that individuals can obtain effective remedies in their domestic legal system when they do not fit within the criteria for standing under Art.230 EC by seeking a reference under Art.234 EC. The remedy though will only be effective where the defendant is the Member State as the national court cannot review acts of the Institutions or annul a Community measure. For Harlow (2002) and Cygan (2003) this position remains unsatisfactory because it leaves a legal vacuum in the EU system of protecting individual rights that the Constitutional Treaty does not adequately fill.

Article 288 EC: The Non-contractual liability of EU Institutions

Under Art.288 EC, which is based on a principle of non-contractual liability, individuals may apply for compensation from an Institution for damage which he/she has suffered. The damage must have arisen out of the acts or omissions of the Institution and is a possible alternative to the lack of a remedy under Art.230 EC. Article 288 EC can be seen within the context of the administrative and legislative activities of the Institutions and falls within a general principle of governance and sound and efficient administration. It is therefore necessary to consider the damage arising out of the conduct complained of and according to Lasok and Bridge (1991) it is "unthinkable that every damage should be made good and every misconduct could lead to compensation".

The Court's judgments have stated that for an individual to be successful he/she must demonstrate:

(a) actual damage to the plaintiff;

(b) a causal link between the damage claimed and the conduct alleged against the institution; and

(c) the illegality of this conduct (*i.e.* a wrongful act or omission on the part of the institution, or its servants).

On the question of wrongful act the Court stated in *Zuckerfabrik Schöppenstedt*[28] that where general legislative measures are concerned then an applicant must satisfy two criteria. Firstly, the applicant must establish that there is a breach of a superior rule of law, for example the principle of non-discrimination or proportionality.[29] Secondly the applicant must demonstrate that the breach is sufficiently serious. This requires that the breach to be manifest and grave. In Joined Cases *Mulder and Others v Council and Commission*[30] the Court held that individuals must show that both the scale of loss and the degree of the Community's breach of the rule of law are both sufficiently serious to warrant the award of damages.

In *Zuckerfabrik Schöppenstedt* the ECJ has restricted the application of Art.288 EC when the nature of the Community's liability in damages is in respect of "legislative action involving measures of economic policy". According to the Court, such legislation involves "choices of economic policy", leaving a large degree of discretion in the hands of the Institution which presumably will seek to act in the public interest. This continues the trend, which is apparent when individuals seek remedies against the EU Institutions, that the Court is reluctant to award any remedy without a high degree of culpability. The remedy under Art.288 EC is independent of any action which an individual may bring under Art.230 EC. If an individual applicant has failed to achieve granted *locus standi* under Art.230 EC it is unlikely he or she will be any more successful in an action for damages under Art.288 EC.

FUNDAMENTAL RIGHTS IN EC LAW AND JUDICIAL ACTIVISM

Defining fundamental rights

The Court has consistently acknowledged the role of the individual in European integration and that protection of individual rights can be identified as one factor contributing to economic integration. Judgments, such as *Konstantinidis* and *Johnson* have referred to Community law as providing individuals with fundamental rights and through the use of this rights based language the judgments have endowed the Treaties with a constitutional quality. The Treaties contain principles which are conventionally considered as fundamental rights, such as non-discrimination under Art.12 EC. Other rights, for example equal pay under Art.141 EC and the economic rights of the Internal Market, are not traditionally within fundamental rights discourse and provide a broader interpretation of rights within Community law by comparison to that of the ECHR.

The description of Community law rights as fundamental rights by the ECJ has elevated Community law rights to a status normally reserved for a domestic Bill of Rights. This has occasionally led to conflict with national constitutional courts that have not perceived Community law rights as having the same constitutional status, or offering an equivalent level of protection by comparison to human rights provisions within domestic constitutions.[31] In *Internationale Handelsgesellschaft* and *Simmenthal* the German and Italian Supreme Courts respectively were concerned that the fundamental rights protection which the constitutions guaranteed could be undermined by Community law. The two Supreme Courts contended that in such circumstances the principle of supremacy should not apply. The ECJ rejected these concerns and held that *every* national court without exception is under an obligation to apply Community law. Furthermore, any national court which sought to reserve for itself this right to resolve such conflicts was itself acting in a manner that is incompatible with Community law. The Court of Justice stated in *Internationale Handelsgesellschaft*:

"the validity of a Community measure or its effect within a Member State cannot be affected by allegations that it runs counter to either fundamental rights as formulated by the constitution of the State or the principles of a national constitutional structure."

Similarly in *Simmenthal* the Court held:

"Every national court must, in a case within its jurisdiction, apply Community law in its entirety and protect rights which the latter confers on individuals and must accordingly set aside any provision of national law which may conflict with it, whether prior or subsequent to the Community rule."

The judgment of the Court in *Internationale Handelsgesellschaft* is noteworthy because it defines judicial attitudes towards fundamental rights in Community law. The case is more commonly referred to as *Solange I*, which translates as "so long as" from German to English. This is because in its judgment the *Budesverfassungsgericht*, the German Federal Constitutional Court (FCC), stated it would only accept European integration "so long as" it was based upon a respect for fundamental rights. The concerns of the FCC were based upon the principle that fundamental rights are entrenched in the German Constitution. Furthermore, the protection afforded to such rights in the Community legal order contained several regulatory gaps. Firstly, Community law as set out in the Treaty of Rome 1957 included no definitive list of fundamental rights. Secondly, the EEC was not a signatory to the ECHR, and in *Opinion 2/94*[32] Advocate General Jacobs confirmed that despite several Treaty developments, the EU still lacked the institutional capacity to sign the ECHR. Thirdly, the FCC was concerned that Community law might be adopted which is in breach of fundamental rights and that there is no remedy within Community law by which to challenge this. Finally, Community law in violation of fundamental rights cannot be challenged within the domestic legal systems because of its supremacy.

The ECJ addressed the concerns of the FCC by adopting rights based language in its judgment, a practice which has become an increasingly common feature of ECJ judgments. The Court stated:

"Respect for fundamental rights forms an integral part of the general principles of Community law protected by the Court of Justice. The protection of such rights, whilst *inspired by the constitutional traditions common to the Member States* (emphasis added), must be ensured within the framework of the structure and objectives of the Community."

The Court applied the ECHR as a benchmark for fundamental rights, which *all* Member States had subscribed to, and which provided a uniform minimum standard of fundamental rights protection across the Community. The ECJ stressed that European integration has its roots in the constitutional traditions of the Member States. This suggests that protection of fundamental rights in the domestic legal order constitutes not only a source of inspiration for the Court but also provides a binding standard (Lenaerts, 2003:877). Lenaerts argues that to form its judgments, the ECJ has regularly adopted teleological techniques, arising from comparative law, to draw upon the legal traditions of the Member States for guidance in the absence of an EU fundamental rights jurisprudence. The reference to legal traditions of the Member States is a mechanism through which the Court seeks to reassure and secure acceptance of its judgments by the Member States. The judgment of the Court in *Solange I* is an early example of this. For Lenaerts such comparative analyses and teleological reasoning in the application of Community law has been a key ingredient to the process of integration. Rather than being classified as judicial activism it is more appropriate to consider this as effective enforcement of Community law rights (Lenaerts, 2003:879).

Although the ECHR remains outside the Community legal order, it continues to be utilised as a point of reference for the ECJ. In *Nold*, the Court stated[33] that an additional source of inspiration for fundamental rights protection in Community law are:

"international treaties for the protection of human rights on which Member States have collaborated or of which they are signatories."

The reference to external human rights documents and comparative law techniques in *Solange I* and *Nold* is not necessarily an example of judicial activism *per se*. The judgments can be considered as the development of a human rights jurisprudence, in which a maturing judicial body draws upon established legal principles to ensure not only that human rights are protected, but that the scope of fundamental rights is extended.

The FCC in *Solange I* accepted the assurances of the ECJ and the obligations which supremacy demand but reserved the right to monitor how Community law was applied by the ECJ. In *Solange II*[34] the FCC referred to various developments in the Community since the judgment of *Solange I*, and particularly the Single European Act 1987 and case law concerning the protection of fundamental rights. It concluded that the protection of fundamental rights in the Community had reached a degree essentially comparable to the standard set by the German Constitution. On this basis the FCC stated that it would no longer exercise its jurisdiction to review secondary EC legislation by the standards of fundamental rights guaranteed by the German Constitution. It did, however, caution against a transfer of sovereign rights which may impinge upon the basic constitutional structure of Germany which encompassed the "federal order" created by the Constitution.

The judgment of the FCC in *Brunner v Maastricht Treaty*[35] signalled a shift in focus with fundamental rights no longer being the primary cause of concern. In this judgment the FCC cautioned against the doctrine of supremacy being used as a justification for the development of the EU in an undemocratic manner. In particular, the FCC was concerned that further integration may alter the separation of powers and federal and institutional structure of Germany. The FCC concluded that the transfer of powers to the EU, and particularly those concerning Economic and Monetary Union, fell within the democratic principle guaranteed by Art.38 of the German Constitution. This provision precludes the transfer of powers to the EU if it leaves the *Bundestag* devoid of sovereign powers and is the decisive factor in the FCC's judgment.

The FCC adopted a cautious stance towards deeper integration and transfer of competence to the Community. It stated that if Germany were to participate in deeper integration then this must have parliamentary approval. Furthermore, any such extension must not offend the principle of subsidiarity in Art.5 EC, which it considered to be a fundamental principle of EU law. The FCC rejected a dynamic interpretation of integration by stating that it will not accept extensions to the Treaty which occur through judgments of the ECJ. In particular the FCC stressed the need for democracy in EU decision-making and adherence to the principle of subsidiarity.

This line of cases in which the FCC engaged in a judicial dialogue with the ECJ over questions of supremacy and integration are noteworthy for several reasons. Firstly, they reinforce the position that the Community operates within a principle of the rule of law and should act where it has express competence. Secondly, Community action does not occur in isolation. It must be acceptable to the Member States and not offend long established principles of fundamental rights protection and democracy. Thirdly, the judicial dialogue in these cases demonstrates a mature legal order where the ECJ fulfils its role to guarantee the supremacy of Community law in partnership with the national courts.

Broadening fundamental rights protection in Community law

For Community law rights to be accessible to individuals they require an elevated status over domestic law which the judgments of the Court have guaranteed by the principle of supremacy. Community law has contributed to the bundle of fundamental rights which individuals enjoy through a process of judicial interpretation. One such example is the Court's judgment in the case of *Defrenne (No.2)*.[36] This case concerned the question of whether Art.141 EC, which provides that "men and women should receive equal pay for equal work", had direct effect. Ms Defrenne was an air stewardess who, during her period of employment, had been paid less than her male counterparts. The Belgian government had failed to ensure the application of Art.141 EC and Ms Defrenne claimed that as a result she had suffered direct and indirect discrimination. The ECJ concluded that while Art.141 EC did not immediately appear to satisfy the criteria of direct effect, on a teleological interpretation, the objective was clear. The aim of Art.141 EC was to prevent discrimination between men and women in employment. The ECJ's reasoning stressed a distinction between direct and indirect discrimination and concluded that only the former was caught by Art.141 EC.

In addition to responding to the formal question of whether Art.141 EC has direct effect, the Court of Justice used the judgment to provide much needed momentum to European integration. Specifically, the Court highlighted that the EEC Treaty was not restricted to merely economic considerations. The Court held that:

"Article 141 EC also forms part of the social objectives of the Community, which is not merely a economic union, but is at the same time intended, by common action to ensure social progress and seek the constant improvement in the living and working conditions of their peoples. This double aim, which is at the same time economic and social, shows that equal pay forms part of the foundations of the Community."

This statement is important as it recognises that European integration is not a self-serving process intended to be for the benefit of a political or economic elite. Community law has at its core the objective of increasing citizens' rights and creating a scheme of protection and enforcement of those rights.

In *Defrenne (No.3)*[37] the Court went further and stressed the importance of guaranteeing individual social rights and in doing so referred to other external documents, namely the European Social Charter (1969) and Conventions of the International Labour Organisation (ILO). This adds weight to the argument of Laenarts that the ECJ applies teleological reasoning and draws upon external legal traditions and norms when doing so.

Ms Defrenne challenged the different retirement ages for men and women, which her employers imposed, as being contrary to Art.141 EC. The Court stated that as this was a working condition it fell beyond the scope of the direct effect of Art.141 EC and remained an issue for national law. The Court did take this opportunity to reinforce and, arguably develop, the statement made in *Defrenne (No.2)*. The Court stated that:

"[t]he respect for fundamental personal rights is one of the general principles of Community law, the observance of which it has a duty to ensure. There can be no doubt that the elimination of discrimination based on sex forms part of those fundamental human rights."

The Court's description of the principle of non-discrimination as a "fundamental right" is noteworthy for two reasons. Firstly, the broad, and arguably less traditional, interpretation of what constitutes a fundamental right demonstrates a difference between the objectives of fundamental rights protection through the case law of the ECJ and that of the ECHR. The reference to other international documents such as the European Social Charter has a definitive integrative effect (Szyszczak, 2000:47). Rights within the European Social Charter, such as rights to collective bargaining, are not directly part of EC law, but they do form part of a wider source of international law protection of employment rights and as such should be recognised by EC law.[38]

Secondly, fundamental rights protection in Community law has a different centre of gravity to that of the ECHR. The ECJ has attached the label of fundamental right to economic and non-economic rights alike and this interpretation is evident in the broader coverage of the EU's Charter of Fundamental Rights. The ECJ's judgments have consistently recognised the need to ensure that Community law does not restrict the fundamental rights protection afforded to individuals through existing domestic and international provisions. By so doing the Court is susceptible to criticisms of judicial activism, but this criticism ignores the argument of Szyszczak and Laenarts that through teleological reasoning the Court has can *broadened* the range of individual rights.

Supremacy is not mentioned explicitly in the Treaty but is the central principle of integration. In the *Solange I* judgment the ECJ held that adherence to the principle of supremacy overrides even domestic constitutional provisions. The next part of this chapter considers supremacy and the techniques that the ECJ has employed to guarantee supremacy in the absence of an EU constitution. The discussion begins by examining Art.10 EC, often described as the principle of solidarity and which acts as a binding force on the Member States in the integration process.

ARTICLE 10 EC: THE PRINCIPLE OF SOLIDARITY

Article 10 EC is the key article of the EC Treaty and closest to which the Treaty comes to refer to the principle of supremacy. This provision requires Member States not to act contrary to the objectives of the Treaty. Article 10 EC states:

"Member States shall take all appropriate measures, whether general or particular, to ensure fulfilment of the obligations arising out of this Treaty or resulting from action taken by the institutions of the Community. They shall facilitate the achievement of the Community's tasks.

They shall abstain from any measure which could jeopardise the attainment of the objectives of this Treaty."

This provision appears to be a rudimentary requirement for Member States who have voluntarily signed the Treaty. Not only does it require Member States to refrain from acting contrary to Community law, but also to take positive steps to ensure that Treaty obligations are fulfilled. Consequently Art.10 EC is referred to as the principle of solidarity. This solidarity is required to achieve the objectives set out in Arts 2, 3 and 14 EC.

Article 10 EC guarantees communitarian action and supremacy at the domestic level and compliments the Community decision-making process. According to Temple Lang (1997:6) Art.10 EC requires both administrative *and* judicial institutions to work actively to secure the observance of Community law and to prevent action which is inconsistent with the attainment of the Treaty's objectives. The ECJ has recognised this is essential for the uniform application of EC law. In *Factortame (No.2)*[39] the ECJ stated that:

"In accordance with the case-law of the Court, it is for the national courts, in application of the principle of cooperation laid down in Art.10 of the EEC Treaty, to ensure the legal protection which persons derive from the direct effect of provisions of Community law." (paragraph 19)

The Court's interpretation of Art.10 EC has given the provision a constitutional quality. The ECJ has recognised that Art.10 EC provides scope for teleological interpretation to secure the supremacy of Community law and there are four key mechanisms which have been developed. The first three principles are direct effect, indirect effect and state liability. These are mechanisms that have arisen out of the judicial dialogue under Art.234 EC and their primary purpose is to ensure the unfettered availability of EC law rights in the Member States.

A final mechanism, namely the principle of effective remedies, requires Member States to compensate individuals in circumstances when their Community law rights have been infringed. The principle of effective remedies, firmly within the ambit of Art.10 EC, operates as a deterrent to discourage Member States from acting contrary to Community law. In circumstances where individual rights have been infringed, for example the failure to transpose a directive within the specified time period, national courts will award damages to the individual against the Member State responsible if a loss has been suffered.[40] The purpose of such an award is to act as a deterrent for future breaches and to compensate the individual for the infringement of their rights. In *Marshall (No. 2)*,[41] the ECJ held that any remedy awarded to an individual must be effective thereby prohibiting national legislation from placing an upper ceiling on the damages which can be awarded.

THE PRINCIPLE OF SUPREMACY

The supremacy of Community law is an objective rather than being a technique developed by the Court when implementing Community law. In this sense it is different from direct effect and the other mechanisms mentioned above. The commitment of the ECJ to the principle of supremacy is the single most identifiable reason why, despite the absence of a constitution Community law has secured sophisticated and deep integration between the Member States.

The principle of supremacy can be explained in the following terms. In situations of conflict between EU law and national law, EU law must prevail. The simplicity of defining the concept hides a rather more complex relationship that exists in the interaction between national law and procedure and the ECJ. Supremacy is now largely taken for granted, though some challenges still occur. In the *Metric Martyrs Case*[42] the applicant challenged a Directive requiring produce that was not pre-packed to be sold in metric and not imperial measurements. The High Court dismissed the applicant's defence, which was based on the argument that as the Weights and Measures Act 1985 entered in to force after UK accession, this later statute impliedly repealed the European Communities Act (ECA) 1972. In such circumstances the defendant argued that UK law takes precedence over EU law. The English court dismissed these arguments and held that the ECA 1972, the primary legislation which provides for UK accession to the EU, has a "constitutional quality" which prevents implied repeal and thereby suggesting a degree of entrenchment.

The ECJ has established a clear body of case law which provides guidance to national courts, regarding their obligations to protect individual rights under Community law. The origins of the Court's commitment to the supremacy principle can be traced to the decision of *Van Gend en Loos* in which the Court stated that the EEC Treaty had "created a new legal order" which, in international law terms, was different both in substance and effect to other treaties, for example the ECHR. The Court stated that the EEC Treaty was intended to:

"..confer rights upon individuals which became part of their legal heritage."

Though not stated expressly by the Court, this declaration would only make sense if EU law were supreme. The Court expanded this logic in *Costa v ENEL*.[43] This case is important because it demonstrates how persons who are often referred to as "opportunistic litigants" have utilised Community law rights. This group can be defined as individuals who enforce Community rights before the ECJ to an extent which may not have been anticipated by the Treaty makers.

In *Costa v ENEL*, Costa was an Italian lawyer and small shareholder in Edison Volta (an Italian electricity company) sought to challenge a 1962 law which nationalised the electricity production and distribution industries. He refused to pay a bill of less than two Euro and was brought before the lowest court in Italy who referred the case to the ECJ for a preliminary ruling under Art.234 EC. The Italian government was adamant that no reference was necessary in such circumstances and that the obligation of the Italian court was to apply national law. The ECJ rejected this view and stated that *any* national court is entitled to seek an interpretation on the application of Community law from the ECJ:

"The integration into the laws of each Member State of provisions which derive from the Community, and more generally the terms and spirit of the Treaty, make it impossible for the States, as a corollary, to accord precedence to a unilateral and subsequent measure over a legal system accepted by them on a basis of reciprocity. Such a measure cannot therefore be inconsistent with that legal system. The executive force of Community law cannot vary from one State to another in deference to subsequent domestic laws, without jeopardising the attainment of the objectives of the Treaty..."

The statement has its roots firmly in the obligation arising out of Art.10 EC. By the reference to the "terms and spirit of the Treaty" the Court goes beyond merely stating that Community law takes precedence over national law. The intention of the Court is, through the use of teleological interpretation, to demonstrate that Art.10 EC provides scope for a dynamic interpretation of the Treaty. European law is to be considered as a new legal order which has a broader objective of integration. The Court places itself at the centre of this integration process and confirms that it will strike down measures which undermine the principle of supremacy.

Accepting the supremacy principle has proved problematic for all Member States. The cases of *Solange I* and *Simmenthal* demonstrate the conflict that national supreme courts have encountered when reconciling obligations of protecting fundamental rights under Community law and guaranteeing domestic constitutional provisions. In the UK the *Factortame* litigation demonstrates how the constitutional principle of parliamentary sovereignty has not always sat comfortably with supremacy (Gravells 1990:180; Craig, 1991:222). In this case the UK incorrectly transposed legislation under the Common Fisheries Policy and required that boats fishing in UK territorial waters were 75 per cent British owned. These requirements *prima facie* infringed Arts 12 and 43 EC. The applicants' sought an interlocutory injunction against the Crown to suspend the Merchant Shipping Act 1988 which implemented these requirements. This temporary injunction was to operate until such time as the question of whether the Act was compatible with Community law had been resolved. At first instance the English High Court rejected the applicants' claim and stated that interlocutory injunctions were not permitted against the Crown by virtue of s.21 of the Crown Proceedings Act 1947.

On appeal, the House of Lords sought a preliminary ruling from the ECJ asking whether it could dis-apply a domestic statute, namely the Crown Proceedings Act, and award an interim injunction. The Court responded:[44]

"It must be added that the full effectiveness of Community law would be just as much impaired if a rule of national law could prevent a court seised of a dispute governed by Community law from granting interim relief in order to ensure the full effectiveness of the judgment to be given on the existence of the rights claimed under Community law. It follows that a court which in those circumstances would grant interim relief. if it were not for a rule of national law, is obliged to set aside that rule."

Lord Bridge in the House of Lords stated in his judgment:

"Parliament has always loyally accepted the obligation to make appropriate and prompt amendments. Thus there is nothing in any way novel in according supremacy to rules of Community law in those areas to which they apply and to insist that. In the protection of rights under Community law, national courts must not be inhibited by rules of national law from granting interim relief in appropriate cases is no more than a logical recognition of that supremacy."

In circumstances where national law inhibited the individual from enjoying the rights granted under Community law, then it is the obligation of the national court to set that law aside. In this case the duty required the House of Lords to dis-apply the relevant provision of the Crown Proceedings Act. Though this challenges the principle of parliamentary sovereignty their Lordships viewed this course of action as being a necessity arising out of UK membership of the Community and based upon the provisions of s.2 (2) and (4) ECA 1972. The ECA while not using the word "supremacy" states at s.2 (4) that:

"The provision that may be made under subsection (2) above includes, subject to Schedule 2 to this Act, any such provision (of any such extent) as might be made by Act of Parliament, and any enactment passed or to be passed, other than one contained in this Part of this Act, shall be construed and have effect subject to the foregoing provisions of this section; but, except as may be provided by any Act passed after this Act, Schedule 2 shall have effect in connection with the powers conferred by this and the following sections of this Act to make Orders in Council and regulations."

The House of Lords in *Factortame* interpreted this section purposively:

"The words 'is to be construed and take effect subject to directly enforceable Community rights' are to be understood *as having the same effect as if a section were incorporated in to the Merchant Shipping Act 1988 which enacted that the provisions with regard to the registration of British Fishing Vessels* (emphasis added) were to be 'without prejudice to the directly enforceable Community rights of nationals of any member state of the EC.'"

The effect of their Lordships' judgment is to impliedly include in to the Merchant Shipping Act 1988, and *all* UK legislation, a proviso that national law does not restrict the fundamental individual rights which are granted by Community law. The statement of the High Court in the *Metric Martyrs case*, that the ECA 1972 has a "constitutional quality" has the effect of entrenching the ECA in to UK law and consequently provides an enduring guarantee of supremacy of EU law within the UK (Wade, 1996).

THE DIRECT EFFECT OF COMMUNITY LAW

Direct effect concerns the content of a legislative provision and refers to its capacity to give rise to rights for individuals which can be enforced before national courts. Direct effect is an important constitutional provision and the means through which individual rights are guaranteed in the domestic law (Pescatore, 1983:158). It is important to distinguish direct effect from direct applicability, which refers to the status of a Community provision in the domestic legal order (Winter, 1972:425). Treaty Articles and Regulations are directly applicable because they do not require any transposition to be implemented in the domestic legal order. Directives do not have automatic direct applicability, as Member States implement these through existing domestic procedures, but do so once the transitional period has expired.[45]

Direct effect is not a universal feature of all Community provisions and this includes Treaty Articles. Individuals can plead a rule of Community law before their national courts but this will only occur if the criteria discussed in Chapter 1 have been fulfilled. Direct effect is arguably the most important mechanism through which the supremacy of Community law is maintained and national courts are under an obligation to ensure rights contained within the legislation are available and should use Art.234 EC when they have doubt. The ECJ has consistently held that both Treaty Articles and Regulations have the potential of direct effect. Through cases such as *Van Gend en Loos*, *Van Duyn* and *Defrenne v Sabena* the Court has established prerequisite criteria for a provision to have direct effect. These are:

- The provision is clear and unconditional,

- The rights contained within the measure are expressed with sufficient precision, and

- In the case of directives only, the date for implementation of the directive has passed.

Application of these principles to Treaty provisions and Regulations raises little difficulty and they will commonly have direct effect. The area of controversy where the ECJ has been most active is with regard to directives. If implemented correctly, individuals can rely upon the rights contained within a directive before their national court. In circumstances where the directive is incorrectly implemented, or not implemented at all, then providing that the transitional period has expired, an individual can rely on the directive itself. This is despite that Art.249 EC addresses a directive at Member States not individuals. In situations of incorrect implementation national courts are required, through Art.10 EC to interpret national law, so far as possible, in a manner which ensures compatibility with the directive. This teleological technique is referred to as indirect effect and is considered below.

In circumstances of incorrect implementation it may be possible to rely on the directive itself, provided that it has fulfilled the three criteria outlined above. The one restriction is that an individual can rely upon the directive in vertical relationships only. That is where the other party is the State, or according to the ECJ in *Foster v British Gas*,[46] an "emanation" of it. The Court has held in *Marshall (No.1)*[47] that directives cannot have horizontal direct effect and be used by one individual against another. The Court's reasoning is based upon the premise that the it is the State's obligation to transpose the directive. Consequently it is the State, and not any private party, which is responsible for the absence of those rights from domestic law. This reasoning has been criticised as restricting the scope of directive (Tridimas, 1994:621; Lenz et al, 2000:512).[48] By contrast to directives, the Court has held that Treaty articles can have horizontal direct effect.[49]

In the context of Directives, the requirement that the other party be the State or an emanation of it is based on the principle that directives are only binding on the State and do not create enforceable rights *inter partes*. Yet since the 1980s the structure and competence of the State has changed profoundly, particularly with many State functions being transferred to the private sector. The modern understanding of the State is one based upon wholesale privatisation of certain sectors, for example utility services. Other structural changes include the development of public/private partnership financing arrangements, quasi-autonomous regulators who ensure competition and protect consumer interests, and contracting out of services which the State traditionally provided, to ensure value for money for the taxpayer. The State has reduced in size and with it the opportunity for individuals to rely upon vertical direct effect.

Foster v British Gas concerned the question of whether a measure could have direct effect against a recently privatised utility company. While no longer part of the State, the Court held that the company remained an emanation of the State. Broadly this suggests that the company retains the exercise of some public function and has organs which are closely linked to the State. The Court highlighted several criteria which may lead to the conclusion that the body in question is an emanation of the State. The body should be:

- Subject to the authority and control of the State;
- Have special powers for that purpose,
- Provide a public service.

It is not clear from the judgment whether the "test" is cumulative or that it is sufficient to satisfy only one of the requirements. Furthermore while some organs may fit within the definition within one Member State, there may be a difference in understanding and application of the criteria in another.

Despite the divergent interpretation of the State, both public sector and privatised entities would appear to fulfil the *Foster* requirements. This raises a number of questions, not least whether it is appropriate for public concerns to be regulated under the same conditions as those within the private sector. The growth of competition within the Internal Market and decline in the role of the State inevitably call in to question the interpretation of the Court in *Foster*. Can the *Foster* criteria remain relevant propositions in an EU where the emphasis has shifted towards deregulation and competition? Szyszczak (1996:352) argues that the Court in *Foster* was primarily concerned with ensuring that Community law rights were available as widely as possible through the principle of direct effect. She suggests that this judgment is part of a wider objective of making Europe more relevant to its citizens by enabling them to actively pursue their Treaty rights.

In *Foster* the Court was not concerned with wider economic and philosophical questions of what the role of the modern State should be. The Court was merely expressing a view on the relationship between the State and a privatised entity a short time after its privatisation. Furthermore, this judgment was delivered at a time when privatisation had not become widespread within the Community. Its sole purpose was to maximise the availability of Community law rights to citizens. It is only in the light of developments within the Member States since *Foster* that the continued relevance of the "test" can be called in to question. Perhaps the most significant point about the judgment is that the Court has not applied the *Foster* criteria since its 1989 judgment, though the Court remains as concerned with the effective protection of EC rights. Judgments such as *Doughty v Rolls Royce* in the English Court of Appeal cast further doubt on the application of the *Foster* test.[50] In this case the Court of Appeal held that Rolls Royce did not provide a public service when it was a nationalised industry.

THE PRINCIPLE OF INDIRECT EFFECT

The provisions of directives which contain specific rights for individuals and are clear and unambiguous may, after the expiry of the transitional period be pleaded against the State. Such rights cannot be pleaded against a private party as directives have vertical and *not* horizontal direct effect.

The result of this is that there is a clear discrepancy in the enjoyment of rights depending upon the relationship the individual enjoys with the State. For example, a woman who is compulsorily retired at the age of 60 by a private sector employer, which is in breach of the principle of equal treatment in Directive 76/207/EEC, cannot rely upon the provisions of the Directive. If the woman were employed by the State she would be able to utilise the rights within the Directive to challenge the decision. Clearly such a distinction is unsatisfactory, particularly as the role of the State in its capacity as an employer has altered.

Interpretation of Community law: The Von Colson *principle*

The Court has addressed these problems through teleological means, using the principle of *effet utile* or effectiveness of Community law. In *Von Colson v Land Nordhein Westfalen*[51] the issue centred on the implementation of the Equal Treatment Directive 76/207/EEC. Two women who had applied for posts in a German prison had been rejected on grounds of sex, despite German transposition of the Directive in to German law. The remedies which were open to the German Labour Court appeared to be limited to the re-imbursement of their travelling expenses to attend the interview at which they were ultimately discriminated against. The German court, using the Art.234 EC procedure, referred questions to the ECJ concerning the adequacy of remedies within the context of the Directive.

The ECJ stated that it is the *duty* of national courts to interpret provisions of national law "in the light of the wording and purpose of the directive".[52] Accordingly, if the national court had the discretion to do so, it should exercise its powers in a manner that remedies for sex discrimination should operate as a deterrent to such conduct. The Court considered this teleological approach as another method through which the objectives of Art.10 EC could be guaranteed.

Von Colson was a case which concerned transposing legislation. But what would be the position in circumstances where existing national legislation conflicted with Community law? In such circumstances do national courts have the same duty to interpret national legislation to ensure compatibility with Community law? Furthermore would the teleological rule apply in circumstances where there was a horizontal relationship? In *Von Colson* the relationship was a vertical one, the defendant was the State and the Directive did not fulfil the requirements of direct effect. The Court addressed the issue of horizontal indirect effect in the *Marleasing*.[53]

Marleasing concerned litigation in Spain between two private parties. The ECJ held that with regard to the question of pre-existing legislation this made no difference to the fact that the litigation concerned two private parties. All national law had to be interpreted to give effect to Community law without exception, even though the State was not a direct party to the proceedings. The Court's argument was that Member States are under an obligation to create the conditions for private parties to exercise their Community law rights. The Court suggested that emanating from Art.10 EC is a requirement for national courts to interpret national law to ensure compatibility with Community law, and according to *Marleasing*, this duty arose irrespective of the source of Community law. The duty of harmonious interpretation was not just a rule to mitigate against the limited scope of direct effect of directives. Interpretation, alongside the principle of direct effect, was a tool of securing supremacy (Hartley, 1998:212).

One question raised by *Marleasing*, which the ECJ did not answer, was what, if any, limits were there to the power of national courts to interpret legislation to ensure conformity? Would there be circumstances where the national legislation and Community law were so far apart that interpretation would not be possible? The Court has refined and narrowed the *Marleasing* principle and addressed this issue through subsequent judgments (Craig, 1997:525).

In *Kolpinghuis* the Court stated that no criminal liability could flow, by reason of interpretation, from the provisions of a directive which a Member State had failed to implement. Similarly a non-implemented Directive could not give rise to obligations for an individual. In *Arcaro*,[54] the Court accepted that there would be limits to interpretation as a correctional tool. National law should, according to the ECJ, not be interpreted to attribute to it a meaning which it clearly was not intended to have. In such circumstances the national court should make a declaration of incompatibility with Community law.

The *Von Colson* judgment has created difficulties which the House of Lords identified in *Duke v GEC Reliance*.[55] This case concerned compatibility of the Sex Discrimination Act 1975 with Directive 76/207/EEC. Their Lordships stated that as the UK Act was passed before the Directive it would "be most unfair to the respondent to distort the construction of the 1975 Sex Discrimination Act in order to accommodate the meaning of the Equal Treatment Directive". Their Lordships were concerned that through interpretative techniques they would adopt the mantle of legislature and provide the Act with a meaning which Parliament had not intended.

The House of Lords has subsequently shown greater willingness to apply a more purposive interpretation to Equal Treatment legislation.[56] In *Webb v EMO Cargo*,[57] the House of Lords interpreted the Sex Discrimination Act to conform with Directive 76/207/EEC on equal treatment in a manner which the Court of Appeal had previously rejected as a distortion of the statute. Their Lordships held that this could not be done if the impact of such purposive interpretation was to alter the meaning of domestic legislation. Following the ECJ judgment in the case of *Wagner Miret*[58] it would appear that the broad interpretative approach of *Marleasing* has been curtailed and in this case the ECJ stated that national courts should only interpret domestic law as far as possible to meet the requirements of the directive. Otherwise the national court should declare the national law incompatible leaving the individual to bring an action for damages against the offending state.

Indirect effect can only be of assistance to a litigant where national legislation exists and it is irrelevant as to whether it pre or post-dates the Community measure. This still leaves one situation outstanding, namely where there is an absence of national implementing legislation and where an individual has suffered a loss resulting from a failure by the State to implement the directive. In these circumstances it appeared as if an individual, notwithstanding Art.10 EC, had no means of recourse. A failure to implement a measure which did not have direct effect also meant that there was no scope for indirect effect. The Court of

Justice filled this legal vacuum, by developing the principle of indirect effect and creating an all-encompassing principle of State liability.

THE PRINCIPLE OF STATE LIABILITY

The Francovich *judgment*

In *Francovich* the ECJ acknowledged a Community law remedy which requires Member States to pay compensation for loss or damage arising out a breach of Community law by the State (Ross, 1993:525). The State liability principle is based upon deterrence, but also, through the requirement to pay compensation, provides tangible proof that Community rights have a real value to EU citizens (Szyszczak, 1996:353). The *Francovich* case is a good example of this principle.

In *Francovich* the Italian government had failed to implement Council Directive 80/987/EEC which required the establishment of a system for guaranteeing to employees the payment of unpaid wages in the event of their employer's insolvency. The Commission had already brought a successful infringement action under Art.226 EC against Italy for its failure to transpose the Directive. Francovich and Bonifaci (the second applicant) had lost wages when their employer went in to liquidation. They commenced proceedings against the Italian State claiming it had a duty to pay their wages either through accepting the guarantees contained within the Directive, or, as compensation for the State's failure to transpose the legislation. The ECJ stated that that Directive did not meet the criteria of direct effect because the provision lacked sufficient clarity and precision by leaving discretion to the State as to *how* the guarantee scheme would operate in practice. Yet the Court stated that the Directive had a clear objective of protecting employees in circumstances similar to those of the applicants. In developing the principle of State liability the Court revisited its previous "constitutional" judgments to support its reasoning.

The Court, drawing upon the judgments of *Van Gend en Loos* and *Costa v ENEL*, reiterated that Community law is a distinct legal order which has created rights for individuals and corresponding obligations for Member States. It is the duty of Member States to ensure that these rights are fully available to all citizens and in these circumstances it would be inconsistent with the principle of full effectiveness of Community law if the applicants were denied compensation for the failure by the Italian State to implement the Directive. The Court held:[59]

"It follows that the principle of State liability for harm caused to individuals by breaches of Community law for which the State can be held responsible is inherent in the system of the Treaty."

Art.10 EC places upon Member States an "obligation to nullify the unlawful consequences of a breach of Community law".[60] It remains a moot point whether the Court in *Francovich* created a new remedy or merely refined an existing one. Either way, the significance of the judgment cannot be understated primarily because of the requirement that each Member State should recognise a Community law remedy for breaches of Community law and not simply the application of a national remedy. The effect is to create a scheme for enforcement of individual rights which is based on Community law principles and judicial dialogue (Harlow, 1996:203). At the Community level the Commission will enforce a failure to implement a measure through Art.226 EC. At the national level an individual will seek compensation for the loss suffered which arises from the breach and this is based on the principle of State liability. Crucially there is no need for a provision to be directly effective for an individual to bring a successful action.

In circumstances where there is a complete failure to implement a directive the Court in *Francovich* stated that three conditions are necessary to give rise to liability. These are:

• The directive grants rights to individuals

• The content of those rights is identifiable form the directive itself

• There is a causal link between the breach of Community law by the Member State and the actual loss suffered by the individual

Though State liability is a Community principle it is for national courts to apply it in the appropriate circumstances. This is commonly referred to as the national autonomy procedure and is part of the dialogue that exists between national courts and the ECJ. Though application of the principle is reserved for national courts, the ECJ has made it clear that State liability is central to ensuring the objectives of Art.10 EC and that national courts have a duty to give effect to Community law. In *Francovich* the Court stated:[61]

"It is in accordance with the rules of national law that the State must make reparation for the consequences of the harm caused. In the absence of any Community legislation, it is a matter for the internal legal order of each Member State to determine the competent courts and lay down the detailed procedural rules for legal proceedings intended fully to safeguard the rights which individuals derive from Community law. . ."

In establishing the principle of State liability *Francovich* left several question unanswered regarding the scope and application of the principle. The principle of direct effect was a clear method through which Community rights could be enforced in domestic courts in all cases, including incorrect implementation and non-implementation. In contrast, the *Francovich* judgment only referred to situations of non-implementation of Community law. Could State liability also apply to situations of incorrect implementation of Community law, or where a Member State had failed to adapt existing legislation? If the answer was "yes" then State liability would be more than just a remedy of last resort. Furthermore in situations of failure to adapt existing legislation, for example as occurred in *Marleasing*, State liability is a *more* effective remedy and deterrence than indirect effect as it dispenses with the need to consider horizontal indirect effect.

The *Francovich* judgment only provided limited guidance as to whether the principle applied only in situations where fault could be established. Would *Francovich* also apply to non-fault situations? Craig argued, and this has been the general approach of the Court that when assessing the concept of fault the Court should seek assistance from the standard of non-contractual liability in Art.288 EC (Craig, 1993:597). In the Joined Cases of *Brasserie du Pêcheur* and *Factortame III*[62] the Court addressed these questions refining and extending the principle of State liability.

Extending the State liability principle

The *Brasserie du Pêcheur* litigation involved a claim by a French brewer against Germany for loss of profits incurred when it was prevented from selling its product because the beer did not meet the German Beer Purity laws. The Court had already held that the purity laws amounted to a breach of Art.28 EC on the free movement of goods.[63] In *Factortame III* the claim was made by Spanish fisherman who were not able to secure access to British fishing quotas and which the Court had ruled breached Arts 12 and 43 EC.

The Art.234 EC reference raised several questions. Firstly did the principle of State liability apply to breaches which arose from legislative measures? Secondly, was direct effect available in situations where the Community legislation in question satisfied the criteria for direct effect? Finally what were the criteria for State liability in these circumstances?

The Court stated categorically that State liability is available in *all* circumstances in which the State causes harm. The presence of the direct effect principle is irrelevant and will include situations, as in these two cases, where there are breaches of the Treaty itself. The Court's judgment expanded upon the basic State liability principle established in *Francovich* where the Court referred to Art.10 EC as a justification for State liability. In these two judgments the Court followed this reasoning and expressly referred to Art.220 EC which requires the Court to ensure that the Community law is observed and Art.288 EC on the non-contractual liability of the EU Institutions.

Article 288 EC provides the foundation for the elaboration of the conditions for liability in *Brasserie du Pêcheur* and *Factortame III*. The Court stated that the three part "test" in *Francovich* is relevant in the cases of non-implementation but reformulated the conditions under which liability will be established (Craig 1993:596):[64]

- The rule of Community law must confer rights on individuals;

- The breach must be "sufficiently serious"; and

- There is a direct causal link between the breach and the damage suffered by the injured party.

The Court held at paragraph 55 that a breach of Community law by a Member State will be sufficiently serious if it "manifestly and gravely disregards the limits of its discretion". The concept of "manifest and grave" is borrowed from the *Schöppenstedt* judgment concerning the application of Art.288 EC. The Court provided some limited guidance as to what amounts to manifest and grave:

". . . a breach of Community law will be sufficiently serious if it has persisted despite a judgment finding the infringement in question be established, or a preliminary ruling or settled case law of the Court on the matter from which it is clear that the conduct in question constituted an infringement."

The Court also examined the basis of liability and the judgment provides that the existence of a "sufficiently serious breach" requires the presence of fault. What actually amounts to a sufficiently serious breach is a matter for national courts to decide. The House of Lords in *Factorame V*[65] provided greater clarity, and their Lordships suggested that a deliberate and prolonged breach, which is not remedied despite being brought to the attention of the Member State, would be manifest and grave and therefore sufficiently serious (Cygan, 2000:124). In *Factorame V* the House of Lords applied significant weight to the fact that the Commission had notified the UK government on numerous occasions that the Merchant Shipping Act 1988 was contrary to Community law. It is therefore necessary to distinguish between a breach of Community law which is inadvertent, or remedied immediately upon being notified to the Member State by the Commission and one where the breach is persistent.

What has been the effect of *Brasserie du Pêcheur* and whether a breach actually gives rise to State liability? In *Denkavit*[66] and *British Telecommunications*[67] a failure to implement a directive where the directive was vague and unclear as to its content did not amount to a sufficiently serious breach. By comparison a complete failure to implement a directive will be very likely to amount to a sufficiently serious breach,[68] as was a restriction of rights under Art.28 EC.[69]

As with the concept of an emanation of the State under *Foster* the Court has adopted a broad interpretation of the State for the purposes of *Francovich* liability. In *Köbler* the Court confirmed, that the principle of State liability extends to national courts including supreme courts. The Court also held that in line with national autonomy procedure it is for the national law of Member States to determine the form of action for claiming damages for a breach of Community law by such a Court. To date the *Brasserie de Pêcheur* conditions are applied but in the case of a national supreme Court the breach must be particularly manifest and grave.[70]

The principle of State liability has arguably contributed more than any other principle developed by the Court to constitutionalise the Treaties. It requires Member States to pay compensation for a breach of Community law and, as suggested by Szyszczak, provides a direct connection between Community law and the citizen who receives compensation for the loss suffered arising from the breach.

The principle of State liability has also ensured the effectiveness of Community law. In *Courage Ltd v Crehan*[71] the Court ruled that an individual could not be prohibited from relying on Art.81 EC because he had been a party to an anti-competitive agreement. The significance of this judgment is that the principle of State liability was applied in circumstances involving two private individuals, a question which had been debated since *Francovich* (Van Gerven, 1996:597). The Court held that a right of action in damages under the State liability principle must be available to an individual before national courts. In this case the Court focussed not on the issue of national procedural autonomy but rather on the nature and importance of the substantive Community law right at issue. The Court declared the hierarchical superiority of free competition as a constitutional norm protected by the EC Treaty and by the Court:[72]

"It should be borne in mind, first of all, that the Treaty has created its own legal order, which is integrated into the legal systems of the Member States and which their courts are bound to apply. The subjects of that legal order are not only the Member States but also their nationals. Just as it imposes burdens on individuals, Community law is also intended to give rise to rights which become part of their legal assets. Those rights arise not only where they are expressly granted by the Treaty but also by virtue of obligations which the Treaty imposes in a clearly defined manner both on individuals and on the Member States and the Community institutions (see the judgments in Case 26/62 *Van Gend en Loos* [1963] ECR 1, Case 6/64 *Costa* [1964] ECR 585 and Joined Cases C–6/90 and C–9/90 *Francovich and Others* [1991] ECR I–5357, paragraph 31)."

The language of the Court is interesting because it has a constitutional quality through reference to the judgments in *Van Gend en Loos* and *Francovich*. These judgments have made a significant contribution to the protection of Community law rights. The Court also refers to Art.81 EC as being a "fundamental right" which reinforces the idea of constitutionality.

The judgment has a broader impact because it also supports the existence of an economic constitution. Economic rights such as Art.81 EC are so fundamental that they must be accessible to individuals in horizontal situations and can be protected through the principle of State liability. In *Courage Ltd v Crehan* the Court has extended the scope of Treaty rights by coming back to first principles for the enforcement of these rights. The judgment reinforces the settled view that Community law is "a new legal order" that provides individuals with a bundle of rights and Member States together with the ECJ are under a positive obligation to ensure individual rights are effectively protected.

A COHERENT STRATEGY FOR ENFORCING COMMUNITY RIGHTS?

The techniques of the Court considered above provide an integrated scheme of principles through which an individual may enforce Treaty rights. In the words of Art.10 EC they provide individuals with the tools to ensure that Member States "take all appropriate measures, whether general or particular to ensure the fulfilment of the obligations". Through this the Court has created a strategy by which the Treaty provisions have become constitutionalised. Consequently, the supremacy of Community law, and access to Community law rights has been achieved through these principles.

The judgments of the Court have reflected the objectives of the Treaty which can be defined as the written will of the Member States. The judgments have also perpetuated closer integration through the Court's us of teleological techniques. Whether the Court has been a judicially activist institution remains a matter of debate. On one level, judgments such as *Von Colson*, *Cassis de Dijon*, *Francovich* and *Courage v Crehan* are intended to give effect to Treaty provisions and permit individuals to enforce their Community law rights. On another, judgments such as *Cassis* and *Courage* have defined the extent of these Treaty rights by stating the basic principles of economic integration in the absence of such statements from the Treaty makers. For example, the principle of mutual recognition established by the Court in *Cassis* formed the philosophical basis of the 1985 White Paper on the Completion of the Internal Market.

The judgment in *Courage* is an expression by the Court of the interconnectedness between the free movement rules and competition law which form the basis of the modern governance techniques of the Internal Market. Consequently, the techniques used by the Court to enforce Internal Market rights have created an economic constitution forming the cornerstone of EU integration. The creation of the Internal Market is inconceivable without the contribution of the ECJ to ensure universal application of the common rules of Community law. The Court has played a central part in upholding the legal order established in the Community and this is a legal order founded upon the pursuit of economic integration.

ECONOMIC INTEGRATION
THROUGH GOVERNANCE

During the early years of the Common Market the original
Member States and the Community Institutions interpreted the
economic aims of the customs union and Common Market
broadly. There was a period of "eurosclerosis", but between the
1960s and the early 1980s the Member States were able, and willing, to develop a wide range of European policies and adopt legislation to create a Common Market in relation to a common
agricultural policy, a competition and state aid policy, an embryonic environmental policy, a consumer policy and, albeit *ad hoc*
in form, an industrial policy and a social policy for the
Community which shored up the four basic economic freedoms
of the Common Market: the free movement of goods, workers,
services and capital. At the Paris Summit of the Heads of State
or Government in October 1972 the political will to move the
then European Economic Community into a wider range of
social activities was expressly acknowledged in the Final
Communiqué:

"Economic expansion is not an end in itself. . . . It should result in
an improvement in the quality of life as well as standards of living. As befits the genius of Europe, particular attention will be
given to intangible values and to protecting the environment, so
that progress may really be put at the service of mankind."

Following on from this declaration of intent, the Council began
to explore how to develop a social policy, a migration policy, as
well as regional and development policy, environmental measures and a health and safety at work legislative programme.
Progress at the European level was hampered by the need for
unanimity voting in the general market building legal base of
Art.100 EC (now Art.94 EC) and the residual legal base of Art.235
EC (now Art.308 EC). In sensitive areas, such as migration policy,
use was made of non-binding measures, for example Council
Resolutions, showing a public recognition of the necessity for

Community-wide action, but a lack of political consensus on *how* this should be achieved and the *content* of any Community law. This is an example of consensus building through soft law.

A link was made between the use of the (old) Arts 100 and 235 EC and the objective set out in Art.3(f) EC of

"the institution of a system ensuring that competition in the common market is not distorted".

The argument was made that different legislation in the Member States would affect production and marketing costs, creating unequal conditions of competition between producers in different Member States. This justified Community intervention to ensure that all producers throughout the Community were bound by the same rules.

Until Opinion 2/94, *Accession by the EC to the ECHR*[1] (on the scope of Art.308 EC) and the *Tobacco Advertising*[2] ruling (on the scope of Art.95 EC) it was presumed that if the political will of the Member States was present (because such legislation was adopted on a unanimous vote under the earlier provisions), then Community legislation could be adopted without too close an inspection as to whether the measure was a necessary component of the market integration project. In one case, concerning an infringement action against Italy, the Italian government attempted to defend its non-implementation of a Directive on detergents by challenging the Community's competence to use Art.94 EC as the legal base for such a Directive. The Court rejected the argument giving its support to the use of harmonisation measures to iron out inconsistencies between national laws even where such inconsistencies did not create an impediment to the trade in goods and services.[3]

If we look at the Preambles to Community legislation adopted during this period there was little detailed evidence adduced to justify Community harmonisation measures. Despite some concerns at the national level on the scope of Community law-making powers[4] the political will of the Member States legitimated the Community's law-making competence and practice.

It was a formative period in developing a culture where European law-making powers were construed in a broad way, once the political consensus had been reached. This allowed the Member States to enhance the role of the Council and achieved a sense of security: control and ownership of the Community decision-making process. The role of consensus building during this era cannot be underestimated. It avoided successfully the resort to litigation which materialised when law-making powers were transferred to qualified majority voting (QMV) and when the European Parliament was admitted into a more active role in Community law-making.

THE SINGLE EUROPEAN ACT 1987

When the SEA came into force in 1987 a sea-change in the evolution of the European integration project occurred (Craig, 2002). The SEA 1987 introduced QMV to a number of existing legal bases for European law-making powers, the most important change being the introduction of what is now Art.95 EC (the old Art.100a EC) to allow for measures to complete the Internal Market. This invigorated an approach to using all the provisions for QMV in the EC Treaty, rather than striving for consensus and unanimity in the Council decision-making process. The Member States were, for the first time, faced with the reality of adopting a *communautaire* approach and accepting that they could be out-voted in the Council and be obliged to implement European leg-islation within their national systems which they objected to in the Council Meeting.

During this period changes in attitude allowed for the begin-nings of an industrial policy for the EU. Equally as important was the beginning of new competences for the integration project in the area of social policy and the environment. Historically there had been attempts using the old Arts 100 and 235 EC to balance the emphasis upon economic market integration issues with a social and citizenship dimension but there was no coherent policy towards this latter dimension.

This was the period when greater focus was placed upon the legality of Community law-making. It can be described as a period of "constitutionalisation" of Community competence and law-making processes. During this period the European Court was called upon increasingly to adjudicate upon the competence of the EU and the legality of law-making processes. But also, the pace and detail of Treaty amendments since 1987 reveals a tension between the Member States' desire for deeper and wider economic, social and political integration, measured against a more careful transfer of power away from the Member States to the Community.

The role of the Court in policing the boundaries between Member State and Community competence is central to this era.

This is a recurring theme through many of the chapters of this book. As we shall see in Ch.4, the Court has interpreted widely the four fundamental economic freedoms, guaranteeing the core of the Internal Market and the integration project. Even where Member States are allowed to derogate from these freedoms the Court has interpreted such derogations restrictively and according to the principle of proportionality. It has also extended the range of available derogations, bringing a number of non-economic values, within the domain of Community law, and transferring competence for the definition and implementation of such policies away from the Member States.

During this era new forms of monitoring and enforcement of Community law were used. In particular the use of the Internal Market Score Board introduced a new form of peer pressure and "name and shame" techniques to coerce the Member States into implementing Internal Market legislation.

THE TREATY OF MAASTRICHT 1993

The Treaty of Maastricht was a major change in direction for the Community, altering the architecture of the integration project from a single EC Treaty to a three pillar structure of the EC Treaty supported by two inter-governmental pillars. Community law-making powers were extended in 1993 when the Treaty of Maastricht came into force. QMV was extended to a number of social and employment issues (but sensitive issues such as social security, employment protection rights continued to be governed by unanimity voting), public health measures, economic sanctions resulting from Common Foreign and Security Policy decisions.

The price for extending QMV, and by implication Community competence, was the UK's opt-out from the Social Policy provisions involving the use of the social partners and opt-outs from the single currency (the third stage of EMU) by the UK and Denmark. This led Curtin to describe the Community as composed of "bits and pieces"[5] and could have led to the disintegration of the European integration project.

Paradoxically, at the time when competence of the Community was expanding, the EC Treaty offered, for the first time, a principle which could restrict, rather than expand, Community competence, the principle of subsidiarity now found in Art.5 EC. In the few cases where the application of the subsidiarity principle has been at issue the Court has interpreted the EC Treaty provisions designed to inhibit the exercise of Community competence narrowly.

Also important in the evolution of the identity of the integration process was the recognition of Union Citizenship in the Maastricht Treaty, now forming Art.17 EC. This is discussed in Ch.4.

Article 102a EC, introduced by the SEA 1987, recognised the European Monetary System which paved the way for the creation of economic and monetary union (EMU) in the Treaty of Maastricht. EMU was dependent upon the single market being achieved. It was introduced in three stages. The first Stage started on July 1, 1990, the date when the free movement of capital was achieved under Directive 88/361.[6] The Treaty of Maastricht contained the provisions to realise Stages 2 and 3. Stage 2 began on January 1, 1994. During Stage 2 the Member States were obliged to meet certain convergence criteria, aimed at keeping public spending and excessive deficits in check (Art.121(1) EC). The Commission monitored the Member States' performance. This system of multilateral surveillance continues under Arts.98 and 99(2) EC. It is regarded as the precursor of the new forms of economic governance, such as the open method of coordination, discussed below, which have emerged to implement the Lisbon Process. Failure to comply with the convergence criteria would bar entry to the single currency. The Member States also were obliged to create independent central banks. The European System of Central Banks came into operation on January 1, 1999. A European Monetary Institute was created to prepare for a single currency in the EU. This was replaced by the European Central Bank on January 1, 1999.

Stage 3 began on January 1, 1999. On January 1, 2002 a single currency, the Euro, became operational for the Member States which had fulfilled the convergence criteria. Multilateral surveillance of the Member States' budgetary discipline continues under Art.99(2) EC. All the Member States are bound by Art.4 EC, Art.98 EC and Art.99(2) EC.

At the Amsterdam European Council 1997 the Stability and Growth Pact was introduced by two Regulations and a Council Resolution.[7] This allows for the continued surveillance of the Member States participating in the third stage of EMU. If a Member State fails to meet the fiscal criteria for EMU there are sanctions which can result in a fine. Some Member States (for example, France, Germany, Ireland, Italy) have been warned by the Commission that they are running excessive deficits but the Commission has been reluctant to impose sanctions. In recent years it has been suggested that the Stability and Growth Pact is a weak compliance tool and should be abandoned before it collapses.

In 2004 the Court was asked to rule upon measures taken to curb the excessive deficit incurred by France and Germany.[8] The ruling is a clear warning to the Member States that they cannot handle breaches of the Stability Pact in a diplomatic way, but are bound by the EC Treaty rules. On a recommendation from the Commission, the Council found that an excessive deficit existed in both Member States and adopted two Recommendations asking France and Germany to reduce their deficits, setting a deadline for the adoption of the corrective measures (based upon Art.104(7) EC). Neither Member State complied with the Recommendations. The Commission asked the Council to give the two Member States notice to take measures (under Art.104(9) EC). But the Council could not obtain a majority to take such action and merely adopted conclusions in which it decided to hold the excessive deficit in abeyance. The Council declared itself ready to take a Decision under Art.104(9) EC should it appear that either Member State was not complying with commitments entered into by it.

The Commission mounted a challenge to the Council's stance. The ECJ held that the failure to adopt acts provided for in Art.104(8) and (9) EC was not an act giving rise to a challenge by way of judicial review under Art.230 EC. But the action was declared admissible. The Council's conclusions were intended to have legal effects in that they held the ongoing excessive deficits in abeyance. This modified the Recommendations previously adopted by the Council under Art.104(9) EC. The Council had not complied with the procedural rules, involving a breach of the Commission's right of initiative, and of the voting rules.

THE AMSTERDAM TREATY 1999

The Treaty of Amsterdam is a watershed in the history of the scope of European integration. One of the most significant extensions of Community competence straddles ideas of citizenship and social rights. Article 13 EC authorises the Council to take action by unanimous vote to combat discrimination based upon sex, racial or ethnic origin, religion or belief, disability, age or sexual orientation. This legal base was taken up soon after the Treaty of Amsterdam came into force. New Directives, as well as soft law programmes and Action Plans, have increased the range of social rights which can be used by citizens against their own Member States and exercised by TCNs.[9]

The Treaty of Amsterdam also introduced the European Employment Strategy (EES) which was based upon the multilateral surveillance systems of the Member States' budgetary discipline. The EES put the fight against unemployment, which had bedevilled the Community since the oil crisis of the 1970s, to the top of the economic agenda (Szyszczak, 2000). The procedures used in the EES provided a template for extending this kind of convergence of policies into new areas. At the Lisbon European Council 2000 the EU set itself an ambitious aim to become the most dynamic competitive global economy by the year 2010. The use of the EES template was proposed for a number of new areas where the Community lacked the political consensus to extend competence, but where the demands of greater and closer economic and political union required closer convergence of Member State policies. The techniques of multilateral surveillance, Score Boards, Annual Reports, National Action Plans, encouraging consensus building and convergence of Member State policies were named the "open method of co-ordination" at the Lisbon Summit 2000.

The Treaty of Amsterdam transferred a number of external frontier issues relating to the free movement of persons (immigration, visas, asylum) from the inter-governmental pillars to the mainstream of Community law-making. Of significance was the realisation that the transfer of such competence to the Community entailed further clarification of the principle of subsidiarity as well as mechanisms to enforce the principle. Thus a Protocol defining subsidiarity, as well as identifying the requirements and procedures for making subsidiarity work more effectively in the legislative process, was included at the behest of the Member States revealing greater concern over controlling the exercise of Community competence.

THE TREATY OF NICE

The Treaty of Nice did not extend Community competence. In sensitive areas, such as tax harmonisation, the UK government held out against any extension of Community competence. This may have been a tactical error, for as we shall see in the next Chapter in the absence of harmonisation the Court has chipped away at Member States' tax laws which may be contrary to the idea of an Internal Market. The Treaty of Nice did transfer some existing Community competences from unanimity voting to QMV, for example, the implementation of citizenship rights of free movement and residence in the host State.

The driving motivation for the Treaty of Nice was to adjust the EU to manage the enlargement of May 2004 when 10 additional Member States of varying demographic size and political and economic importance were admitted to the EU. The focus of the Treaty of Nice was upon the *rules* for QMV, setting the number of votes necessary for Community measures to be adopted. The Declaration on The Future of the Union annexed to the Treaty of Nice addressed the problem of *how* to establish and monitor a more precise delimitation of powers between the European Union and the Member States, reflecting the principle of subsidiarity".[10]

If the Constitutional Treaty is not ratified the Treaty of Nice provides a fall back position to keep the process of European integration on-going.

THE DIFFERENT APPROACHES TO HARMONISATION

The EC Treaty confers no competence to harmonise *per se* (Weatherill, 2002). Article 5(1) EC states that the EC is competent only where so provided by the EC Treaty. A number on "non-economic" activities of the Member States remain outside of the scope of Community law, for example, the provision of State education, health care services. Where the laws of the Member States differ, the creation of an Internal Market will be impeded. The differences between the Member States which may impede or hinder the development of an Internal Market may be addressed by a process of *negative integration.* This is where the Member States' laws are challenged either by using the direct effect of Community law in the national courts or through the enforcement processes of the Commission, using Art.226 EC or more rarely, other Member States using Art.227 EC.

From the *Cassis de Dijon*[11] ruling, and the various derogations allowed in the fundamental freedoms, as well as services of general economic interest in Art.86(2) EC, the Member States may continue with laws and policies which *prima facie* infringe

Community law. But these are seen as a justified *derogation* from the aims of creating an Internal Market. Any derogations are to be interpreted narrowly and are subject to the principle of proportionality. Member States may not a plead a derogation from the EC Treaty rules where the Community has occupied the field and adopted harmonising measures.

Where the Member States laws and policies are divergent, and this divergence poses a threat to the Internal Market, the EC Treaty allows for *positive integration* to take place. This takes place through the creation of Community policies which harmonise the Member States' divergent practices and leads to the re-regulation of markets. The spill-over effect from what is a functionally broad programme of harmonisation is to extend Community law competence into a number of areas which are now seen as distinctive Community law disciplines: private law, consumer law, environmental law, social policy law, labour law, health care law, family law. In some instances these disciplines have been raised to the status of values within the Community and are to be mainstreamed through all Community policies. Article 3(2) EC mainstreams equality between men and women; Art.6 mainstreams environment concerns and Art.127 EC states that a "high level of employment" shall be taken into consideration in the formulation and implementation of Community policies and activities. Thus the integration programme, which is presented as an exercise in securing market freedoms through the creation of an Internal Market, has not only explicitly recognised the need for horizontal or flanking policies to support the four freedoms but has inevitably spilled-over into a number of broad policy areas and has committed the Community to a sustained commitment to rule-making at the Community level (Egan, 2001).

As a result of this expansion of objectives and competences there can be conflicts between the central Internal Market objectives of integration and the other recognised objectives of the Community. Article 95(3) EC recognises that non-market objectives should be given recognition in the legislative process. In recent cases the Court has recognised the objectives of social legislation over internal market legal base objectives on which the legislation was justified.[12]

The breadth and expansion of Community objectives may also result in conflicting aims being present in one piece of legislation and the Court has ruled that where there are market and non-market objectives present which are not necessarily consistent with each other there needs to be a balanced interpretation of such legislation. In *Bodil Lindqvist*[13] the Directive on the free movement of personal data has the aim of ensuring the free flow of personal data *and* the aim of safeguarding the fundamental rights of individuals. The Court recognised that these objectives may be inconsistent with each other but also that the Directive itself provided mechanisms allowing for the different rights and interests to be balanced.

EXHAUSTIVE HARMONISATION

The original approach of the EU of sectoral harmonisation, with a top-down centralised approach, proved to be unworkable especially after the Member States retained the power to block Commission proposals in the Council through the threat of the veto where a national interest was at stake. The idea of exhaustive harmonisation also spawned ridicule in the media and the popular imagination. Stories emerged of the "Euro-sausage" and images of the Commission: "If it moves – harmonise it!". But there are still some examples where exhaustive harmonisation is used where the Member States are able to agree that there is a need for common uniform rules.

Once the Community has entered the field the Member States are pre-empted from imposing their own standards and rules.[14] In a harmonised area the Member States may not use the justifications for derogations to the fundamental economic freedoms.

OPTIONAL HARMONISATION

Some harmonisation Directives provide for the option for producers to follow the provisions of the Directive. This approach is not used often and it creates problems for intra-Community trade. The idea of optional harmonisation is that producers need only follow the provisions of a Directive where they intend to trade the goods across an EU Member State frontier. If they do not intend to export the goods they have the option of complying with the Directive.

MINIMUM HARMONISATION

Minimum harmonisation is the most popular form of harmonisation, and represents a compromise, or half-way house for the

Member States. The Member States agree to minimum intervention through Community harmonisation techniques and are free to adopt or retain higher levels, for example, in the fields of environmental protection, consumer protection and, especially, social policy. Minimum harmonisation became the routine approach after the ruling in *Cassis de Dijon* paved the way for a less intrusive form of regulation of the Internal Market: mutual recognition.

MUTUAL RECOGNITION: THE NEW APPROACH

The necessity to reach consensus for unanimous voting in the Council meant that even where consensus was reached technological change had often over-taken Community harmonisation processes. A breakthrough in the integration process came as a result of a ruling of the Court's using a principle called "mutual recognition" (Armstrong, 2002). In *Cassis de Dijon*[15] the German authorities refused to allow a French liquor, Cassis de Dijon, to be sold as a liquor in Germany because it was weaker than the minimum alcohol content of liquors marketed as such in Germany. German liquor had to have at least 25 per cent alcohol content whereas Cassis had between 15–20 per cent alcohol content. The German authorities claimed the rule was to protect consumers.

The Court introduced the idea of "home State control" stating that

"... in the absence of common rules it is for the Member States to regulate all matters relating to the production and marketing of alcohol and alcoholic beverages in their own territory".

Thus where a product was lawfully marketed in one Member State there was a presumption that it could be sold in other Member States without any further impediments to free trade. This was the idea of mutual recognition. A Member State was allowed to rebut this presumption if it could show that there were certain interests to be protected by the receiving State which had not been protected in the State where the goods were produced: public health, fairness in commercial transactions, fiscal supervision, consumer protection.

The final limb of the *Cassis* principle was that home state control and mutual recognition reduced the need for exhaustive harmonisation at the Community level and the Community could

move towards greater use of minimum harmonisation to harmonise Member State rules which resulted in continuing trade
barriers.

The Commission reacted quickly to the *Cassis* ruling and pushed
for the greater use of mutual recognition, which was already recognised in the EC Treaty in Art.49 EC (the mutual recognition of
diplomas) and Art.220 EC (the mutual recognition of companies).
Mutual harmonisation became the backbone of the Commission's
White Paper on Completing the Internal Market in 1985.

The approach of mutual recognition is essentially a horizontal
approach setting general principles across a range of sectors. A
good example is seen in the Directives which provide for the
mutual recognition of educational and vocational qualifications
which are discussed in Ch.4.[16] Differences between the Member
States constitute a real barrier to the free movement of persons,
and yet, the Member States are reluctant to allow the Community
to interfere in so sensitive an area as education and vocational
training in order to harmonise such qualifications. Where such
intervention has been allowed it has been slow and piecemeal.
Therefore the idea that comparable qualifications acquired in one
Member State should also be recognised as an equivalent qualification in another Member State is a solution to a pervasive barrier
to market integration.

Another aspect of mutual recognition is that it relies upon private bodies to establish voluntary standards. This has raised concerns that the Commission is delegating its law-making powers.
But the Commission argues that the standards are voluntary
codes, not binding legislation A number of organisations, CEN,
CENELAC, ETSI, acting on a qualified majority vote on a mandate from the Commission, establish essential technical specifications which are necessary for each mutual recognition Directive.
A manufacturer has a choice whether or not to conform with the
specifications, but where the goods conform they will be tested
and certified. Not surprisingly some of these decisions take time.
There has also been criticism of the new approach to harmonisation from the perspective of quality in EU governance. The lack of
accountability and transparency in the decision-making process,
as well as the fear that the bodies may be influenced by powerful
lobbying by interested groups while denying the opportunity for
consumers to have a say, or participate, in the decision-making
processes, ("regulatory capture") are all criticisms.

The most well known technical specification mark is the "CE"
found on many goods, for example, toys, and is therefore a kite

mark signifying the product satisfies EU standards. But many consumers also see the technical specification mark as a guarantee of the *quality* of the goods. (Weatherill, 1995). Products manufactured in accordance with the technical standards are presumed to comply with the requirements of the harmonisation Directive[17] Under the minimum harmonisation approach the Community is concerned only with harmonising essential safety requirements. Once goods conform to these standards they are free to move freely throughout the Community. There are incentives for goods produced outside of the EU to conform also with the technical requirements as this will also allow for free movement throughout the EU, and this is why toys made in China, for example, will often bear the "CE" mark.

The new approach to harmonisation has also been questioned as to whether it will lead to a "race to the bottom". This is the idea that there will be a tendency for producers to move to the Member State which has the lowest standards. But in fact what has happened is a form of competitive regulation. Member States with higher standards provide a quality "kitemark" for goods and services produced under the higher national standards.

A final aspect of the mutual recognition and minimum harmonisation approaches is that the Member States are under an obligation to provide information concerning national measures which derogate from the principle of free movement of goods.[18] In order to provide greater transparency and an early warning system for any measures which impose technical requirements on goods.[19] This allows the Commission and other Member States to raise objections to such national measures before they can cause harm to the functioning of the Internal Market.

REFLEXIVE HARMONISATION

Reflexive harmonisation is a newer harmonisation process which have been identified as part of the move away from the top-down, exhaustive harmonisation approach. Reflexive harmonisation is explained as a process which is procedural in approach, allowing various new political actors in the integration process to use procedures established by the EU to promote a variety of local ("bottom-up", as opposed to "top-down") prescriptions for regulatory problems in the EU (Deakin, 1999).

Reflexive harmonisation also allows scope for experimentation at the local level, allowing a wider range of political actors to be involved in decision-making and implementation processes. It therefore resembles some of the ideas behind other forms of new economic governance, such as the open method of co-ordination. Examples of reflexive harmonisation are seen especially in the area of employment law and industrial relations where it has proved difficult to secure Community competence, for example, in the information and consultation provisions for workers and their representatives of The European Works Council Directive,[20] and also the European Company.[21] Similarly the role of the social partners and the resulting Framework Directives adopted under the provisions relating to social law in Arts 138 and 139 EC are examples of a newer form of harmonisation, linked with ideas of subsidiarity.

New Forms of Economic Governance: The Open Method of Coordination

The phrase the "open method of coordination" (omc) was coined at the Lisbon Summit of March 2000. A legal base, for what is now generically identified as the omc, is seen in the use of new methods of co-ordinating policy in the arena of economic and monetary union, (BEPG) introduced in the Maastricht Treaty 1991 (now Art.98 EC) and later, in the arena of employment policy (EES), introduced in the Amsterdam Treaty 1997 (Arts 125–130 EC).

It is arguable that the advent of the omc in EU policy making and governance models is not so novel, or so recent, but merely builds upon the long tradition of soft law processes used in policy making (Senden, 2004). The experimentation with new forms of governance includes the commitment to proportionality, subsidiarity, the use of comitology, framework legislation networked administrative agencies, drawing upon the success of Commission monitoring of traditional hard law Directives and the peer review, "name and shame" mechanisms utilised in the implementation and monitoring of the Internal Market programme.

The omc may be viewed as yet another aspect of experimental governance without entailing a systemic change to the underlying constitutional settlement of 1957 (Szyszczak, 2002). In this respect firm boundaries are drawn between "old" governance, or the Community method, and "new" governance which, to some extent exists outside the legal constitutional structures of the EU. The omc may also be characterised as part of an inherent logic within the EU of political actors switching from traditional to "better" or more "efficient" regulation in areas where some level of EU regulation is necessary but where it has been difficult to reach consensus on *what* level and *how* this should be achieved.

A uniting characteristic of new governance[22] is that it is seen as an experimental form of governance and decision-making; a response to the various regulatory shortcomings of the EU which manifested themselves in the last century. Such shortcomings include the limited decision-making capacity of the EU, buttressed by political concerns of the Member States to retain a residual sovereign capacity to direct and implement economic and social policies which are not seen as central to the integration project, the Court's continued role to set legal limits to the competence attributed to the integration project,[23] and the various criticisms of the powers of the EU, questioning the legitimacy of the decision-making processes and the powers attributed to the EU (Schmitter, 2000).

One normative analysis of the problem is provided by Scharpf (1999) who argues that the EU is bedevilled by systematic limits, or black holes, of non-decision. Regulatory competition forces Member States into a downward spiral and European decision-taking tends to end up lower than that of any single Member State. In his analysis a solution to the problem emerges by estimating the degree to which decision-making should be decentralised. But within the EU deadlock in decision-making is also reached because of institutional factors. The EU is a multi-level decision-making polity, with very few institutional mechanisms to achieve hierarchical cooperation and this contributes to the decision-making deadlock. The situation is exacerbated by the creation of new institutional models of decision-making giving bodies such as the European Parliament greater powers of co-decision and attaching importance to the views of other Institutions such as the Economic and Social Committee, the Committee of the Regions, the Economic and Policy Committee, the Employment Committee and the Social Protection Committee. For Scharpf a way out of this deadlock is to emphasise the horizontal and vertical *differentiation* of decision-making and to put in place mechanisms to determine the proper *choice* of decision-making arenas or patterns of linkages between the arenas, to prevent decision-making breakdown.

A different approach to analysing the normative dimension of new governance in the EU is seen in the work of Joerges (1999). He argues that the Member States, and the political interests of the elites, as well as stakeholders in the EU decision-making processes of the EU, can break the decision making deadlock by *transforming* interests. This thesis argues that the Member States' preferences are influenced by continual discussion and exchange of arguments. An example of this is seen in the academic analysis of the use of comitology in the EU (Joerges and Vos, 1999). The outcome, it is claimed, is that expert deliberation in committees leads to Community-compatible interests.

These developments have shifted the focus of academic study of the EU away from the substantive issues of European integration towards a greater emphasis upon inquiry as to *how* the EU is emerging as a system of governance.

Soft law processes have played an important role in the governance of the Internal Market. Following quickly on the Court's ruling the Commission issued a Communication on *Cassis* followed by the White Paper of 1985,[24] which was an important policy document setting the agenda for next stage of economic integration. The Commission continued with a number of strategy papers, action plans which continued to outline the objectives of the Internal Market, setting targets and commenting on progress made, and the future direction of the Internal Market.

The Implementation of the SEA 1987 and the 1992 project also led to greater monitoring of the Member States' implementation of the measures introduced to complete the Internal Market through the use of the Internal Market Score Board. This is a form of peer group review whereby Member States are "named and shamed" by the Commission. It has subsequently been used in other areas such as State Aid, the modernisation of social protection, immigration policy, where a lighter touch is needed to persuade the Member States to align their national policies towards the aims of European integration.

The Lisbon process has used a variety of new governance tools to encourage the coordination of Member States' policy in an attempt to achieve a softer persuasive approach from the more heavy-handed harmonisation approach. Each year targets are set for certain goals and Member States' progress is judged by benchmarking processes, peer review and a process of iteration: learning from each other.

The omc is not confined to a limited set of economic and employment, social protection policies, but has been extended into the flanking policies of the EU. The Commission is exploring its use in developing immigration policies, an area fraught with political sensitivity for the Member States,[25] environmental policy[26] and taxation.[27] It is ironic that the Member States have guarded their national competence in these sensitive areas while allowing incursions into that competence through the use of the new forms of economic governance (Szyszczak, 2002).

The use of the new approach to harmonisation, reflexive harmonisation and the new approaches to economic governance such as the omc reflect the fact that the Community uses multiple tools and a variety of political actors at various levels in the Community to implement its goals: multi-level governance. The goal of the Community today is first, to co-ordinate the new tools of economic governance, namely the Internal Market Strategy, the Broad Economic Policy Guidelines of the Member States and the Community and the European Employment Strategy. These are now streamlined and adopted on the same day. The second goal is to address the continuing pervasive barriers to market integration (taxation and procurement being two of the most problematic areas) as well as continued emphasis on the monitoring and enforcement of Community law, and the improvement in quality and the simplification of the Community rules: the regulatory environment in which the Internal Market operates (Weatherill, 2000).

HARMONISATION AND THE CHOICE OF LEGAL BASE

Article 95 EC, introduced by the SEA 1987, provided a new legal base for harmonisation measures for the Internal Market using qualified majority voting. The Maastricht Treaty changed the procedure to the co-decision procedure, making greater use of the involvement of the European Parliament. Article 95 EC allowed measures to be adopted which have as their object the establishment and functioning of the internal market, as defined in Art.14 EC. The growth in areas of EU competence has led to a number of disputes over the correct legal base for Internal Market measures. Paradoxically, the incremental growth of specific sectoral bases for Community-based measures had the effect of reducing the scope for general Internal Market legislation. But the situation was complicated by the fact that prior to the SEA the Internal Market legal base had been used to adopt a number of measures not strictly addressing the market-building focus of Art.94 and 308 EC.

At the heart of the initial disputes was the issue of democratic participation in decision-making. Article 95 (1) EC is a residual legal base, to be used only where there is no other suitable EC

Treaty base. But where the procedures under different legal bases are the same, the ECJ has allowed a dual legal base for measures.[28] The Court gave a broad interpretation to the scope of Art.95(1) EC in *Titanium Dioxide*[29] where the use of Art.95(1) EC was contested against the use of Art.175 EC in a measure relating to the disposal of waste in the titanium dioxide industry. The Court argued that since environmental and health measures were a burden on undertakings, competition within the Internal Market could be distorted if the Member States' laws were not harmonised. The ruling was criticised for giving too broad an interpretation to Art.95 EC: nearly all measures have a cost implication leaving the legal bases for other policies in a residual role. It was also felt that the Court was paying attention to procedural factors (Art.95 EC involved the European Parliament in the co-operation procedure) over the actual *form* and *content* of the contested measure.

In contrast where a measure relating to the disposal of waste was adopted under Art.175 EC the Court looked to the main objective of the Directive and concluded that its purpose was the protection of the environment and that Art.175 EC was a suitable legal base for such a measure. Article 95(1) was not suitable as the Directive had only an incidental effect on harmonising market conditions within the Internal Market.[30] In the later case concerning *Beef Labelling*[31] the Court puts aside considerations of inter-institutional balance and greater democratic participation in decision-making for a more functional approach. The dispute was between the legal bases of Art.95(1) EC and Art.37 EC concerning an agricultural Regulation. The Court ruled that the aim of the Regulation was to re-establish stability in the beef and beef product market after the BSE crisis and that Art.37 EC was the appropriate legal base. It was not relevant that the European Parliament wished to participate in the decision-making process.

In addition to the choice of a legal base, the Institutions must also take account of the principles of subsidiarity and proportionality. Initial academic discussion of whether subsidiarity was justiciable was not reinforced by rulings from the Court which has continued to show a reluctance to investigate whether the subsidiarity principle has been followed, preferring instead to focus upon formal procedural issues[32] or the necessity for Community-action.[33] Only recently in *ex parte BAT*[34] did the Court investigate *why* there was a need for a Community-wide Directive on tobacco products designed to remove the disparities which existed between the Member States.

LIMITS TO COMMUNITY COMPETENCE

Article 95 EC does not vest the Community legislator with "a general power to regulate the internal market".[35] Any measures based upon Art.95 EC must actually and genuinely contribute to eliminating obstacles to trade and removing distortions of competition thus putting a limit upon unlimited exercise of Community competence and jurisdiction. The recognition of the need for horizontal or flanking policies to support the Internal Market project, as well as the desire by some Member States to harmonise rules relating to social policy, migration, the environment, agriculture, health and safety, consumer protection has created tensions within the EU as to how far non-economic objectives can also be the subject of harmonisation within the EU using Art.95 EC rather than a specific sectoral legal base for such measures. Some areas specifically reject the use of harmonisation, for example, health (Art.152(4)(c) EC) and employment (Art.129 EC).

In *Tobacco Advertising* the Court held that where there were two competing legal bases for a measure[36] the principal rule is that the Internal Market base should be used where the aim is to improve the functioning of the Internal Market. Where the aim is to achieve another policy goal (for example, the protection of the environment, social policy etc) then the appropriate specific legal base should be used. Where there is no competence for the latter, then the Internal Market legal base can be used irrespective of whether the Internal Market is ancillary to the objective being sought. Thus Internal Market issues cannot be disregarded when pursuing other ancillary goals of market integration.

There are arguments that the spill-over of competence from Internal Market integration has led to the incidental expansion of Community competence into new areas of regulatory activity (Weatherill, 2004; 2005). This has been labelled "competence creep".

THE ROLE OF "NON-ECONOMIC" VALUES IN THE INTEGRATION PROCESS

An important question today is how far the Community is, or should be, only concerned with economic issues relating to the functioning of the Internal Market, and how far other values should be a concern for the Community. A number of non-economic values were recognised in the original EEC Treaty, for example, in the derogations to the four freedoms, (expanded in the mandatory requirements of *Cassis de Dijon* and subsequent case law), as well as in Art.86(2) EC (which recognises public services ("services of general economic interest")). We see that the Member States are allowed to plead a number of non-economic interests which may be balanced against the imperatives of market integration.

In the formation of legislative proposals the Commission is instructed to aim for a high level of protection for health, safety, environmental protection and consumer protection in its proposals based upon Art.95(3) EC. A number of Community objectives must also be mainstreamed through Community policies: the environment, employment and gender equality. Other policies are not mainstreamed but have acquired a legitimacy in Community policies, for example, consumer policy, education and vocational training. Cultural policy is less openly articulated or developed; it is not a mainstreaming activity but Art.151(4) EC states that:

"The Community shall take cultural aspects into account in its action under other provisions of this Treaty, in particular in order to respect and promote the diversity of its cultures.".

Yet culture is a wide concept and has made an impression in many aspects of Community policy and litigation (Craufurd-Smith, 2004).

More recently it has been accepted that the Community can include (and indeed must include) other values in the integration process. Ideas of citizenship and fundamental, or human rights are present in the Court's case law. Community law, for example, can be held invalid if it fails to give sufficient protection to a fundamental right or infringes such a human right.[37] In the Constitution values are given a prominent role (Millns and Aziz, 2005).

DEROGATIONS FROM HARMONISATION MEASURES

The move towards qualified majority voting in Internal Market matters was softened for the Member States in Art.95(4) and (5) EC by allowing a Member State to derogate from a harmonisation measure adopted under Art.95 EC. But such derogations are carefully controlled and monitored by the Community governance

process. Initially Art.95(4) EC confined this derogation to measures existing at the time the harmonisation Directive was
adopted. Where a Member State deemed it necessary to maintain
national provisions on grounds of "major needs" referred to in
the justifications set out in Art.30 EC or relating to the protection
of the environment it could notify this request to the Commission.
Under the original provisions of Art.95(4) EC the Commission
had to authorise this derogation before the Member State could
continue with the national measure. For example, Sweden
applied for a derogation from a harmonisation Directive,
Directive 94/36,[38] under Art.95(4) EC to continue with a prohibition against the use of an "E-additive", E124 cochineal red, in
foodstuffs. Unfortunately the Commission failed to respond to
the request. When litigation occurred in the national courts, the
Court ruled that Sweden could not rely upon a national law
which was inconsistent with Directive 94/36/EC unless it had
been specifically authorised to do so by the Commission.[39]

In fact the Member States have made little use of this derogation. Derogations sought related mainly to the use of certain
chemicals and additives in foodstuffs. But in one case France was
successful in annulling a Commission Decision granting a derogation to Germany from Directive 91/173/EC.[40] The case was
focused upon procedural issues, with the Court finding that the
Commission had not investigated the impact of the derogation
properly under Art.95(4) EC.

The Treaty of Amsterdam extended the derogation to national
measures adopted *after* the adoption of Community harmonisation measures. Under Art.95(5) EC Member States may introduce
new provisions based upon new scientific evidence relating only
to the protection of the environment or the working environment
on grounds of a problem specific to that Member State arising
after the adoption of a Community harmonisation measure. The
reason for the limited scope of the derogation in Art.95(5) EC is
given in *Commission v Denmark*.[41] When a measure is adopted
under Art.95(4) EC the Institutions are aware of the national provisions and choose to override them, or not take them into
account, whereas the adoption of *new* national measures under
Art.95(5) EC is more likely to jeopardise the attainment of the
Internal Market.

The Treaty of Amsterdam changed the procedural rules relating to the use of Arts 95(4) and (5) EC. Under Art.95(6) EC the
Commission has six months to approve or reject national provisions after verifying whether or not the national measures are a

means of arbitrary discrimination or a disguised restriction on trade between the Member States and whether they will jeopardise the attainment of an Internal Market. The six month period can be extended to twelve months in complex cases. But the Commission must respond to the notification within six months of the notification. If it does not, then Art.95(6) EC states that the national measures are deemed to be approved. This overturns the ruling in *Kortas*.[42] Where the Commission approves of a Member State's derogation Art.95(7) EC states that the Commission may also examine whether there should be a modification of the original harmonising Directive, especially where the Member State's derogation provides a higher level of protection than the Community harmonisation measure.[43] Article 95(8) EC provides for special provisions in relation to any problems a Member State may encounter in the public health field which has already been the subject of harmonisation.

Article 95(9) EC introduced an expedited procedure, by way of derogation from Arts 226 and 227 EC, to bring a Member State directly before the Court if the Commission, or another Member State, considers that a Member State is using the derogations in an improper manner. Finally, Art.95(10) EC states that the harmonising measures shall, in appropriate cases, include a safeguard clause authorising the Member States to take for one (or more) of the non-economic reasons referred to in Art.30 EC provisional measures, but these must be subject to a Community control procedure.

GOVERNANCE AND THE CONSTITUTION

Weatherill (2005) categories the governance approach to the use of Community powers as one based upon *ex ante* restraint by the political Institutions and *ex post* review by the Court. This has not proved to be an effective or acceptable constitutional mechanism to delimit the powers of the EU against the Member States and the constitutional principles governing the EU. The Constitutional Treaty was set the task to clarify and re-organise the EC Treaty rules governing competence and also to institutionalise new political actors, particularly the national parliaments, to monitor the exercise of Community powers.

4

INTEGRATION THROUGH THE LIBERALISATION OF MARKETS: FOUR FUNDAMENTAL ECONOMIC FREEDOMS

Article 2 EC gives special prominence to the task of the Community of creating a Common Market and an economic and monetary union. A number of other tasks are also mentioned in Art.2 EC. By implementing common policies or activities, which are referred to in Arts 3 and 4 EC, the Community is charged with promoting a harmonious balanced and sustainable development of economic activities. This includes a high level of employment and of social protection, equality between men and women, sustainable and non inflationary growth, a high degree of competitiveness and convergence of economic performance, a high level of protection and improvement of the quality of the environment, the raising of the standard of living and quality of life, and economic and social cohesion and solidarity among Member States. Article 14 EC provides the constitutional basis for the establishment of an Internal Market through the liberalisation of four basic factors of production: the free movement of goods, persons, services and capital.

The four freedoms were the central economic constitutional foundation stone of the Common Market with other policies seen as supplementary to the economic priorities of market building. The Single European Act 1987 created greater possibilities for the development of horizontal or flanking policies to the Internal Market, for example, an environmental policy, a consumer policy, a social policy, a vocational training policy. The creation of an economic and monetary union in the Maastricht Treaty 1993 led to a greater spill-over of Internal Market policies into a wider range of areas, many intruding into traditional areas of State sovereignty which had not been transferred to the Community. Since the Treaty of Maastricht 1993 the EU has faced opposition, at the grass roots level as well as at the Member State level, to expanding the competence of the Community. Economic and monetary union also created new challenges for the governance of the Internal Market. There was a greater need for common horizontal policies and the Commission was obliged to re-organise its policy-making strategies away from a vertical division of organisation to allow for the horizontal co-ordination of EU policies. This explains why new techniques of economic governance, such as the open method of coordination, have emerged during the 1990s to fulfil the ambitious aims set out in Art.2 EC. We have seen how, from the SEA 1987 onwards, Community competence has increased into a number of these areas. The Court's case law has also extended the reach of Community law where national measures constitute a hindrance to the attainment of an Internal Market. The change of pace and governance techniques in the post-Lisbon era has allowed for greater co-ordination of a number of national policies without head-on legal clashes between the Member States and the Community Institutions over competence issues.

The four freedoms are distinct provisions in the EC Treaty and have evolved in different ways and at a different pace. There is now a tendency to use similar techniques in identifying barriers to market integration across the four freedoms as well as some convergence in the interpretation of the permissible derogations which can be raised by the Member States to justify the continuance of barriers to market integration. The convergence of the four freedoms is not without criticism (Snell, 2002; 2004). Are people really like goods? Can doctors be treated like bananas? The free movement of persons in the EU presents a special and complicated task for the Community, especially in the new culture of human rights and Citizenship protection and the aims in the post 9/11 world of creating an area of freedom, security and justice.[1]

Securing an Internal Market has two dimensions: an *external* dimension which sets the economic boundaries, as well as the geo-political boundaries, to the area regulated by the EU and an *internal* dimension which is the aim of the Internal Market to dismantle internal frontiers and create a level playing field in relation to trade and competition within the geo-political area of the EU. It has not been easy to secure either the external or internal dimension to the EU across the four freedoms, with free movement of persons presenting special difficulties. There is a greater interest in securing EU competence to define the boundaries of the EU after the enlargement of 2004.

THE FOUR FREEDOMS AS FUNDAMENTAL RIGHTS

The Court refers to four freedoms as "fundamental" principles and "foundations" of the EC Treaty. The free movement of workers has been referred to as a fundamental right,[2] as has the free movement of goods.[3] New ideas of fundamental rights have emerged as substantive rights in EU legislation and the Court's case law. Such rights may complement and enhance the enforcement of the four fundamental economic freedoms but they may also act as a restraint upon the operation of the freedoms.[4] For example, emphasis is placed in Art.I–2 of the Constitution on the values of the Union.[5] Article 7 of the Charter of Fundamental Rights of the European Union (CFR) now forming Art.II–67 of the EU Constitution, provides for the right to respect of the individual's private and family life. Article 15 of the Charter (now Art.II–75(2) of the Constitution) provides for the freedom to work in any Member State. The Court has recognised the freedom to conduct a business;[6] this right is also recognised in Art.16 CFR (now Art.II–76 of the Constitution).[7] The Court also refers to the ECHR when determining Community-based rights to free movement, especially in cases relating to the free movement of persons.[8]

Neither the Community legislator, nor the Court, has accepted that the creation of an Internal Market or the liberalisation and free trade are ends in themselves (Szyszczak, 2000). The tasks and aims of economic integration must be balanced against other rights and values recognised in Community law *and* in the Member States' laws. This balancing act is seen in the scope for derogations from the four economic freedoms, contained in the EC Treaty: Art.30, 39(3) and (4) EC, Art.45 EC and in Art.86(2) EC, which protects public services (known as "services of general economic interest") from the full rigour of market competition.

The Court has increased the range of derogations which are available describing such national measures as "mandatory" or "imperative" requirements designed to protect new values which have emerged since the EEC Treaty was adopted in 1957. Such mandatory requirements have involved consumer protection;[9] the protection of the environment;[10] the protection of culture[11] improvement of working conditions[12] protection of plurality of the media.[13] In the Constitution fundamental rights, citizenship and a range of values set out in Art.I–2 play a prominent role along side the aims of an Internal Market.

The recognition of derogations to the fundamental freedoms has forced the EU to acknowledge that the right to trade is not absolute. This is illustrated in *Schmidberger v Austria*.[14] The Austrian authorities had authorised an environmental demonstration which had closed a motorway for nearly two days forming part of the Bremmer pass linking Germany and Austria. A road haulage company attempted to claim damages for loss of business, claiming the Austrian authorisation contravened the free movement of goods provision, Art.28 EC. The Court found the Austrian measure fell within Art.28 EC but the Court and the Advocate General accepted the justification that the Austrian authorities were protecting the fundamental rights of expression and assembly, as guaranteed under Arts 10 and 11 ECHR:

"It follows that measures which are in compatible with observance of the human rights thus recognised are not acceptable in the Community . . .
Thus, since both the Community and its member states are required to respect fundamental rights, the protection of those rights is a legitimate interest which, in principle, justifies a restriction of the obligations imposed by Community law, even under a fundamental freedom guaranteed by the Treaty such as the free movement of goods." (paras 73 and 74)

Despite the limitations to the fundamental freedoms, it is accepted that the four fundamental economic freedoms play a central role in European integration: they are seen as political rights and as constitutional rights. The four freedoms are an example of *negative integration* in that Member States are obliged to remove, and not put in place, any measures which will hinder the four freedoms. This is a concrete application of the fidelity or solidarity clause in Art.10 EC. But the process of negative integration is also de-regulatory, dismantling Member States' laws and regulations which are obstacles to the creation of an Internal Market. There is a need for some re-regulation at the Community level to protect legitimate interests such as consumer protection or the protection of the environment.

It is also possible for the Member States to use a variety of *positive integration* techniques to secure the Internal Market through the use of the general Internal Market legal bases of Art.94 EC and 95 EC, the residual legal base of Art.308 EC as well as specific legal bases pertinent to each individual freedom. Over the years the Community competence has expanded to create flanking policies in areas such as the environment, social policy, consumer policy. Combined with litigation, using the direct effect of the EC Treaty provisions, as well as the secondary legislation fleshing out the bare bones of the EC Treaty, these processes of market building have deepened the *quality* of market integration.

We have seen that the role of individuals, and civil society generally, was downplayed in the early years of decision-making in the EU. But when we start to analyse *how* the four economic freedoms work, and the way in which they have been *made* to work, in favour of individual rights against the Member States we see the importance of the role of litigation using the concept of direct effect. This has led to ideas that the four fundamental freedoms confer basic rights of *economic citizenship* on natural and legal persons who are able to use these rights in the EU. But litigation has also exposed weaknesses in relying upon the four freedoms as the sole source of citizenship rights in an Internal Market. The major limitation of creating citizenship rights from the Internal Market provisions is that there must be some element of economic cross-border activity in order to trigger the rights. The Court has refused to entertain the idea of what is known as "reverse discrimination". This is where an individual seeks to rely on Community law against his or her own Member State without exercising any of the free movement rights. Thus while the practical, and sometimes inadvertent, spill-over of Community law into other areas outside of the core freedoms created the need for horizontal or flanking policies these policies have also contributed to the development of basic layers of citizenship rights which can be used against the home Member State. In some of these areas the litigation has contributed to the development of Community procedural rights and remedies. This is seen in the references to the European Court using the social policy provisions.

HORIZONTAL DIRECT EFFECT OF THE FOUR FREEDOMS

The EC Treaty rules relating to the four freedoms are addressed to the Member States. The competition rules of Art.81 EC and 82 EC were designed to address the barriers to market integration which could be raised by private actors operating in the market. Today it is recognised that barriers to market integration may be raised by regulatory power and *private power* as much as by the public power held by Member States. Competition law has addressed the abuse of market power by private firms and in the liberalisation process has placed positive duties upon the actors in the liberalised sectors. The effects of liberalisation and privatisation, the so-called "rolling back the frontiers of the State", which have been felt in Europe from the 1980s, has placed a number of duties upon private actors to provide goods and services previously provided by the State. A growing interest in placing public duties on private power has led the ECJ to explore, albeit tentatively, the horizontal direct effect of the fundamental freedoms[15] since the rules of the Internal Market are far-reaching in terms of negative and positive duties to promote market integration.

In a series of cases[16] the Court ruled that Arts 28 and 29 EC were addressed to the Member States and not private persons. But in *Dansk Supermarked*[17] the Court gave an indication that private persons should be bound directly by Art.28 EC. This is seen as an *obiter dictum*, and in a later case the Court has expressly denied the horizontal direct effect of Art.28 EC.[18] The Court has applied Art.28 EC to the delegation of State powers to private bodies, otherwise it would be easy for a Member State to evade the application of Art.28 EC.[19]

In contrast to the case law under Art.28 EC, the Court has explored the use of the horizontal direct effect in the are of free movement of workers and applied Art.39 EC to a horizontal situation in *Bosman*[20] and *Angonese*.[21]

THE FOUR FUNDAMENTAL ECONOMIC FREEDOMS

THE FREE MOVEMENT OF GOODS

The Customs Union

The customs union forms the economic basis of the integration project in relation to goods. The legal nature of the customs union is set out in Art.23 EC. A customs union is differentiated from other forms of economic integration in that it creates an external frontier for goods entering the EU based upon a Common Customs Tariff (CTT) allowing foreign goods to enjoy rights to free movement within the EU once they have entered the EU legally. This is called the right of free circulation and also allows for the free movement of goods originating *within* the Member States of the EU.

The existence of a CTT entails the development of a common commercial policy for the EU. Otherwise trade policy between the EU and the rest of the world may not be beneficial for certain Member States and an uneven trade policy conducted on a unilateral basis between a Member State and third countries may not be of benefit to the EU as a whole.

The evolution of a Common Commercial Policy for the EU is seen as another layer of the economic constitution of the EU, but it has been slower in developing (Cremona, 1990). Article 133(1) EC gives the Community power for

"the conclusion of tariff and trade agreements, the achievement of uniformity in measures of liberalisation, export policy and measures to protect trade such as those to be taken in the event of dumping or subsidies."

Proposals are made by the Commission and can be adopted by the Council by qualified majority vote (Art.133 (2) and (4) EC). Under these powers measures have been taken to adopt a Common Customs Code[22] as well as protective measures to protect the EU against what are seen as unfair trade practices by third country importers such as dumping[23] and subsidies by third country governments.[24]

The ECJ defined the concept of "goods" for the purposes of Community law as products which "can be valued in money and which are capable, as such, of forming the subject of commercial transactions."[25]

The Common Commercial Policy

Article 25 EC prohibits customs duties (tariffs) and charges having an equivalent effect on goods crossing an internal frontier of the EU; customs duties are allowed at the EU's external frontier, but once goods have passed through this external frontier they are deemed to be in free circulation. Article 25 EC applies to all fiscal measures, however small, which make imported products more expensive, and therefore less competitive, than home produced products. Statistical levies, charges for health inspections, taxes on the export of art works have all been found to be covered by Art.25 EC.

In *Van Gend en Loos*[26] the ECJ ruled that Art.25 EC was directly effective against a Member State (vertical direct effect).

Article 25 EC does not provide for any justifications, exemptions or derogations from its provisions but in *Commission v Germany*[27] the Court outlined three situations where a fiscal charge would fall *outside* of the scope of Art.25 EC. First, where the charge relates to an internal system of dues applied systematically and in accordance with the same criteria to domestic products and imported products; second, where the charge constitutes payment for a service in fact rendered to an economic operator of a sum in proportion to the service; finally where the charge attaches to inspections carried out to fulfil obligations imposed by Community law.

The first situation refers to another tool within the EC Treaty which addresses common internal policies of the EU aimed at combating measures which may act as trade barriers and result in unfair competition between domestic products and imported products, Art.90 EC.[28] Article 90 EC is directly effective and addresses *indirect taxation*. Although various inroads into the area of domestic taxation have been made through litigation using the free movement provisions, taxation continues to be an area where Member States have the autonomy to determine their own taxation schemes. Article 93 EC provides the means to harmonise legislation concerning turn-over taxes, excise duties and other forms of indirect taxation, to the extent that such harmonisation is necessary to ensure the establishment and functioning of the Internal Market. Article 90 EC allows the Member States to adopt taxation systems which are based upon objective criteria, unrelated to the origin of goods. But Art.90 EC captures both direct discrimination[29] and indirect discrimination.[30]

The application of Art.90 EC is not always easy. Goods which are subject to different taxation levels must be shown to be *similar* to fall within Art.90(1) EC; or to be *in competition* with each other to fall within Art.90(2) EC. The Court abandoned its initial formal approach, asking if the goods fell within the same fiscal, customs or statistical classification[31] and now uses an approach which looks at the factual comparison of the goods combined with an economic analysis.[32]

Many of the cases concern the different taxation of alcoholic beverages. Is beer similar to wine or whisky? Is beer in competition with other alcoholic beverages? These are crucial questions, not only to trigger the use of Art.90 EC, but also in relation to remedies. If goods are *similar*, then any discrimination must be eliminated by the equalisation of taxes imposed on domestic and imported products. Where goods are *in competition* the State must remove the protective aspects of the taxation system, that is, the tax may continue to be different for both products provided that it reflects objective differences between the two goods.[33]

Additionally, to ensure the effectiveness of Community law, Member States must allow for the repayment of any charges which are contrary to Art.90 EC, subject to a limitation where there would be unjust enrichment.[34] A damages claim is available using national procedural rules, subject to the proviso that the claims based upon Community law rights must be not less favourable than those governing similar national law actions and do not make the exercise of Community law rights virtually impossible or excessively difficult.

Measures Having an Equivalent Effect to a Customs Duty

The free movement of goods also addresses non-fiscal barriers to trade. These are measures which concern both imports and exports such as quotas, export/import bans or may cover measures which concern the marketing, presentation or content of goods. These are called measures having an equivalent effect to a customs duty. A Member State may have good justifications for controlling the import and export of goods through non-fiscal measures based upon public policy, consumer, or environmental concerns. Articles 28 EC (imports), 29 (exports) and 30 EC (justifications) address the permissible scope of this balance between a Member State's legitimate interests to control the movement of goods in and out of its territory and the liberalisation of the flow of goods in the EU.

In 1983 the Community attempted to trouble shoot any possible disruption to trade between the Member States by adopting a Directive[35] which required the Member States to notify in advance to the Commission any new technical standards. The Commission would then consult with other Member States as to whether the proposed new standards would produce obstacles to trade. The Court gave this clearance system added weight in *CIA*[36] when it ruled that a Member State could not apply technical standards to individuals in the home state where such standards had not been notified under the Directive. Non-notification was a substantial procedural defect rendering such technical regulations inapplicable.[37]

The Court moved away from ideas of only looking at measures which may be *discriminatory* against foreign imports to adopting a broad test, set out in of *Dassonville*:[38]

"All trading rules enacted by Member States which are capable of hindering, directly or indirectly, actually or potentially, intra-Community trade are to be considered as measures having effect equivalent to quantitative restrictions."

This cast the net of Art.28 EC wide. In *Cassis de Dijon*[39] the Court took the *Dassonville* test a step further by identifying *indistinctly applicable* rules which may also be caught by Art.28 EC. An indistinctly applicable rule is a measure which applies to domestic and imported goods, but in fact imposes a greater burden on imported goods. This is because an importer must comply with the home state rules on production and marketing as well as the rules of the importing State. Where these rules are different this creates a double burden and imposes extra costs upon the importer to adapt the products to the requirements of the importing State. The fact that an exporter may now have to conform to 25 Member States' requirements underlines the need for harmonisation of essential laws and standards, but also reinforces the reason why the Court in *Cassis* introduced the idea of home state control and mutual recognition. In *Cassis de Dijon* the Court ruled that:

". . . in the absence of common rules it is for the Member States to regulate all matters relating to the production and marketing of alcohol and alcoholic beverages in their own territory.".

But in relation to *indistinctly applicable* rules the Court saw the need to allow the Member States a wider margin of discretion in the justifications they might raise in order to take the potential restriction of trade outside of the application of Art.28 EC: a rule of reason. The Court in *Cassis* accepted that:

"Obstacles to movement in the Community resulting from disparities between the national laws relating to the marketing of the products in question must be accepted in so far as those provisions may be recognised as being necessary in order to satisfy mandatory requirements relating to the effectiveness of fiscal supervision, the protection of public health, the fairness of commercial transactions and the defence of the consumer."

Unlike the derogations contained in Art.30 EC, discussed below, the list of mandatory requirements is not exhaustive and has been added to by the Court in relation to, *inter alia*, protection of the environment, working conditions, protection of national and regional socio-cultural objectives, financial equilibrium of a social security system, the protection of fundamental rights and freedom of the press. The Court has also applied the proportionality principle.

As we saw in the previous chapter, the Commission used *Cassis*, and the principle of mutual recognition, to form the basis of a new regulatory approach to kick start the integration project in the 1980s.[40]

In many cases the source of the barriers to trade within the Internal Market will be "product requirements". In *Rau*[41] a Belgian requirement that margarine was to be sold in cubes (in order to avoid confusion with butter) was found to be an indistinctly applicable measure having an equivalent effect to a customs duty because imported margarine would need to be repackaged, adding to costs, in order to be sold in Belgium.[42] But the Court was also asked to rule on the compatibility of Member States' rules regulating the "marketing" of products. For example, restrictions on advertising, the way goods are produced and sold. In the *"Buy Irish"* case[43] the ECJ held that the national measures need not be legally binding.

The wide scope of this test allowed for a period of opportunistic litigation testing how far Art.28 EC could become an economic due process clause, allowing for challenges on *all* domestic measures which impinged upon commercial freedom (Maduro, 1997). There was, for example, no *de minimis* test built into the application of Art.28 EC and therefore virtually any form of State regulatory activity, or even policy, could be caught by Art.28 EC. For some commentators this was seen as an abuse of the free movement provisions (Steiner, 1992). It allowed for Community law to be used to challenge policies made by democratic, elected governments governing their own territory (Szyszczak, 2000). For example, in the UK challenges were made by traders (usually large DIY stores) challenging the legislation which prevented stores from trading on a Sunday (Rawlings, 1993). Not all commentators are critical of this litigation strategy. Weatherill (2002) argues that it is a useful modernising device and allows for challenges to protectionist national rules.

The extension of Art.28 EC to the marketing rules of a Member State appeared to take the scope of Art.28 EC too far into the autonomy of the Member States, but also undermined the principles of home state control established in *Cassis de Dijon*. The Court of Justice was deluged with preliminary references from the national courts using Art.234 EC to question and challenge regulatory aspects of national law. This in turn created an academic environment where the search was on to create limits to the scope of Art.28 EC (White, 1989).

The Court re-appraised its post-*Cassis* case law in *Keck and Mithouard*.[44] Two traders sold goods at a loss, contrary to French law. In their defence they pleaded Art.28 EC making the tenuous claim that the French law restricted the volume of sales of imported goods. The Court continued with the *Cassis* test in relation to "product requirements", but in relation to "selling arrangements" the Court stated that such arrangements would be caught by Art.28 EC where only where there was discrimination, *in law and in fact*, against the foreign products. Thus Member State regulations which apply to the conditions under which a good is produced, for example, employment and social law, town planning, criminal law, environmental legislation are considered to be too incidental to the effect on inter-state trade and are not caught by Art.28 EC unless discrimination can be shown.

Some commentators criticised the lack of reasoning in *Keck*, and saw the formal differentiation between product requirements and selling arrangements as artificial.[45] Advocate General Jacobs pointed out in his Opinion in *Leclerc*[46] that a total ban on advertising a certain kind of product would be a marketing rule and therefore using only a discrimination test would be inappropriate. More recently, Advocate General Fennelly[47] and Oliver and Roth[48] have argued that *Keck* does offer an appropriate mechanism for the operation of the four freedoms in an Internal Market. It is argued that *Keck* reflects the different effects of product-related and selling rules. The former affect *access* to a market, whereas marketing rules do not impede access to the market but Member States may still discriminate against foreign produced goods. Oliver and Roth acknowledge that there is still little clarity as to when, and how, market access is impeded, and the Court seems to continue addressing the application of Art.28 EC on a case by case basis. In two cases decided in 2004, the Court looked at the German system of coping with environmental problems created by drinks packaging. Producers and distributors of drinks in non-reusable packaging are subject to the obligation to charge a deposit and take back packaging. These provisions can be complied with by participating in a global collection scheme. This option is withdrawn if for, two consecutive years, the percentage of drinks marketed in reusable packing in Germany falls below a certain threshold. An infringement action was brought against Germany and two Austrian exporters of soft drinks to Germany challenged the rules in the German courts, as being contrary to Art.28 EC. In a preliminary ruling, Case C–309/02 *Radlberger Getranke and S. Spitz*,[49] the Court found this was an indistinctly applicable rule and that it incurred costs for all producers. But producers established outside of Germany use considerably more non-reusuable packaging than German producers. Therefore the German rules hinder the marketing of drinks from other Member States. The Court accepted the German justification for the rules: the protection of the environment. But found that this must satisfy the principle of proportionality. This would be satisfied only if there is a reasonable transitional period which ensures that every producer and distributor can actually participate in the system. This was a matter for the national court to assess. In the infringement action, *Commission v Germany*[50] the rule required that mineral water must be bottled at source. The Court held that the German legislation did not satisfy the principle of proportionality because the transitional period was only six months.

The Court is willing to apply Art.28 EC when a distortive effect on competition can be shown, and will also look at statistical evidence.[51]

The Court has not applied the *Dassonville* test to the *export* of goods, a situation which is covered by Art.29 EC. Instead the Court applies a discrimination test.[52]

Reverse Discrimination

One limitation of the rules on the Internal Market is that they do not cover examples of what is known as "reverse discrimination" (Shuibhne, 2002). In the previous Chapter we saw that Art.95 EC may only be used as a legal base for Internal Market measures where there is a sufficient inter-state element.[53] Reverse discrimination is the situation where the national measures discriminate against domestic goods. The immunity of reverse discrimination from the reach of the Internal Market rules reflects a level of national autonomy reinforced by the *Cassis* doctrine of home state control. In *Mathot*[54] a Belgian law requiring butter produced in Belgium to conform to certain packaging requirements, without similar requirements imposed upon imported butter was held not to infringe Art.28 EC. The *Cassis* principle and the principle of reverse discrimination allows for competition between products to continue and allows the Member States to give a competitive edge to domestic products by insisting on different, and higher standards, for domestically produced products.

In a discrete group of cases the Court has applied the free movement of goods provisions to situations which are wholly internal to a Member State where goods move from geographically distinct territory to another part of a Member State's territory[55] and in *Pistre* the Court applied Art.28 EC to a situation which was wholly internal to France.[56] In subsequent cases the Court has applied Art.28 EC in cases where there was no inter-state element to the free movement of goods.[57] This corresponds with tentative developments in other areas of free movement, for example, persons,[58] services,[59] capital.[60]

Justifications and Derogations From the Free Movement Rules

Article 30 EC provides a set of justifications for the Member States to derogate from the principle of free movement of goods. This is an exhaustive list, drawn up, and un-amended since 1957. The list is based upon classic public policy concerns: public morality, public policy, public security, protection of health and life of humans, animals, plants, the protection of national treasures possessing artistic, historic or archaeological value or the protection of industrial and commercial property.

The Member States' scope to use the derogations is circumscribed by the fact that the derogations can only be invoked in the absence of Community measures in the field.[61] Member States' discretion is also curtailed by the application of the principle of proportionality and by the fact that derogations from a fundamental Treaty principle should be interpreted strictly. The Court has ruled also that the derogations cannot be used to serve economic objectives,[62] although in some of the more recent cases relating to the organisation of health care schemes in relation to the free movement of services the Court appears to re-work economic justifications into acceptable heads of justification.[63]

In recent years the Court has not always adhered to the strict distinction between distinctly applicable measures which can be justified by reference to Art.30 EC and indistinctly applicable measures which may be justified by reference to the *Cassis* mandatory requirements principle.[64] But in other cases the Court adheres to the formal distinctions.[65] In the case law of the other fundamental freedoms the Court has started to blur the distinction between distinctly applicable and indistinctly applicable rules, speaking of hindrances to trade or market integration. The time may come whereby the distinctions in terms of the justifications are abandoned and we see the emergence of a generic "public interest" justification across the case law of all four freedoms (Szyszczak, 2002).

Derogations are often seen as "special pleading", protecting national interests of the the Member States. There are arguments to suggest that the Community has an interest in recognising a range of public interest, non-market values both in the adoption of harmonising measures and in the justifications in Art.30 EC and the Court's case law under *Cassis*. To recognise a wider range of Community values other than purely economic concerns precludes the use of the special pleading derogations by the individual Member States and creates a consensus on Community values.

A procedure for the exchange of national measures derogating from the principle of free movement of goods has also been established in Decision 3052/95.[66] In response to a number of protests against foreign goods where farmers blocked roads and ports in France, the Member States introduced Regulation 2679/98 and a Resolution on the free movement of goods.[67] Where there is an obstacle or a potential obstacle to the free movement of goods the Member State concerned must inform the Commission of the obstacle and explain what it is going to do to remove the obstacle to free trade. The Commission may request the Member State to take measures to remove obstacles to the free movement of goods.

THE FREE MOVEMENT OF PERSONS

Citizenship of the Union

The free movement of persons is an extensive economic right, a social right, a fundamental human right and a citizenship right in Community law. This multidimensional range of rights has grown from a fragmented legal base in the EC Treaty and secondary legislation as well as the case law of the European Court. The Court of Justice has stated that common principles should apply across the rights to free movement of persons[68] but the various rights have evolved at a different pace. Attempts were made to de-couple rights to free movement from the necessity to exercise a cross-border *economic* activity in a set of Residence Directives adopted in the early 1990s.[69] A right of residence in another Member State could be claimed provided that the person was financially self-sufficient.

Today the EU is focusing upon consolidating these rights. But at the same time, the Court is building the right of Citizenship as the fundamental legal basis for free movement rights:

"Union citizenship is destined to be the fundamental status of nationals of the Member States, enabling those who find themselves in the same situation to enjoy the same treatment in law irrespective of their nationality, subject to the expressions as are expressly provided for."[70]

The original EC Treaty had ideas of "citizenship" scattered across it, based upon the non-discrimination on grounds of nationality principle in Art.12 EC and developed by the Advocates General and ECJ.[71] The Treaty of Maastricht 1993 introduced a limited set of *ad hoc* Citizenship rights. The initial reaction to the paucity of the rights attached to Union citizenship led many commentators to see the concept as an embarrassment. After a tentative start, the right to free movement (now found in Art.18 EC) combined with the non-discrimination principle in Art.12 EC has provided the basis for the new approach to Citizenship.[72] The Citizenship concept, linked with fundamental human rights concepts, is extending the right to free movement to areas previously thought to be outside of the scope of Community law.[73]

Article 18 EC is a weak legal basis for Citizenship to become the "fundamental status" of nationals of one of the Member States of the EU. Citizenship is only granted to nationals of one of the Member States. Yet, with the development of a range of flanking policies, it is now possible for third country nationals, legally resident in the EU, to rely upon a set of citizenship based rights, such as the right to equality of treatment, consumer rights, employment rights. Article 18 EC does not outline what other migration and non-discrimination rights might be available for family members who are not EU Citizens. The Court has created these rights through its case law in *Baumbast* and *Chen*. But in *Baumbast* the Court constructs an argument which carefully avoids ruling upon the exact scope of family rights derived from Art.18 EC (Szyszczak, 2004). Article 18 EC does not detail what limits there are the right to free movement. Under the economic rights to free movement the Member States are allowed some discretion to refuse admission and deport EU migrants. The Court relies upon Art.12 EC and equality of treatment in order to create substantive rights for EU migrants deriving rights from Art.18 EC, but as Maduro (2000) points out, in order to achieve true equality of treatment, and integration of persons into the host State, positive measures may also be necessary.

The new ideas embracing Citizenship as the fundamental status for nationals of the Member States may be capable of making inroads into the concept of reverse discrimination. The Constitution states that there are a number of common values in Art.I–2, which presumably can be relied upon by all citizens legally present in the EU. Article 4 and Art.II–21 of the Constitution provide that "any discrimination on grounds of nationality shall be prohibited." Can this be construed to cover discrimination by one's own Member State? The language of *Grzelczyk* is sufficiently wide to cover reverse discrimination. But in a later case the Court goes further:

". . . a citizen of the Union must be granted in all Member States the same treatment in law as that accorded to nationals of those member States who find themselves in the same situation. It would be incompatible with the right to free movement were a citizen, in the Member State of which he is a national, to receive treatment less favourable than he would enjoy if he had not availed himself of the opportunities offered by the Treaty."[74]

The Constitution makes extensive reference to Citizenship and Citizens' rights suggesting that this will be the generic concept for rights in the future. A new Citizenship Directive, Directive 2004/38/EC,[75] which will come into force on May 1, 2006, confers benefits on *all* EU Citizens, whether economically active, or not. These rights amend Regulation 1612/68/EEC which formed the core of the rights attached to free movement of workers and repeals, *inter alia*, Directives 64/221/EEC and 68/360/EEC, which facilitated free movement of persons in the EU. The new Directive enhances the rights of family members, irrespective of their nationality and registered partners and non-married partners can be recognised as members of the family. Family members will be able to retain their residence rights in the EU in the event of divorce, death or departure from the Member State of the European Citizen. After five years of residence citizens will have the right to permanent residence in the host State.

This creates an inherent tension between the historical development of rights which was associated with an economically active migrant and the new basis of rights which are de-coupled from economic activity. Arguably the sophisticated set of rights which have developed from the free movement provisions will continue to reward the economic migrant and provide incentives for people to move in the EU to create an active labour market. The Citizenship Directive continues to differentiate between economically active Citizens and other persons who move between the Member States. For example, Art.7(1) grants workers and their families a right of residence in the host State beyond the three month guarantee given to Citizens. This residence is protected if the worker becomes incapacitated, suffers involuntary unemployment or takes up vocational training. Rights of family members are also secured even if the worker goes to work in another Member State (Art.17). Under Art.7(3) the worker cannot be expelled from the host State even if he/she becomes a burden on the social security system, although the Member State may legally expel the worker and his/her family on public policy/security grounds.

Securing the External Frontier of the EU

One of the European Union's objectives is to create an area of freedom, security and justice. The aim of this objective is to secure internal free movement for Citizens of the Union and third country nationals (TCNs) who have entered the EU legally.[76] Recent case law of the ECJ and Opinions of the Advocates General have extended the rights of TCN family members sometimes using human rights concepts (Szyszczak, 2004a). Some TCNs have limited economic rights to enter the EU to exercise an economic activity under international agreements made between the EU and third States, for example the EEA agreement, the Europa Agreements leading up to the 2004 enlargement of the EU in May 2004, Agreements with Turkey, Morocco, Algeria, or Russia.

Admission of TCN migrants has always been a sensitive economic and political issue for the EU. Some Member States encourage such migration as it is an essential part of the economy and allows for flexibility within labour markets. Indeed, managed migration at the Community level is seen as an important aspect of the European Employment Strategy and attaining the Lisbon Strategy goals.[77] Other Member States, particularly States with economic problems, or forming part of the external frontier of the EU, are concerned to retain control over migration flows, especially from irregular migrants (Bogusz *et al.*, 2004). Historically this issue has been a major site for a battle of competence between the Member States, who wish to retain sovereignty in the area of immigration control and the treatment of TCNs in their own territory, and the Community, which claims to have a collective economic and political interest in managing migration and the treatment of TCNs.[78]

Community competence over matters relating to the external borders of the EU and for the control of the free movement of persons has developed in a slow, incremental fashion, but in recent years political events and the threats posed by the migration of legal and illegal migrants have compelled the Member States to co-operate more closely on securing the external frontiers of the EU.

Some of the Member States were willing to cooperate on removing the internal frontiers to free movement and attempting to secure an external border through closer co-operation on visa policy for TCNs as well as co-operate on law enforcement. In 1985 the Schengen Agreement was signed by a sub-group of EU States and was implemented through a Convention in 1990. This was essentially an inter-governmental agreement, operating outside of the Community-law framework. Although the crossing of the internal "frontiers" between the Member States of Schengenland has become easier, the price for the abolition of such formalities has been tougher checking of TCNs at the external frontier of Schengenland and closer police co-operation which has had a number of implications for civil liberties (Curtin and Meijer, 1995).

The Treaty of Maastricht introduced a third intergovernmental pillar (Title VI TEU) which included co-operation in relation to Justice and Home Affairs matters. For example, the crossing of external borders, immigration, asylum, drug addiction, fraud, judicial co-operation in civil and customs matters, police co-operation. The discussion of such sensitive matters outside of the judicial and democratic control of the main body of Community law raises concerns over secrecy, lack of transparency and accountability.

A new Art.100c EC was introduced which allowed the Council to determine which TCNs should have a visa in order to enter the EU. Labour market issues relating to conditions of employment for TCNs were addressed in Art.137(1)(g) EC. The Treaty of Amsterdam built upon this method of co-operation by transferring a number of areas relating to the free movement of persons (asylum, immigration and the crossing of external borders) into the EC Treaty in what is currently Title IV of the EC Treaty. This area has been brought within the more normal channels of EU decision-making and also the jurisdiction of the ECJ. But only courts or tribunals against whose decision there is no judicial remedy can make references to the ECJ (Art.68(1) EC).[79] The ECJ does not have jurisdiction on measures relating to the crossing of internal borders, the maintenance of law and order and safe-guarding internal security (Arts 62(1) and 68(2) EC). The UK, Ireland and Denmark opted-out of some of these provisions.

The Treaty of Amsterdam incorporated the Schengen Agreement and Convention into the main body of EC law. The UK and Ireland continue to remain outside of the Schengen arrangements although they have been allowed to cherry pick participation in some of the Schengen measures such as police and judicial co-operation on criminal matters. This has led to a fragmentation of the legal base for handling the external dimension of free movement of persons as well different priorities in relation to the aims of securing a common external frontier and the aims of securing internal free movement under the Internal Market aims. The Constitution brings all areas relating to the external dimension (police-co-operation and judicial co-operation) into the main body of EU competence. But already the EU has moved towards a better managed external frontier in relation to visas, asylum and refugee policy, the control of irregular migration, trafficking and a policy of returning migrants to the home State. There is now a Directive on Family Reunification[80] and a Directive on Long Term Residents.[81] But other immigration matters in relation to TCNs remains within the competence of the Member States.[82]

Free Movement of Workers

Article 39 EC was intended as a dynamic right, to allow workers to move freely to take up jobs where there were labour and skills shortages. The right is broad in scope, allowing for a number of positive social rights, as well as family migration and family social rights, in addition to the principle of non-discrimination on grounds of nationality. Such rights are seen as embryonic fundamental social rights and have been built upon in the Court's jurisprudence, extending the basic right to have both *vertical*[83] and *horizontal*[84] direct effect in the national courts. In *Angonese* the Court applied Art.39 EC to a situation where a private bank required of applicants a certificate of bilingualism from a local authority. The Court drew an analogy with the horizontal direct effect of the equal pay principle in Art.141 EC. The Court ruled that Art.39 EC should apply to private parties as well as public authorities, otherwise there would be inequality in the application of the free movement principle.

The right to free movement for workers is one of the core economic rights of the Internal Market contained in Art.14 EC. It is also accepted as a fundamental right in the 1989 Community Charter of the Fundamental Social Rights of Workers. Article 4 of the Constitution guarantees the free movement of persons; Art.III–18 restates the current Art.39 EC. The right to seek employment and work in any Member State is a recognised freedom in Art.II–15.

As a substantive economic right, the right to free movement of workers is subject to detailed Community law regulation. To fall within the concept of a "worker" for the purposes of Art.39 EC brings with it the right to non-discrimination on grounds of nationality (Art.12 EC) and triggers access to a number of economic, social and political rights within the host State,[85] as well as rights to family migration which are found in Regulation 1612/68/EEC. Some of these social rights are now recognised in the EU Constitution. Article II–34 states that everyone residing and moving legally within the Union is entitled to social security benefits and social advantages. Article II–35 states that everyone has the right of access to preventative healthcare and medical treatment.

In order to take advantage of the right to free movement a person must possess the nationality of one of the Member States. The Member States retain the right to determine their own nationality laws and this, therefore, is a limitation on the right to free movement. But the ECJ has ruled that since free movement is such a fundamental economic right the Member States must *apply* their nationality laws so as to give effect to the right to free movement.[86]

A second condition is that the person must be a "worker". There is no definition of a worker in the EC Treaty but the definition has implications for the scope of a wide range of Community employment and social law rights. The Court has ruled that the concept of a worker is a Community law concept. To rule otherwise would mean that the trigger for such a fundamental economic right will vary from Member State to Member State and would undermine the principle of free movement of workers.[87]

The Community law test is a functional test, summarised in *Lawrie-Blum*,[88] that:

"for a certain period of time a person performs services for and under the direction of another person in return for which he receives remuneration."

It is for the national court, as a matter of fact, to decide if the test is satisfied. But the concept of a worker, drawn from the economic right to free movement is also relevant for applying rights to free movement under agreements with third countries as well as Community-based employment rights.[89] As a result a wide range of economic activity falls within the scope of Art.39 EC. Various sporting activities such as football[90] have been held to fall within the scope of an economic activity, as well as an apprenticeship, prostitution, community-based work, part-time work, a retired worker[91] and work-seekers.[92] In *Collins*[93] an Irish-American national, had moved between the UK and America, working intermittently. When he entered the UK to look for work he was refused a social benefit, a job seekers' allowance which was available to UK nationals looking for work. The Court acknowledged that Collins was not a "worker" within the meaning of Art.39 EC and had no right of residence in the UK. But the Court argued that in the light of his status of an EU Citizen he could rely upon the prohibition on the grounds of nationality contained in Art.12 EC and Art.39(2) EC to claim a social benefit intended to facilitate access to employment.

The Article 39 EC concept of a worker is also being used as a basis for the concept of a "worker" under the social policy law provisions, even though the legislation in this area usually allows for national law definitions of a worker.[94] This is an indication that the Court is extending the fundamental rights concept into areas of social policy creating new ideas of the "citizen-worker" (Szyszczak, 2000).

The final trigger for Art.39 EC is that the worker, or work-seeker, must have crossed a Member State frontier. Thus Art.39 EC cannot be used to trigger more favourable rights to a situation which is wholly internal to a Member State.[95] Community law may provide more favourable immigration rights, especially for members of a migrant workers' family, when the free movement principle has been triggered legally.[96]

If these three conditions are met a worker has the right to move to another Member State to accept offers of employment or to look for work. He/she is protected by the principle of non-discrimination on grounds of nationality and, in addition, the migrant worker acquires a number of positive rights. For example, the migrant worker is entitled to move freely within the territory of a Member State, to stay in the Member State for the purposes of employment, to bring his/her family to the host state and for the family to be admitted to education and vocational training schemes, the right for the family members to stay in the home state to continue the education, alongside a primary carer who may be a third country national, the right to take up employment without encountering discrimination on the grounds of nationality and the right of the worker and his family to remain in the Member State after the work has ended as a result of retirement or illness/invalidity. This right does not extend to the TCN family members where the worker dies and death is not linked to an industrial disease, within two years of entering the Member State[97] The fact that a migrant worker derives positive rights from Community law leads to the possibility of reverse discrimination taking place where migrant workers receive more rights than the nationals of a host state.

The right to leave the home state and enter and reside in the host state

The economic right to free movement is based upon a fundamental right to leave a Member State. Any provisions which *preclude or deter* a national of a Member State from a Member State are incompatible with the EC Treaty.[98] The free movement of workers differs from the free movement of goods because, as we saw above, since the ruling in *Groenveld*, the Court has applied only a *discrimination* test to the export of goods from a Member State.

Under Directive 68/360/EEC nationals of a Member State, and their families may leave a Member State by producing a valid identity card or passport which confirms the nationality. A Member State is obliged to issue or renew such a document. The passport must be valid for all Member States. A Member State may not demand an exit visa but Art.10 allows for derogations on grounds of public policy, public security and public health.

Direct discrimination is an obvious barrier to free movement of workers.[99] The Court has also recognised that indirect discrimination may also be a barrier to free movement. For example, in *Heylens*[100] a Belgian national with Belgian qualifications challenged a French rule which required football trainers to possess a French football trainer's diploma.

The Court has moved beyond a discrimination approach to investigate barriers to free movement which may *hinder* the right to free movement. In *Bosman* rules drawn up by the European Football Association (UEFA) restricting the number of foreign footballers who could play in football teams in the national football league and allowing for transfer payments when a player's contract had expired fell foul of Art.39 EC since Art.39 EC would be

". . . deprived of its practical effect and fundamental right of free access to employment which the Treaty confers individually on each worker in the Community rendered nugatory."[101]

The host state must allow workers and their families to enter its territory on the production of an identity card or passport. In interpreting Art.14 EC the Court has ruled that the Member States may not carry out border checks in a systematic, arbitrary or unnecessarily restrictive manner.[102] But a Member State may continue to check that people invoking the right to free movement have the necessary qualifications, the most fundamental qualifying condition being possessing the nationality of a Member State.[103] Members of the worker's family who are TCNs may be asked for additional visas; the list of TCNs who need a visa when crossing an external border is set out in Council Regulation 539/2001.[104]

In *MRAX*[105] the Court stated that where a TCN spouse did not have a visa, a refusal of entry would be disproportionate if the TCN spouse could prove his/her identity and marriage and there was no evidence of risks covered by derogation on grounds of public policy public health or public security. *MRAX* may be confined to the situation where the TCN spouse joins the migrant *directly* from a non-EU State. In *Akrich*[106] the Court limited the right to free movement of spouses where a TCN spouse had not entered the Community external frontier in a lawful manner.

Once admitted to a Member State a worker and his/her family may be required to obtain a residence permit but this must be granted free of charge and renewed automatically. But the right of residence is a fundamental right derived from the EC Treaty and Member States may not ask migrant workers to provide evidence of residence in order to secure rights and benefits in the host State where they do not require such evidence from their own nationals. Any penalties for failing to comply with local residence regulations must not be disproportionate.[107]

Family Migration Rights

Under Regulation 1612/68/EEC a migrant worker may bring his/her immediate family to the host state and the family, even if TCNs, enjoy a number of positive rights as well as the right not to be discriminated against on grounds of nationality. Dependants of a migrant worker and his/her spouse may also be admitted. There is an overriding duty upon the Member States to ensure the integration of the migrant worker and his/her family into the economic and social fabric of the host State.

Community law provided a liberal model of labour migration, which was ahead of its time. Normally a receiving State would admit only a migrant worker, often on a "guest worker" basis". Family members were seen as "uneconomic" migrants who could be a potential drain on housing, social services health and education systems and were, therefore, not welcome. But Community law provided a basis for an embryonic citizenship model where migration was seen as an important aspect of the economic and political integration model. In *Güll*[108] a Cypriot spouse of a British migrant worker was entitled to a permanent practising certificate as a doctor in Germany. The most far-reaching set of children's rights is seen in *Baumbast*.[109] The Court interpreted Art.12 of Regulation 1612/68/EEC in the light of Art.8 ECHR, to allow children of a migrant worker to remain in a Member State to continue their studies, together with the right for the TCN primary carer to remain to look after them, even after the migrant, the primary right holder, had lost the status of migrant worker.

Derogations from the Right to Free Movement

The right to free movement is not absolute. It is subject to a number of derogations which Member States may invoke on a case by case basis. Art.39(4) EC allows the Member States to exclude *access* to posts in the public service from the free movement and non-discrimination principle. Article 39 (3) EC, Arts 46 and 55 EC allow the Member States to use public policy, public security and public health grounds to prevent foreigners from entering their territory. The public security and public policy grounds may be used to deport foreigners.

These are classic derogations drawn up in 1957 and which the Court has ruled are exhaustive, unlike the derogations to the free movement of goods which were expanded upon in *Cassis*.[110] This reflects the protection of the sovereignty of the Member States in sensitive areas. But EU law has made inroads into that sovereignty. The derogations relate to a fundamental economic right of the EC Treaty and must be interpreted restrictively and are subject to the principle of proportionality and the principle of respect for fundamental human rights. For example, the derogations cannot be used to serve economic ends and there are procedural rights contained within Community law and the general principles of Community law. The Member States' traditional

executive powers are also subject to judicial review.[111] These derogations were developed in Council Directive 64/221/EEC, which
will be repealed when Directive 2004/38 comes into operation on
May 1, 2006.

Free Movement of Services

The free movement of services is a residual category of free movement (Art.50 EC). As a result of changes in technology, the industrial base and the liberalisation of global services the provision of
services is now a dominant form of economic activity, contributing some 70 per cent of GDP in the EU. The industrial base of
Europe has changed with greater reliance upon the service sector
for the creation of jobs and economic activity. The rise in the
importance of services to the European economy is matched by
an increasing interest in regulating services at the Community
level and a body of case law exploring the scope of this freedom.

The free movement of services is a complicated concept as it
may be triggered by a variety of economic activities: a person
may move to another Member State to *provide* services; a consumer may move to another State to *receive* services; both the
service provider and the consumer may move; the service itself
might move (for example a fax, telephone, internet, electronic
commerce services, satellite TV); or neither the service provider
nor the consumer may move. Another feature of the provision of
services is the *range* of activity caught by the provision. It can
include the self-employed, for example a taxi driver or hair-
dresser, as well as organised business in the banking, financial
commercial sectors. Some sectors have received closer attention
from the Community, for example, the creation of a Financial
Services Action Plan.[112] At the time of writing the Commission is
proposing to introduce a controversial Directive on Services[113] in
an attempt to liberalise this sector even further. This is because
the Community secondary legislation and the case law on services, while creating general principles, does not address in detail
the remaining barriers to free markets.

The free movement of services has made inroads into narrow-
ing down the scope of the reverse discrimination principle by
finding that economic activity is not wholly internal to a Member
State.[114] The most far-reaching, and controversial ruling is that of
Carpenter[115] where the free movement of services protected the
right to family life of a service provider. A Philippine wife of a
British man who provided services in other Member States was

able to resist a deportation order. It was argued that she stayed at home to look after the service providers' children from a previous marriage. If she was deported this would impair the husband's ability to provide services in another Member State. The case has been criticised, in the broad interpretation given to a *hindrance* to provide services in another Member State. There was no discrimination present, and the effect upon the provision of services was incidental. The *Carpenter* case is seen as analogous to the case law pre-*Keck* in the area of free movement of goods.

Services are not defined in detail in the EC Treaty. Article 50(1) EC states that services are "normally provided for remuneration".[116] Changes in the State provision of many public services, through contracting out, public-private finance partnerships and the use of economic, market-based principles has brought a lot of traditional State provision of services within the potential scope of the free movement rules of the EU. The Court has not produced a workable "bright line" to distinguish when State activity is caught by the Internal Market and competition rules of the EC Treaty and when State activity is "non-economic" and remains outside of the reach of Community law (Szyszczak (2004b). A number of cases have arisen where restrictive rules on the availability of social and public services provided on an economic, market footing have been tested against the free market principles.[117]

Gebhard[118] provided some clarification of the definition of services, distinguishing them from the right of establishment. Services are provided on a temporary basis and should be distinguished from establishment by reference to the duration of the service, its regularity, periodicity or continuity. Although the Court was realistic to recognise that in order to provide services in a Member State the establishment of an infrastructure, for example, offices, staff, consulting rooms, chambers, is not incompatible with the nature of a service where such an infrastructure is necessary to perform the service.

Recipients of services are free to travel to another Member State in order to receive services by virtue of Directive 73/148.[119] It is this right which has been used in the "health care tourists" cases where individuals travel to another Member State to receive immediate and/or superior medical services (van der Mei, 2002; Davies, 2004).

The Court has treated the export of services in the same way as it has approached the issue in relation to workers in *Bosman*. In *Alpine Investments* Dutch restrictions on cold calling for financial services which were framed in a neutral manner and were non-discriminatory, were scrutinised as impeding the free movement of services since they restricted access of the service provider to the markets of other Member States where cold calling was permitted.[120] Exporters of the service would be subject to a double burden, of having to obey two or more sets of national regulatory rules, making the service less competitive. This approach, however, makes a significant inroad into the principle of "home state control" and highlights the need for Community harmonisation of such regulatory measures.

Directive 73/148/EEC extends the rights of immigration and residence in relation to services by requiring the Member States to abolish restrictions not only in the provision of services but also for providers of services. A number of cases have concerned workers employed by service providers who are then sent to another Member State to work. The lack of harmonisation of social and labour laws in the Community allows for competition between regulatory systems of the Member States with incentives for employers to establish themselves in a Member State with lower labour and payroll costs.

In *Commission v Belgium*[121] the Court held that a Belgium law requiring service providers to carry an identity card issued by the Belgian Ministry of the Interior was in breach of Art.49 EC. The right of residence is only available for the corresponding time that a service is being provided, or received. More far-reaching cases are *Rush Portuguesa*[122] and *Van der Elst*[123] where the Court ruled that a service provider may take a workforce composed of workers not entitled to the right of free movement under Art.39 EC to another Member State provided that they have been admitted to the home state by legal means. At that time, the harmonisation of the Member States' labour and social laws was very underdeveloped. In order to avoid a "race to the bottom" in terms of lowering labour standards the Court ruled that the host State may apply its own labour standards to the migrant posted workforce.[124] These cases reveal the necessity for Internal Market law to "spill-over" into the areas of harmonising Member States' employment and social laws. The cases led to the adoption of a Directive on posted workers Directive 96/71/EC[125]

Many of the issues relating to free movement of services involve the elimination of *discriminatory* measures which act as barriers to free movement.[126] In the same way as the Court approached "distinctly applicable" and "indistinctly applicable" obstacles to free trade in relation to goods, the Court has also recognised such a distinction in relation to the freedom to provide services. The leading judgment on indistinctly applicable measures is an infringement action, *Commission v Germany* known as "the insurance cases" (White, 2004).[127] Here the Court found that German rules requiring insurance companies to be both established and authorised in Germany was a double burden, increasing the costs of insurance services provided by non-German service providers and therefore in breach of Arts 49 and 50 EC. The Court accepted that insurance services were a sensitive sector and that there were good mandatory requirements of consumer protection justifying a continued interest in the German regulation of insurance services where such interests were not adequately protected in the home State. While the authorisation requirement was a proportionate response to such needs, the residence/establishment requirement was not.

The free movement of services follows the other freedoms in relation to handling issues of equality of treatment in the *exercise* of the right to free movement. Issues of direct discrimination on grounds of nationality, which is contrary to Art.12 EC, have arisen in relation to social advantages[128] and also indirect taxation.[129]

As with the other freedoms the Court has increasingly looked to *market access* as a criterion for determining whether or not a breach of the free movement provisions has occurred.[130] In *Mazzoleni*[131] the Court refers to a:

"restriction . . . which is liable to prohibit, impede or render less advantageous the activities of a provider of services."

In other cases the Court has also used ideas of tackling measures which hinder or impede access to a market[132] or deter recipients from using a service.[133]

The Court has accepted that Member States may justify such measures by imperative reasons in the public interest where the home State does not provide adequate protection.[134] The Court will scrutinise these reasons for proportionality[135] and also for legitimacy.[136] This wider justification, based upon the *Cassis* approach, has modernised the rather limited EC Treaty justification contained in Art.45 EC which reflects the 1957 public policy/public interests justifications of that era. In *Omega*[137] the police authorities in Bonn, Germany, issued a prohibition order against Omega, a company which had introduced a laser sport which targeted humans by using sensory tags. A British company supplied the equipment and the technology for the laser sport. The police took the view that games for entertainment which simulated killing were contrary to human dignity and constituted a danger to public order. The Court took the view that the prohibition order affected the freedom to provide services under Art.49 EC. But the Court acknowledged that the Community and the Member States are required to respect fundamental rights. The protection of fundamental rights was a legitimate interest which could be used to justify a derogation from Community law obligations, even if the Community law obligations guaranteed a fundamental freedom under the EC Treaty. Provided that the German measures were necessary and proportionate they could be used to restrict a service even though another Member State had chosen a different way of protecting human rights. In this case the protection of human dignity, which was being protected by the prohibition order, corresponded to the level of protection the German Constitution aimed to guarantee within Germany and the order banned only human targets in laser games. It was, therefore, proportionate.

The Court will allow a Member State to justify rules which are restrictive where they are designed to prevent an abuse of rights.[138] But the Court is careful to balance the freedom to provide services against a Member State's claims that the freedom has been exercised merely to abuse local regulatory laws when in fact a legitimate service is being provided in another Member State.[139]

Of significant political importance is the litigation often known as "health care tourism" where nationals of a Member State have taken advantage of the right to move receive services as a way of avoiding inadequate medical care, or waiting lists, in the home state.[140] The Court has applied Art.49 EC to hospital treatment and also to a medical benefits in kind.[141] The ECJ ruled that patients could rely upon Art.49 EC to challenge rules which prevented or made it more difficult to seek appropriate health care in another Member State, for example, the need for prior authorisation before travelling to receive health care services. The Court accepted that a Member State could justify such rules where considerations of planning and the financial equilibrium of healthcare schemes are taken into consideration. These justifications are perilously close to economic considerations which the Court has ruled are not valid justifications for impeding the four fundamental freedoms (Snell, 2005). It may be that the time has come for the Court to reassess this justification in the light of the expanding scope of Community law and the changes in State and private provision for various services. The Court seems to take a softer line on such sensitive public services, and the provision of social facilities for a Member State's population as a whole. The rise of such litigation begs the question as to whether there should be more specific Community law rules handling such sensitive issues. The omc is being used to co-ordinate a dialogue between the Member States to reduce the disparities in the way health care services are provided. This would minimise the *ad hoc* litigation which is gradually chipping away at the Member States' sovereignty in sensitive areas.

PROCUREMENT

The State continues to be a huge buyer of a number of goods and services, and also must supply certain services and create tangible objects to supply services, for example, the building of a transport infra-structure (roads, bridges, railways), hospitals, schools. The procurement of these goods and services still occupies a large part of Community GDP: 16.3 per cent. States tend to favour their own nationals, either openly or covertly by creating procurement conditions which make it easier for national firms to comply with. Thus tackling discrimination on the grounds of nationality was one of the first tasks of a Community procurement policy. Surprisingly the original EEC Treaty did not address procurement as a separate issue. It was only after the completion of the Internal Market, that greater attention was placed on the regulation of State procurement activity.

The lack of a Treaty base entailed the use of the general Internal Market base of Art.95 EC to provide a detailed set of tools to regulate procurement. (Trepte:2004). Directives were adopted regulating procurement in works, supply and services contracts as well as public utilities in water, transport, telecommunications. In addition a Directive on review procedures (remedies) was adopted. More recently the Community has had to adopt policies on defence procurement, e-commerce and address the special forms of public-private financing initiatives. In 2004 the procurement Directives were modernised to take account of developments in markets, especially the effects of liberalisation and two new Directives were adopted on the public sector and for utilities.[142]

FREEDOM OF ESTABLISHMENT

The right of establishment is available to natural persons who are nationals of a Member State and also to legal persons. Thus, the right applies to companies and to the self-employed. Article 43 EC bases the right of establishment on the right to take up and pursue activities in another Member State without discrimination. In the *Factortame* litigation the Court of Justice described the right of establishment as

"the actual pursuit of an economic activity through a fixed establishment in another Member State for an indefinite period."[143]

As with other fundamental economic freedoms the concept of establishment is not defined in the EC Treaty and it has been left to the Court of Justice to provide working definitions of the concept. In *Gebhard*[144] the Court stated:

". . . the concept of establishment within the meaning of the Treaty is therefore a very broad one, allowing a Community national to participate, on a stable and continuous basis, in the economic life of a Member State other than his State of origin and to profit therefrom, so contributing to social and economic penetration within the Community in the sphere of activities as self-employed persons.".

The right of establishment can be exercised by being a shareholder[145] or a director of a company.[146] More recent cases brought under the Europe Agreements have added to the concept of self-employment. These cases arose because, under the Europe Agreements and under the terms of Accession Treaty 2004, some Member States were concerned that there would be a flood of migrant workers from the Central and Eastern European accession States and restricted the rights to free movement of workers. But loopholes were created in the lack of restrictions on the right to provide services and the right of establishment. In *Jany*,[147] a case concerning Czech and Polish prostitutes, offering services in The Netherlands, the Court distinguished the "self-employed" from "workers" in that the self-employed work outside of the relationship of subordination and take economic risks not taken by workers and they are paid directly, and in full, for their services. In *ex parte Barkoci and Malik*[148] the Court stated that a self-employed person could conduct "activities of an industrial or commercial character, activities of craftsmen, or activities of the professions of a Member State."

Freedom of Establishment and Individuals

The right of establishment is a complicated right as it may give rise to claims by individuals as well as companies. Starting with individuals, the rights under Art.43 EC embrace the right to take up activities as a self-employed person on the same terms as nationals of the host State and also the right to exercise an activity, as well as family residence rights and the right for the self-employed and their families to remain in the host State.[149] Many of the issues mirror the problems faced by migrant workers under Art.39 EC. Immigration and residence rights are granted under Directive 73/148/EEC[150] and such rights are extended to a self-employed person's family. In *Roux*[151] a requirement to register with the relevant authorities in the host State and the penalty for failure to register, deportation, were held to be inconsistent with the rights conferred by Art.43 EC.

Problems have arisen in exercising the right to freedom of establishment. Often a person in business may wish to set up a second office, a secondary establishment, in order to exercise economic activities in more than one Member State. Some Member States forbid secondary establishment, arguing that they wish to maintain local regulation over business and professional activities. In *Klopp*[152] the Court ruled that a ban on secondary establishment used by the Paris Bar was contrary to Art.43 EC. This was a forward looking judgment in that the Court held that while it was legitimate for the Paris Bar to want to exercise control over lawyers practising locally a *ban* on secondary establishment, forcing lawyers to give up their primary establishment, was out of proportion given that lawyers were able to maintain contact with their clients and the French courts through modern methods of transport and telecommunications. Where there is indirect discrimination the State may be able to justify rules which are objective.[153] Other cases have involved more overt forms of discrimination based upon nationality which is contrary to Community law.[154]

The Court has moved on from considering rules based only on nationality discrimination to consider rules which are non-discriminatory but nevertheless prevent access to the local market. This is very similar to the indistinctly applicable rules considered in relation to goods in *Cassis de Dijon*. In *Gebhard*[155] the Court ruled "national measures liable to hinder or make less attractive the exercise of fundamental freedoms guaranteed by the Treaty must fulfil four conditions: they must be applied in a non-discriminatory manner; they must be justified by imperative requirements in the general interest; they must be suitable for securing the objective which they pursue; and they must not go beyond what is necessary in order to obtain it . . ."

The Court has imposed some limits on this test where the alleged impediment and the allegation of restricting access to a market is too remote.[156] But other cases, for example, prior authorisation for a trade fair[157] a language requirement imposed upon dentists[158] and a restriction on multi-disciplinary partnerships between lawyers and accountants[159] have been held to be restrictions on the freedom of establishment. As with the other fundamental economic freedoms, such restrictions may be justified by the Member State, subject to the principle of proportionality.

One of the major obstacles for individuals wishing to provide services or establish themselves within another Member State is the requirement of professional qualifications. The development of an education policy for the EU has been a contested area since the Member States still seek to maintain control over such a fundamental area of national identity. In the Constitution Art.I–17 is a new provision giving the Union competence to carry out supporting, co-ordinating or complementary action in the field of education and vocational training. Vocational training has also been part of the omc processes relating to the European Employment Strategy.

The principle of mutual recognition of qualifications has underpinned the Community legislative approach and has been used by the Court to liberalise free movement in the professions. Art.47 EC allows the Council to adopt Directives on the mutual recognition of diplomas using the Art.251 EC procedure. Directives have been adopted over the years, for example dentists, vets, doctors, nurses, lawyers services, architects. The sectoral approach to mutual recognition proved to be too slow and so the Community adopted two horizontal mutual recognition Directives. Council Directive 89/48/EEC[160] covers the mutual recognition of qualifications gained through tertiary education of at least three years duration and not covered in a specific sectoral Directive. Council Directive 92/51/EEC[161] extended the principle to diplomas and qualifications obtained through work or a course of study post-secondary education of less than three years duration. As part of

the ongoing modernisation process the Commission has proposed a new Directive (COM (2004) 317) to streamline the sectoral
Directives.

The mutual recognition process was slow in developing, partly
because the original Art.47 EC required unanimity voting. As a
result case law has produced far-reaching principles which may
be used to remedy the barriers to integration which different education and training systems create. In *Thieffry*,[162] an early case
recognising the principle of mutual recognition, the ECJ ruled
that Member States were bound by the principle of solidarity, as
set out in Art.10 EC and the principle of non-discrimination, as set
out in Art.12 EC. In the later case of *Vlassopoulou*[163] a Greek
lawyer with Greek and German qualifications did not satisfy the
exact qualifications for the mutual recognition approach to be
applied. Nevertheless the ECJ accepted that national rules on
qualifications may have ". . . the effect of hindering nationals of
the other Member States in the exercise of their right of establishment" guaranteed under Art.43 EC. The Court invoked
Art.10 EC, ruling that Member States were under a duty to co-
operate in the exchange of information to allow comparisons to
be made to determine the equivalence of qualifications. The
Court affirmed the duty to give reasons for decisions, allowing
such decisions to be reviewable by the courts to ensure that any
national rules and regulations were compatible with Community
law.[164]

An example of the extensive protection provided by
Community law to facilitate the free movement of persons is seen
in *Bobadilla*. Here a Spanish national was refused a permanent
post at a Spanish museum on the ground that her English post-
graduate qualification was not equivalent to a Spanish qualification. The English qualification fell outside of the scope of the two
horizontal mutual recognition Directives and was not covered by
a sectoral Directive. Nevertheless the Court ruled that the
museum was obliged to assess whether Bobadilla's knowledge
and qualifications were of an equivalent standard required under
the Spanish regulations for the post.[165]

The kinds of issues which have arisen in exercising the freedom
of establishment go beyond pure market access issues and
embrace the need to extend the principle of equal treatment to the
exercise of professional activities, for example the ability to rent
property to exhibit artistic works,[166] access to social housing[167]
equal treatment in relation to taxation, especially taxation based
upon residence requirements[168] as well as rules which may lead

to the double payment of social security contributions in the home state and the host State.[169]

Freedom of Establishment and Companies

Turning attention to issues relating to the freedom of establishment and legal persons (companies) the issues are exacerbated by the fact that companies may want to retain their registered head office (the "seat") in the home State but establish branches, agencies or subsidiaries in other Member States in order to conduct business at the local level. Company law in the Member States of the EU is not fully harmonised (Edwards, 1999; Wouters, 2000).

One fundamental difference between the Member States is the approach taken to deciding *where* a company is actually located: the place of incorporation or the place where the economic activity really takes place. Some States take an approach which identifies where the predominant economic activity is exercised. Other States use a more formal "place of incorporation" approach. The harmonisation of company law in the EU has been slow and the Member States are anxious to impose restrictions upon the movement of companies where they suspect that migrating companies may try to evade local laws and regulations.

One example is the case of the *Daily Mail*.[170] This company, which produces a national newspaper in the UK, wanted to move its central management and control to The Netherlands but also to maintain its legal personality and status as a company in the UK. There were a number of tax advantages to this, plan. It needed the prior approval of the UK Treasury to do this but relocated to The Netherlands before receiving such approval. The ECJ dismissed the argument that the requirement of prior approval for such a relocation was contrary to Arts 43 and 48 EC. The Court recognised that a company must be anchored in at least one Member State for regulatory rules to apply and that in the absence of harmonising measures Member States were able to regulate the movement of companies. Thus, if the Daily Mail had wanted to establish a subsidiary in The Netherlands the UK would have had to justify rules which prevented the partial emigration of the economic activities of the Daily Mail. It would still be open for the UK to raise a justification based upon public policy considerations of combating tax evasion.[171]

The case can be viewed as the ECJ prompting the Member States to move forward on the harmonisation of company law; a hint which was ignored by the Member States. Later developments suggest that the ruling in the *Daily Mail* case may be at odds with the developments in relation to the free movement of services and capital, and the more general shift towards looking at rules which are a "hindrance" to free movement. This has led to the ECJ chipping away at the Member States' national laws governing company law.

The change in approach is seen in two cases, *Centros* and *Inspire Art*. *Centros*[172] concerned two Danish nationals who were shareholders in a private company incorporated in the UK. The shareholders applied to have a branch of the company registered in Denmark where the economic activities of the company took place. The company had never traded in the UK but had taken advantage of the more lenient incorporation rules of the UK which, *inter alia*, did not require minimum capital requirements. The Danish authorities refused to register a branch of the company arguing that the device was being used to evade the tougher Danish regulation of companies. The Court found the refusal to register the branch, the secondary establishment, was an obstacle to free movement of establishment, since it was not an attempt to evade the Danish rules. This was a legitimate *exercise* of the right to free movement within the EU. Although the Danish regulators could take steps to counteract fraudulent use of the free movement provisions; the outright refusal to register the secondary establishment was a disproportionate response.

Inspire Art[173] concerned Dutch rules on minimum capital requirements and Directors' liability which prevented foreign companies from exercising economic activity in The Netherlands except through a branch. The Court accepted that any justifications for the rules to prevent abuse of Dutch laws and regulations could only be carried out on an individual basis. A general rule, impeding the right of establishment, was disproportionate.

In *Überseering*[174] the Court was faced with a more complicated issue. In a private dispute a Dutch company, Überseering, sued a German company for defective work carried out in Germany. All the shares of Überseering had been acquired by two German nationals before the litigation commenced. Under the German law, Überseering had transferred its centre of administration to Germany, it did not satisfy the German rules relating to incorporation and therefore did not have the legal capacity to bring proceedings. Überseering was still legally incorporated in The Netherlands. The ECJ ruled that the requirement to re-incorporate the company under German law in order to obtain access to the German legal system was a double burden, "an outright negation of freedom of establishment". These cases reveal that the Court is willing to allow regulatory competition to encourage free movement.

A host State cannot insist that a company's business be conducted through a primary establishment.[175] In *Factortame*[176] the ECJ ruled that a nationality condition on the owners of ships or the shareholders and directors was a breach of Art.43 EC and was also contrary to Art.294 EC. The residency and domicile rules were unjustified forms of indirect discrimination, but the requirement that a vessel had to be managed and its operations directed and controlled from within the UK was compatible with Community Law since it essentially coincided with establishment which implies a fixed establishment. But this could not preclude the registration of a secondary establishment in the UK.

In addition to barriers to market access companies have also faced problems in access to economic activities,[177] and validation of qualifications provided by an education establishment[178] and relating to equality of treatment in relation to tax treatment.[179] Direct taxation is an area jealously preserved by the Member States, but as with company law, successive ECJ rulings relating to the four freedoms are gradually chipping away at this autonomy. In *Marks and Spencer plc v David Halsey (HM Inspector of Taxes)*[180] a challenge has been made to the UK's corporation tax scheme which allows for group relief under which a company may surrender its losses to another company in the same group carrying on trade in the UK. This allows the company to deduct those losses from its taxable profits. Marks and Spencer plc argue that the rules are incompatible with the freedom of establishment. Advocate General Maduro states that the rules are an "exit restriction" which creates obstacles dissuading companies from establishing subsidiaries in other Member States, and restricts the freedom of establishment. The Advocate General examines the justifications for the rule, rejecting the argument that by taking into account foreign losses would reduce the amount of tax revenue leading to budgetary difficulties in the Member States. The Advocate General argues that the territorial principle is not satisfied. There is nothing to prevent the UK from extending tax relief to parent companies with non-resident subsidiaries. Finally, the Advocate General examines the justification of preserving the coherence of a tax system. He argues that there must be a direct connection between the grant of a fiscal advantage and the offsetting of that advantage by a specific charge to tax. The UK government argued that the tax scheme was aimed at fiscal neutrality, avoiding a situation where a company with a foreign subsidiary may gain advantages where the subsidiaries losses might be offset in another Member State as well, giving the group a double advantage. The general prohibition on offsetting losses far exceeds what was necessary to preserve the cohesion of a group system. Each case must be taken on an individual basis. The benefit of tax relief should be available where subsidiaries are not able to receive advantageous tax treatment in the Member State where they are resident. Consequently companies would not be at liberty to choose the place of imputation of their losses and this would avert the risk of "trafficking in losses" at the Community level.

FREE MOVEMENT OF CAPITAL

Capital should be one of the easiest commodities to move freely within the EU. In practice the Member States have been less reluctant to liberalise this economic freedom, and the free movement of capital continues to be the least developed of the four economic freedoms (Peers, 2002). The original free movement of capital provisions did plan for the liberalisation of capital by the end of the transitional period, and the EEC Treaty provisions were not complete as they envisaged liberalisation of capital to take place in stages through Directives adopted under Art.69 EC. The EEC Treaty provisions were drafted in what the Court in *Casati* called "less imperative terms".[181] In this case the Court ruled that complete free movement of capital could undermine the economic policy of the Member States or create an imbalance in the balance of payments. Therefore Art.67(1) EC was not directly effective and free movement of capital should be available only to the extent necessary to ensure the proper functioning of the then Common Market. As a result, the free movement of capital differs from the other three freedoms in that it has developed from detailed secondary legislation into a directly effective EC Treaty principle (Usher, 2005).

Council Directive 88/361/EEC[182] brought about the full liberalisation of capital movements and in its Annex set out a list (a nomenclature) of the capital movements which includes current payments covered by the Directive which is still referred to in the case law.[183] Thus loans and mortgages, the taxation of dividends, guarantees linked to the provision of services, the use of golden shares by governments when publicly owned companies are privatised have all been held to fall within the scope of the Directive. Shortly after this Directive was adopted the Maastricht Treaty introduced new rules on capital movements and payments which were broad in nature, and legally complete, allowing for the direct effect of the relevant EC Treaty provisions.

Article 106(1) EC required the Member States to authorise means of payment as consideration for trade in goods, persons, services or capital. This therefore distinguishes the means of payment from the free movement of goods. In *R v Thompson*[184] the Court stated that Art.106 EC was perhaps the most important provision in the EC Treaty for the attainment of a Common Market and Art.106(1) EC was declared directly effective in *Luisi and Carbonne*.[185]

The Court explained the distinction between Art.106 and Art.67 EC.[186] Current payments covered by Art.106 EC involved such transactions as the transfers of foreign exchange as remuneration for a service whereas Art.67 EC covered free movement of capital such as the investment of funds. This distinction became less important after the Treaty of Maastricht

Articles 56–60 EC are the backbone of the second stage of EMU, applying to all of the Member States, not just those States which have moved to the second stage of EMU. Article 56 EC is directly effective and applies to movements within the EU as well as movements to, and from, third countries. This raises the question as to whether the overlap between the capital movement rules open up the other freedoms to third country nationals who are operating in the Internal Market, where the free movement of workers, services, goods and establishment overlap with the free movement of capital rules.

Article 67 EC uses a discrimination model to establish the free movement of capital prohibiting discrimination on the grounds of nationality, the place of residence and the place where capital is invested. The issue of direct discrimination has dominated the case law.[187] In the *Golden Shares*[188] cases the Court has recognised the concept of indirect discrimination and followed the ideas seen in the services and goods case law of looking for a hindrance to free movement of capital. Such hindrances may be justified by public interest defences, subject to the principle of proportionality.[189]

Article 58 EC contains two derogations from the principle of free movement of capital. The first derogation applies to tax payers. Member States may distinguish between tax payers who are not in the same situation with regard to their place of residence or where their capital is invested.[190] The second derogation is a broader derogation using the traditional grounds of public policy or public security.

In *Manninen*[191] a challenge was made to Finnish legislation which did not allow shareholders to benefit from a tax credit on dividends where the company is established in another Member State. The Court recognised that direct taxation remained within the competence of the Member States. But the Court found that the Finnish rules involved a restriction on the free movement of capital within the meaning of Art.56 EC. Looking at the justifications for the rules the Court rejected the argument based upon Art.58(1)(a) EC. This should be interpreted restrictively and was limited by Art.58(3) EC which is directed at arbitrary discrimination and disguised restrictions. In order to fall within Art.58(1) EC it must be shown that the difference in treatment must concern situations which are not objectively comparable, or be justified by overriding reasons in the general interest, and comply with the principle of proportionality.

One overriding reason which may be raised by the Member States is the need to safeguard the cohesion of the tax system.[192] But to date a Member State has not satisfied the principle of proportionality when applying the derogation to a fundamental Treaty freedom. In *Manninen* the Court shows how a less restrictive approach could be taken to preserve the cohesion of the national system. A direct link must be established between the tax advantage concerned and the offsetting of that advantage by a particular tax deduction The objective pursued by the tax legislation should also be examined. In the Finnish case the objective was to prevent double taxation. The Court saw the link between the tax advantage and the offsetting tax deduction and why the Finnish rules were necessary to achieve this. But granting to a shareholder in a company established in another Member State a tax credit calculated by reference to the corporation tax paid by the company in the Member State would be a less restrictive measure while at the same time not threatening the cohesion of the tax system.

COMPETITION LAW
AND POLICY

The competition rules complement the rules relating to the four freedoms which form the core of the Internal Market. The four freedoms and the competition rules, together with directly enforceable individual economic rights combined with the guarantee of competition as an economic value bestow a quality of a liberal economic constitution upon the EC Treaty. Article 4 EC charges the Member States and the Community to conduct their economic policies

". . . in accordance with the principle of an open market economy with free competition.".

In relation to economic and monetary policy Art.98 EC states that

"The Member States and the Community shall act in accordance with the principle of an open market economy with free competition, favouring an efficient allocation of resources, and in compliance with the principles set out in Article 4."

The importance attached to Art.4 EC is seen in *CIF* where it is used as a "fidelity clause".[1]

In recent years the competition rules have also influenced the development of an industrial policy for the EU. Although the Commission has developed an industrial policy through the use of soft law it was not until the Treaty of Maastricht 1993 that such a policy was included in the EC Treaty (Sauter, 1997).

The competition rules of the EC are found in Arts 81–89 EC. Competition policy addresses the barriers to market integration which can be raised by the State and non-State actors, particularly private firms. The competition rules of the EC Treaty are interpreted in a teleological way by the European Courts. Competition is one of the *tasks* of the Community set out in Art.2 and is also mentioned as an *activity* in Art.3(g) EC.[2] Also of importance in understanding EC competition law is the principle of subsidiarity in Art.5 EC and the fidelity clause of Art.10 EC. The principle of non-discrimination on the grounds of nationality contained in Art.12 EC plays a role in many cases dealing with access to markets and distribution of goods and services. Overall, the principle of proportionality underpins the approach of the Court in reviewing anticompetitive acts of the State and private parties and the Commission's response to such conduct.

The founders of the Common Market recognised that it was pointless to create a Common Market where State barriers to market integration were dismantled but private barriers continued. A multinational firm operating across a number of Member States can cause as much damage to free trade and market integration by dividing up its operations along national lines as can a State. Market power may also disrupt the competitive conditions of a market, denying customers choice and denying competitors entry to the market. Similarly, collusion and agreements between smaller firms can also divide up the Internal Market and create an anti-competitive market.

The State may actively encourage this form of collusion by regulating how certain goods and services are delivered. Ownership of intellectual property rights is an important tool in promoting innovation, research and development but the exercise of such rights may prevent market access and divide up the Internal Market along territorial lines. Although aimed primarily at private undertakings, the Court has argued that Art.81 EC and Art.82 EC may also be applied to State activity. This explains why, there is a need to create a complementary approach between the rules of trade, the Internal Market, and the rules of competition (Mortelmans, 2001; Baquero-Cruz, 2002; Szyszczak, 2004).

In 1957 few Member States had a developed system of competition law. The EC Treaty coincided with the new system of competition law established in post-war Germany at the behest of the United States. Germany led the evolution of Community competition law in the 1960s and 1970s, therefore the early development of a Community competition system was influenced by the US antitrust system. Over time the EU and the individual Member States have created a distinctive *European* system of competition law[3] which may sometimes clash with the operation of US anti-trust policy in the globalised economy.

EC competition law and policy is different from other competition and antitrust regimes in two particular dimensions. First, it is aimed at promoting the public and private integration of

European markets. Alongside the free movement provisions of the Internal Market the competition rules form a central plank of the economic constitution of Europe. A second dimension is that EU competition law and policy recognises that alongside European integration it pursues a variety of aims beyond the narrow view of promoting efficiency in markets. Other goals have been articulated: ensuring consumer welfare, protecting social interests and protecting the competitive structure of markets. Another concern of modern competition law in the EU has been the prevention of the abuse of excessive market power, either by the State or private parties. The focus upon the restraint of private power in the market has been seen by Amato (1997) as a part of the process of upholding the fundamental freedom of individuals: a foundation stone of liberal democracy.

Article 81 EC addresses agreements and other forms of co-operation between private parties which may affect competition within the EU and segment markets, in the same way that national boundaries may present obstacles to the free movement of goods, persons, services and capital. The Court also developed a doctrine which imposed restraints upon the economic policy of the Member States. Using Art.10 EC, the fidelity or solidarity clause, the Court ruled that the Member States were prevented from depriving the competition rules of their *effet utile*, that is, their effectiveness.

In *Au Ble Vert*[4] the Court suggested that State legislation which makes anti-competitive behaviour redundant, and thus restricting competition, would infringe Art.81 EC. This was extended to cover, firstly, any State measures (even including a mere policy) which imposed, or facilitated or reinforced the effects of restrictive agreements[5] and, secondly, where the State delegated to undertakings the responsibility to take measures of economic policy which restricted, or had the potential to restrict, competition.[6] This approach coincided with the era pre-*Keck* where the Court gave an expansive interpretation to Art.28 EC. In a series of rulings delivered at the same time as the ruling in *Keck* the Court reigned in this expansive approach to the application of Art.81 EC to State activity.[7] This self-imposed judicial restraint towards State intervention where there was no Community interest at stake was called the "November Revolution" by Reich (1994). Reich argues that these cases were a significant turning point in the Court's constitution building of the EU, with an implicit rejection of a liberal economic Constitution. The Court continues to accept that Art.81 EC can apply to State activity but will find legislative and regulatory activity of the State acceptable, provided that the principles of subsidiarity and non-discrimination are observed.[8]

Article 82 EC addresses the abuse of a dominant position in the EU. This is where a dominant firm, often a foreign multinational company, exercises its market power, segmenting markets or affecting the way competition between firms develops, for example, by unfair pricing, attaching unnecessary terms to market transactions. The activities of the State, where it creates a public monopoly, or assigns special or exclusive rights to an undertaking to provide goods or services on the market, may also be caught by Art.82 EC. This Article is used in conjunction with Art.86 EC and Arts 10 and 12 EC and has resulted in many Member States adapting and even dismantling public monopolies in Europe in the wake of the creation of an Internal Market post-1992. The use of Art.81 EC and 82 EC in this way is seen as a procedural approach (Harm, 2002). The Court is careful not to criticise a particular Member State's policy but finds certain behaviour contrary to the competition rules of the EU.

States may create barriers to economic integration by using policies and tools which are related to competitive conditions of the market in their own territory. This may produce spill-over effects which affect trade between Member States by preventing access to domestic markets. But the effects may be wider where the State activity disrupts the competitive structure of markets by the use of the extraordinary political and economic power it enjoys in the Internal Market. In 1957 there was no clear policy towards regulating State intervention in the market. The Member States were divided as to how far State intervention could, and should, be tolerated in a Common Market. Many States were continuing to use, and to believe in active State intervention in the market in order to re-build the war torn economies of Europe. Particularly in networked sectors (utilities, telecommunications, transport) there are economies of scale in placing the production and delivery of certain services in one co-ordinated owner. Many States continue to see State owned undertakings, and even whole sectors, as national champions and find it difficult to accept that the goods and services produced can also be supplied by private actors. One feature of the role played by competition policy is how sharp divisions between the Member States on the *role* of State intervention have been ironed out by the use of the competition rules. This has led to the creation of an industrial policy for the EU (Ehlermann, 1992; Sauter, 1997).

Recognition of the role of the State in the market is seen in the belief that States are free to choose between public and private ownership in Art.295 EC:

"This Treaty shall in no way prejudice the rules in Member States governing the system of property ownership."

The Member States have attempted to use this clause to protect State intervention in sensitive areas. But the ECJ has refused to allow Art.295 EC to be used to shield economic activity and direct intervention in the market, from the scrutiny of, and compliance with, Community law.[9] Nevertheless, cases continue to arise where the State argues that the activity in question is non-economic and therefore not subject to the rules of the EC Treaty at all.[10] The Commission has attempted to draw some bright lines between "non-economic" activity and "economic" activity caught by the EC Treaty.[11] These bright lines are not always consistent, or always followed by the European Courts, who continue to use a number of legal tests to decide if State activity is caught by the EC Treaty rules (Szyszczak, 2004b). The European Courts appear to be using an approach analogous to the pre-*Keck* approach used under Art.28 EC, drawing the net of Community law as wide as possible, but then allowing exemptions or justifications from the application of the free movement and competition rules where there is a public interest at stake. The difficulty with this approach under competition law is that the competition rules were not drafted in a way which allows for the range of justifications, exemptions and derogations which are available under the four economic freedoms.

Particularly since the Treaty of Maastricht, the extent of the *balance* between free market ideas and legitimate public interests of the Member States has been part of an ongoing debate within the EU. The balance between economic concerns and social concerns has always been in the background in the political processes of the EU, as well as the case law of the European Court. The Lisbon Process, while recognising the need for a balance between what are see as *competing values* of the EU, has emphasised the need for a competitive economy, and this has tipped the balance in favour of economic priorities.

With the liberalisation of markets, and the tendency of some Member States to continue to provide traditional State provision of goods and services ("public services") in competitive markets, a number of issues have arisen which involve the application of the competition rules and the Internal Market rules. In the Constitution Art.I–13 (b) gives the Union exclusive competence in establishing the competition rules necessary for the functioning of the Internal Market. There is also a new provision in the general Part of the Constitution, Art.III–115, stating that

"The Union shall ensure consistency between the different policies and activities referred to in this part, taking all of the Union's objectives into account."

Competition and free movement rules are thus seen as the basic layer of the *economic constitution* of Europe, further layers being economic and monetary union (discussed in Ch.3) and the common commercial policy (discussed in Ch.8). In *Maizena v Council (Isoglucose)*[12] and *ADBHU*[13] the constitutional nature of freedom of competition alongside the free movement of goods was recognised by the Court. In *ADBHU* the Court was asked whether a Directive dealing with the disposal of waste oils was compatible with the principles of free trade, free movement of goods and freedom of competition. The Court responded by stating:

". . . it should be borne in mind that the principles of free movement of goods and freedom of competition, together with freedom of trade as fundamental rights, are general principles of Community law of which the Court ensures observance."

The ECJ has declared the hierarchical superiority of free competition as a constitutional norm protected by the EC Treaty and by the Court:[14]

". . . according to . . . Article 3(1)(g) EC), Article 85 [now Article 81 EC] of the Treaty constitutes a fundamental provision which is essential for the accomplishment of the tasks entrusted to the Community and, in particular, for the functioning of the internal market. The importance of such a provision led the framers of the Treaty to provide expressly, in Article 85(2) [now Article 81(2) EC] of the Treaty, that any agreements or decisions prohibited pursuant to that article are to be automatically void."

In a later case[15] the Court refers to the fundamental political constitutional building blocks of Community law to stress the role of competition policy in European integration:

"It should be borne in mind, first of all, that the Treaty has created its own legal order, which is integrated into the legal systems of the Member States and which their courts are bound to apply. The subjects of that legal order are not only the Member States but also their nationals. Just as it imposes burdens on individuals, Community law is also intended to give rise to rights which become part of their legal assets. Those rights arise not only where they are expressly granted by the Treaty but also by virtue of obligations which the Treaty imposes in a clearly defined manner both on individuals and on the Member States and the Community institutions (see the judgments in Case 26/62 *Van Gend en Loos* [1963] ECR 1, Case 6/64 *Costa* [1964] ECR 585 and Joined Cases C–6/90 and C–9/90 *Francovich and Others* [1991] ECR I–5357, paragraph 31).

Secondly, according to Art.3(g) of the EC Treaty (now, after amendment, Article 3(1)(g) EC), Art.85 of the Treaty constitutes a fundamental provision which is essential for the accomplishment of the tasks entrusted to the Community and, in particular, for the functioning of the internal market (judgment in Case C–126/97 *Eco Swiss* [1999] ECR I–3055, paragraph 36)."

The idea of the *inter-relationship* between competition law and the four economic freedoms is increasingly prominent, especially as liberalisation allows for goods and services previously supplied by the State to be opened up to competition. The complementary nature, as well as the inter-relationship, between the four economic freedoms and competition policy, was grasped early on by the lawyers involved in the litigation where private traders challenged the regulatory power of the State. These cases sparked the controversial emergence of Art.28 EC as the dominant free market constitutional tool, empowering private traders to invoke its far-reaching provisions in the national courts.[16] A similar form of litigation is occurring today using the free movement of services *and* competition law provisions to challenge the healthcare and social protection schemes organised by the Member States. These issues were discussed in Chapter 4.

Many of the early cases used Art.28 EC *and* the competition law provisions against the Member States, particularly Art.86 EC, but also the combination of Arts 10, 81 and 82 EC. The Court was hesitant to use the competition law provisions against the Member States perhaps because, with the exception of Art.86(2) EC, there was no scope to allow a State's economic activity to be justified or exempted from the application of the full force of the rules of the market. This explains why Art.28 EC was the chosen route of the Court in the initial cases exploring the boundaries of the constitutional division of power in the market.[17]

NEW GOVERNANCE

The competition provisions have remained untouched by the various amendments to the original EEC Treaty, largely because the day to day implementation of the competition policy and rules has been allowed to operate in a flexible manner, with the Commission enjoying, until recently, an almost monopolistic role in policy making and enforcement of the competition rules. The modernisation of competition law has been achieved through soft law processes and introducing new modernising pieces of secondary legislation rather than major EC Treaty revisions.

Over the years the increasing recognition of the need to regulate State economic activity in the market has led to greater application of the competition rules to State activity, especially the liberalisation of the traditional State monopolies. This has made a number of incursions into the traditional role of the State, especially where it provides public services. The EC Treaty rules address only the extreme forms of State intervention in the market. The Commission has utilised soft law processes to create coherence and continuity to the application of the competition rules to the State. Such processes have allowed discussion of sensitive areas outside of the Community's competence, for example in demarcating the lines between economic and non-economic activity in the provision of public services.[18] These activities continue, despite the Court of Justice signalling that there are limits to economic integration.[19] Soft law processes have evolved into new forms of economic governance, taking the form of Score Boards, Soft Law, Block Exemptions for State Aid, Press Releases and Speeches by the various Commissioners responsible for competition and the Internal Market. It is through these processes that the regulation of State intervention in the market has been modernised in recent years.

The new forms of economic governance which have emerged as a result of the Lisbon process are similar to the tools used to maintain the Internal Market project. Using a variety of different political actors, the Member States are persuaded to co-ordinate policy goals rather than rely on the heavy-handed "top-down"

Brussels centred law-making. Exchanges of best practice, peer pressure, Scoreboards, Annual Reports, State Aid Register are also part of the ideas of new and modern governance: openness, transparency, accountability.

It is also possible to speak of new economic governance in terms of *how* the State must conduct itself on the Internal Market. This has emerged in the liberalisation Directives and has been underpinned by rulings from the European Courts. For example, in two cases discussed in Chapter 7 we see how *ad hoc* litigation has contributed to a new normative dimension to direct State intervention in markets. In *Hofner*[20] the Court finds that a public undertaking may be abusing a dominant position when it fails to act efficiently and meet the demand for the services it has a monopoly in providing. In *Altmark*[21] the Court sets out prescriptive criteria as to when, and how, the State may use public finances to provide services in the market (Szyszczak, 2004 a or b).

Another feature of new governance is the role of new actors in decision-making processes. This has occurred in the use of expert committees and the new trans-national committees to ensure consistency in competition law policy-making and enforcement at the national level. Increasingly EU competition law has relied upon third party litigation: litigants bringing claims in the national courts as a means of ensuring the monitoring and enforcement of competition law and litigants challenging the Commission's discretion to apply the competition rules. The Commission and the Courts have encouraged private enforcement of competition law, both against the State and private parties, but there are arguments that as a matter of public policy competition law should be monitored and enforced by public bodies, not private litigants (Wils, 2003); (Reich, 2005).

ENFORCEMENT OF COMPETITION POLICY

In 1957 the Commission was placed at the centre of the enforcement of the rules applying to State economic activity. Even today, the European Courts recognise that the Commission has a broad economic discretion to monitor and enforce competition law.[22] The Commission was also the principal enforcer of Arts 81 and 82 EC. Regulation 17/62 provided the Commission with a central and monopolist role to regulate Arts 81 and 82 EC. Because the competition rules also produce direct effect within the national legal order there is sometimes a conflict in the respective powers

of national courts and the Commission, especially where a justification or exemption from the non-application of the competition
rules is pleaded. By using the preliminary ruling procedure,
national courts have contributed to the growth of a body of case
law which refines the principles upon which the EU competition
policy is built. Thus the body of policy-making and decision-
taking built up by the Commission has acquired a normative
status and provided the legitimacy for the competition policy of
the European Union.

The Commission has attempted to lessen its workload in the
monitoring and enforcement of competition law by adopting
Block Exemptions and guidance on policy through soft law
Notices and Communications. Special rules have also been developed to regulate mergers. The most dramatic change came on
May 1, 2004 when Regulation 1/2003/EC[23] introduced the de-
centralisation of the enforcement of Arts 81 and 82 EC to the
national level, repealing Regulation 17/62/EEC. This has liber-
ated the Commission from its excessive workload, allowing it to
focus upon the real "trouble cases" for the EU. It has also led to
the creation of new actors, committees of experts to advise on
competition policy and a network to co-ordinate developments in
the Member States to ensure that there is not too much divergence
in the application of competition law at the national level.

6

THE APPLICATION OF
THE COMPETITION RULES TO
PRIVATE UNDERTAKINGS

ARTICLE 81 EC

Article 81 (1) EC prohibits any kind of agreement or collusion between undertakings which has the object *or* the effect of preventing, restricting or distorting competition. Article 81(2) EC makes any agreement which infringes Art.81(1) EC void. This was a clever self-policing device. Until Regulation 1/2003 came into force it was possible for undertakings to notify their agreements to the Commission and for the Commission to grant a negative clearance, or, if the agreement infringed Art.81(1) EC but was beneficial to the integration project, to be granted an individual exemption. The work load of the Commission became so great that a number of Block Exemptions were introduced allowing firms to mould agreements into business practices which did not require prior approval from the Commission. The option of notification is now lost. Under Regulation 1/2003/EC firms must self-assess whether the agreement is caught by Art.81(1) EC and whether it would satisfy the conditions for an exemption under Art.81(3) EC.

Definition of an Undertaking

The use of the word undertaking in competition law is a deliberate attempt to include as many economic actors as possible within the ambit of competition law. The definition of an undertaking has also been one of the devices used in EU law to create a bright line between State activity which is economic and should be subject to the rules of the Internal Market and competition law and activity which is purely public or social in nature and remains within the autonomy of the State. (Szyszczak, 2004). As with other definitions such as the concept of a "worker" under Art.39 EC, the Court has ruled that the definition of an undertaking is a Community law concept and it is irrelevant as to the national definition of legal status and the way in which the under-taking is financed. In *Höfner and Elser v Macrotron*[1] a Federal Employment Placement Office in Germany was held to be engaged in economic activity. At para.21 the ECJ states that:

"the concept of an undertaking encompasses every entity engaged in an economic activity, regardless of the legal status of the entity and the way in which it is financed."

Thus artists, inventors, a pension fund, the International Federation of Football Association, customs agents and even members of the Amsterdam Bar have all been held to constitute "undertakings" for the purposes of EU competition law. On the other side of the bright line examples of cases where a body has been held not to be an "undertaking" include a French municipal authority with a concession to supply funeral services, *Bodson v Pompes Funèbres des Régions Libérés SA*,[2] and compulsory sickness funds created by statute in Germany, *AOK Bundesverband and others v Ichthyol-Gesellschaft Cordes, Hermani and Co.*[3]

Article 81 EC requires an agreement or collusion between undertakings. One issue is whether Art.81 EC can apply where undertakings are sufficiently linked to form one economic entity, for example, a parent and its subsidiary. In *VihoEurope BV v Commission*[4] Parker Pen Ltd sold stationery products through local subsidiaries. Parker Pen Ltd refused to deal with Viho, a Dutch office equipment wholesaler. Viho complained that the dis-tribution system was a set of agreements between undertakings which divided up the EU market. On appeal to the ECJ the Court noted that Parker Pen Ltd held 100 per cent of the shares in the subsidiaries and that sales and marketing were directed by the parent company. Thus Parker Pen Ltd and its subsidiaries formed a single economic unit within which the subsidiaries did not enjoy real autonomy. The Court makes the point, however, that the large undertaking may run the risk of infringing Art.82 EC. Articles 81 EC and 82 EC are not mutually exclusive.[5]

Agreements and Concerted Practices

In the absence of a clear written agreement the CFI has held that there must be a "concurrence of wills" between at least two par-ties. In *Commission v Bayer*[6] the Commission argued that there was a tacit agreement between Bayer and its wholesalers to partition the Internal Market and maintain high prices. There was no

Internal Market in pharmaceutical products and in one product, Adalat, the price was fixed by health authorities in France and Spain at a level around 40 per cent less than the price in the UK. Wholesalers began to import Adalat into the UK to exploit the price difference. Bayer's subsidiaries began to impose caps on the amount of Adalat supplied in France and Spain. Bayer argued that this was unilateral conduct and that the Commission has stretched the concept of an "agreement" too far. The CFI annulled the Commission Decision. On appeal the ECJ accepted that the use of measures which prevented or hindered parallel imports is not *per se* evidence of an agreement. The policy did not require co-operation between wholesalers but in certain circumstances it may be necessary to look at the intention of the parties.

Article 81 (1) EC also prohibits decisions between associations of undertakings which produce anti-competitive effects. This may encompass the constitution of the association[7] or the code/regulations under which the members of the association operate,[8] even if the code is non-binding,[9] and also professional regulations.[10]

Concerted practices are also brought within the scope of Art.81(1) EC. This has created controversy since firms operating in oligopolistic markets argue that they behave in parallel by reacting to the same market conditions. In *ICI v Commission (Dyestuffs)*[11] the Court explained that there was a difference between an agreement and a concerted practice, providing a definition of the latter as:

". . . the object is to bring within the prohibition of [Art.81(1) EC] a form of coordination between undertakings which, without having reached the stage where an agreement properly so-called has been concluded, knowingly substitutes practical cooperation between them for the risks of competition.

By its very nature, then, a concerted practice does not have all the elements of a contract but may inter alia arise out of coordination which becomes apparent from the behaviour of the participants."

In the later case of the *Sugar Cartel*[12] the Court added to this definition with the words that the participants:

". . . knowingly substituted for the risks of competition practical cooperation between them, which culminated in a situation which did not correspond to the normal conditions of the market."

Proving a concerted practice may be difficult. In *Sugar Cartel* the Court stated that the facts must be looked at as a whole, but in *Hüls AG v Commission (Polypropylene Cartel)*[13] the Court made the Commission's task easier by stating that the anticompetitive effects of the concerted practice on the market do not have to be shown.

Preventing, restricting or distorting competition

To be caught by Art.8(1) EC an agreement must have as its object *or* effect a restriction of competition (Odudo, 2001). Some illustrations of the kinds of agreements potentially caught by the competition rules are found in Art.81(1) EC, for example, price fixing, market sharing. In *Consten and Grundig v Commission*[14] the Court held that the effect on competition does not necessarily have to be detrimental. This allowed for a broad interpretation of Art.81 (1) EC, casting the net of Community competition law wide.

The agreement must be analysed in the totality of the economic and legal context within which it operates.[15] The Commission has codified its own practice and the Courts' case law. In 2004 the Commission produced a set of Guidelines as part of the implementation of the Modernisation programme related to Regulation 1/2003/EC. In one of these Guidelines, *Guidelines on the Application of Article 81(3) EC*, at paragraphs 21–27, the Commission explains how the words "object or effect of restricting, preventing or distorting competition" operate.[16]

May Affect Trade Between Member States

This part of Art.81(1) EC has traditionally been interpreted as the dividing line between Community competence to regulate competition and national competence. The Commission and the European Courts look at the effects of an agreement or concerted practice. Even a local agreement within one Member State may affect competition in the Internal Market. The language used in one of the earliest rulings on this phrase echoes the language of free movement of goods used in *Dassonville*:[17]

"For the requirement to be fulfilled it must be possible to forsee with a sufficient degree of probability on the basis of a set of objective factors of law or of fact that the agreement in question may have an influence, direct or indirect, actual or potential, on the pattern of trade between Member States."[18]

In the Guidelines associated with Regulation 1/2003 there is a document entitled *Guidelines on Effect of Trade Between Member States* which summarises the Courts' case law.[19]

De Minimis

The Court[20] and the Commission have accepted a *de minimis* principle in relation to the effects on competition and the effects on trade between Member States. The Commission Notice of 2001 restricts the principle to the *competition* aspects of the infringement of Art.81(1) EC[21] and the 2004 Guidelines explain the application of a *de minimis* approach on the effects on trade between Member States.[22]

Article 81(3) EC

The wide application of Art.81 (1) EC caught many agreements and business practices of undertakings. The Commission was not willing to use a "rule of reason" and preferred to use the possibility of an individual exemption under Art.81(3) EC as the process for deciding if certain kinds of agreement could be beneficial for the Internal Market (Monti, 2002).[23] There are four conditions to be met for Art.81(3) EC to apply, with the applicant bearing the burden of showing all four conditions are met.

The agreement must: (1) lead to an improvement in the production of goods or services; (2) lead to an improvement in the distribution of goods and services; (3) promote technical progress; and (4) promote economic progress.

Efficiency gains can be included in the consideration of Art.81(3) EC and other benefits such as social benefits, for example, improving the stability of the labour market or environmental concerns have been used to justify an exemption under Art.81(3) EC. The Commission provided guidance on the scope of Art.81(1) EC through soft law. Under the new decentralised regime of enforcement of competition law undertakings must assess the balance between Art.81 (1) and (3) EC on their behaviour. The Commission has issued Guidelines on the Application of Art.81(3) EC.[24]

ABUSE OF A DOMINANT POSITION

Article 82 EC addresses the competition issues which arise where a firm has the capacity to behave unilaterally on the market because of the strength of its economic power. Holding a monopoly or a dominant position is not *per se* a problem for EU law; it is the way the dominance is used, the abuse of market power which attaches a special responsibility for dominant firms. Article 82 EC addresses the power held by corporate groups, multinational companies[25] as well as collective dominance of a market by more than one undertaking. The idea of collective dominance is controversial since where there are a few firms operating in an oligopolistic market, such firms will argue that they react in a similar way to the same market conditions. This is no excuse, and indeed, may be evidence of a collective dominant position.

The CFI[26] has defined collective dominance as where two or more independent economic entities are:

"... united by such economic links that, by virtue of that fact, together they hold a dominant position."

In later cases the ECJ ruled that contractual or other links in law are not essential for a finding that there is collective dominance, but other connecting factors could be taken into account in an economic assessment and in particular in an assessment of the structure of the market in question.[27]

Even more far-reaching is the ruling in a case under the Merger Regulation,[28] where the CFI held that evidence of a collective dominant position may be found where the economic links between the undertakings are formed only by:

"... the relationship of interdependence existing between the parties to a tight oligopoly within which, in a market with appropriate characteristics, in particular in terms of market concentration, transparency and product homogeneity, those parties are in a position to anticipate one another's behaviour and are therefore strongly encouraged to align their conduct in the market."

Article 82 EC is skeletal in form. There must be a dominant position in the Common Market, or a substantial part of the Common Market; there must be an abuse of that position, with Art.82 EC providing a set of illustrations as to how abuse might occur, and there must be an effect on trade between Member States. There has been less case law on Art.82 EC and it has been used predominantly against non-EU multinational firms. The Commission has produced less soft law guidance on Art.82 EC.

In contrast to Art.81 (3) there is no possibility of an "exemption" from an abuse of a dominant position. Over the years the

Court has accepted that an objective justification for an alleged abuse of a dominant position may be made, subject to the principle of proportionality. The difficulty with Art.82 EC is that it has been applied *ex post* and undertakings may not realise that they are in a dominant position or that their behaviour is an abuse of a dominant position. In *Continental Can*[29] the Court applied Art.82 EC to changes in the *structure* of the market. Over time it was realised that Art.82 EC was not an adequate tool to deal with the competition problems emerging from the increase in take-overs and mergers in the EU and in 1989 a separate Regulation was adopted to handle mergers.

What is a Dominant Position?

It was left to the ECJ to define dominance. Dominance does not exist in the abstract; it is tied up with the relevant market in which the firm trades. In some instances the State will create a legal monopoly, especially where an undertaking is given exclusive rights to perform a service or produce goods. During the 1990s greater emphasis was placed upon tackling the abuse of such monopolies as ideas of liberalisation of State regulated markets swept across Europe.

A central idea in the Court's definition of dominance is the ability of a firm to act independently. At para.65 of the ruling in *United Brands*[30] the Court provides the classic definition of dominance built up through its case law. A dominant position:

"... relates to a position of economic strength enjoyed by an undertaking which enables it to prevent effective competition being maintained on the relevant market by giving it the power to behave to an appreciable extent independently of its competitors, customers and ultimately of its consumers."

In *Hoffman-La Roche*[31] the ECJ emphasised that a dominant position did not preclude some competition, but to attract Art.82 EC the dominant firm must be able to influence the conditions of competition on the market.

The test for the relevant market for these conditions to exist in has given rise to controversy and criticism. There are two relevant markets to consider. The first is the product market; the second is the geographical market. The Commission would like to define relevant markets narrowly in order to show that the firm is dominant. Whereas the accused dominant firm(s) would like to draw the markets as wide as possible to show that there are other competitors. The issue is how far are products interchangeable so that if a dominant firm exploits its economic position (for example by raising prices) consumers will have the opportunity to switch to alternative products? The Commission will look at the use of the product, price, characteristics. This kind of test is not always easy to apply. If the price of draught beer is raised what does the seasoned beer drinker do? Switch to lager? Or wine? Is he or she just thirsty and will drink mineral water?

In relation to the product market a dominant firm is keen to show that products within a market are interchangeable and that it is competing alongside a number of different products. The facts of *United Brands* illustrate the point. United Brands was a vertically integrated firm. It owned banana plantations in Central and South America and also distributed the bananas under a trade mark protected name "Chiquita". It held between 40–45 per cent of the market share of branded bananas and held sufficient economic power to control the way its bananas were sold by wholesalers. United Brands argued that the "relevant market" was fresh fruit in general.

The Commission and the ECJ took a much narrower view arguing that the banana was a separate market because the banana had unique physical, functional and economic characteristics. Using studies by the Food and Agricultural Organisation, it was argued that there was a low cross-elasticity between bananas and other fruit. Bananas were available all year; the only other fruits which were available all year were apples and oranges. Other fruits such as peaches or grapes were seasonal. Consumers did not substitute other fruits for bananas; other fruits were not interchangeable.

What caused most controversy and criticism of this decision, however, was that the Court recognised a distinct *separate consumer market* which would not substitute other fruits for the banana: the very young, the old, and the sick. This group of consumers, was not the whole of the market, and neither the Commission nor the Court showed *how* United Brands was able to exploit the banana market (for example, charging high prices to this group of consumers). The Commission, in the face of the criticism of the decision, refined its ideas that a distinct group of customers will be relevant for market definition to cover the situation where such customers constitute a separate market and the dominant firm is able to exploit this separate market.[32] But other cases show the tendency of the Court to uphold the narrow view taken by the Commission of the relevant market. For example, in

Michelin[33] the CFI upheld the Commission Decision finding an abuse of a dominant position in the market for new replacement tyres for lorries, buses and similar heavy vehicles. These are perhaps extreme examples, but they show the intuitive approach taken by the Court and the Commission towards controlling excessive power in the market.

The geographical market test determines the Community jurisdiction. In the *Sugar Cases* the Court stated that:

"the pattern and volume of the production and consumption of the said product as well as the habits and economic opportunities of vendors and purchasers must be considered."[34]

It is the *volume* of trade which is a significant factor. This has meant that a number of ports and airports have been held to fulfil the "substantial part of the Common Market" criteria.[35] In some cases a single Member State has also been held to occupy a substantial part of the Common Market.

The Commission and the Court also use various indicators in order to show that a firm is dominant in a particular market.[36] The most obvious indicator to look for is the *amount* of the market share the dominant firms holds in the relevant market. The higher the market share, with "very large shares", are taken by the Court as indicative of dominance, or at least a presumption of dominance, unless the alleged dominant firm can show that there are "exceptional circumstances".[37] The market share should be held over a period of time. Looking at the case law, 50 per cent appears to be threshold for determining that there are very large market shares when the rebuttal of the presumption of dominance comes into play.[38]

Where market shares are lower, then other factors, or indicators are used. These factors relate predominantly to *access* to the market. These will include the structure of the market: what are the shares of competitors? Vertical integration of the undertaking's activities bringing about economies of scale and control over the production and distribution process is an important indicator. This may also lock in customers and consumers to the particular brand or a secondary market such as spare parts, after sales services. Other examples from the case law include ownership of intellectual property rights; state regulation, for example the creation of a legal monopoly; superior technology and efficiency; access to financial resources; raw materials or "key inputs" (for example, airline slots); advertising; overall size; strength and range of products: the ability to cross-subsidise or engage in predatory pricing. In some cases it is the dominant firm which supplies the evidence, either from internal documents used by the Commission, or from claims made by the firm itself. For example, AKZO described itself as "the world leader in the peroxides market".

Abuse

Article 82 EC lists *examples* of what constitutes an abuse of a dominant position. These examples show how a dominant undertaking may exploit its market power against other competitors and also to the disadvantage of consumers. Many cases involve the pricing policies (unfair purchase or selling prices) of dominant firms (Bishop, 1991). By and large, the attack has been upon the *supply* of goods/services on the market, but it is recognised that a dominant firm may be a monopsonist, one example might be where a supermarket in a dominant position exploits its buying power against suppliers. But neither the Court, nor the Commission, can act as a price regulator. There are arguments that in the absence of barriers to entry and legal restraints, competition law should not intervene to regulate prices. A successful firm should be allowed to reap the benefits of efficiency and success otherwise there are disincentives for innovation. Excessive prices may force customers to change brands and attract new competition to the market.

One concern over pricing policy is the issue of predatory pricing. This is where an undertaking prices its product so low that competitors are forced out of the market. When this occurs with goods coming from outside of the EU this is called "dumping" and the Commission has the power to impose duties on such imported products to raise the price and protect home produced goods. A dominant firm may target certain customers with low prices to fend off a competitor. It can do this by squeezing profit margins or cross-subsidising products. A dominant firm may also use pricing strategies to divide up the Internal Market along geographical lines, maintaining the divisions with other measures (which have also been examined under Art.81 EC) such as preventing parallel imports, limiting supplies, using intellectual property rights to prevent access to the market, or divide the Internal Market along territorial lines. The Court has allowed dominant firms to refute such allegations of abuse by showing that there are objective market conditions which explain price differences between the geographical areas. These would include transport costs, costs of licensing or intellectual property rights.

Another form of differential pricing strategies which has come under scrutiny is the use of loyalty rebates and discounts which tie in customers.[39] Rebates are a common business practice. The dominant firm will argue that there are cost savings where discounts are given for quantity buying but there must be a correlation between the discount and the saving. In contrast loyalty discounts are seen as problematic since they prevent customers from obtaining supplies from competitors and will usually prevent competitors from offering their goods at a price which can induce the customer to switch supplier.[40]

Tying

A dominant firm may lock in customers of a primary market by limiting the choices of goods or services on a secondary market. It may be that the primary market is competitive but the dominant firm may not allow for competition in, say, after sales care, or servicing, or spare parts for its products which are not be interchangeable with spare parts from competitors. This ties the customers to buy these products from the dominant firm. The issue of finding abuse from tying or lock-ins is therefore bound up with the definition of the relevant market. In *Van den Bergh Foods Ltd v Commission*[41] a manufacturer of ice cream products included an exclusivity clause in its distribution agreements for the "impulse buying" market of ice cream. Freezer cabinets were made available at a nominal sum and maintained by the manufacturer on condition that they were used for the exclusive use of its products. In *Hilti*[42] a supplier of nail guns engaged in a number of practices to ensure its customers of the nail gun also bought nails from it. This included *inter alia*, discounts where guns and nails were bought together but also refusing to supply customers who bought nails from other suppliers. In *Hugin*[43] the Court held that the relevant market for establishing dominance was the spare parts for Hugin cash registers. Hugin was the sole supplier of the spare parts and therefore abused a dominant position by refusing to supply the spare parts to a small firm which sold, leased, serviced, repaired Hugin cash registers. In *Digital*[44] the Commission found that there were two separate markets for the maintenance of Digital computers: maintenance of hardware and software. The services were not interchangeable. *Microsoft* concerns the tying in of software markets.[45]

Refusals To Supply

In *Commercial Solvents*[46] the Court found that Commercial Solvents was using its dominant position on the raw material market to affect competition, and to drive a competitor out of business by refusing to supply a derivative product. Commercial Solvents wanted to vertically integrate its operations and enter the derivatives market. The Commission ordered Commercial Solvents to resume supplies of the products in order to keep a competitor in the market. Interestingly most of the supplies of the product, which was used to make drugs to fight tuberculosis, were exported outside of the EU. The Commission and the Court were concerned to maintain the competitive structure of the market. United Brands refused to supply a long standing customer who had advertised competing brands of bananas. While the Court accepted that a dominant firm can protect its commercial interests, it found the cutting off of banana supplies to be a disproportionate response. In *Hugin* the dominant firm cut off supplies of spare parts to a customer.

Essential Facilities

From the refusal to supply cases the Commission began to entertain the idea of an "essential facilities" doctrine. This concerns *access* to a facility supplied or controlled by a dominant undertaking in an upstream market rather than the supply of products (Doherty, 2001). The early cases concerned access to transport facilities especially in sea ports.[47]

An essential facilities doctrine using competition law has been greeted with much comment and criticism. As we have seen in relation to abuse of a dominant position, courts cannot step in and act as a regulators. Too much intervention in markets will destroy incentives for efficiency, innovation and investment (Areeda, 1990). If there is a breakdown in the competitive structure of a market this is better handled through regulation rather than litigation. In the liberalisation process access to networked services and the infrastructure is regulated specifically.[48]

In *Oscar Bronner*[49] access to a newspaper distribution system created by a dominant firm was sought by a small distributor. The Court referred to its earlier case law on refusal to supply. It did not refer to the concept of "essential facilities. The Court took a narrow approach. Arguing that before an abuse of a dominant position could be found for failing to grant access to a facility

owned or developed by the dominant undertaking, three conditions should be met: first, the refusal should be likely to eliminate
all competition in the downstream market; secondly, the refusal
must be incapable of objective justification; thirdly, the access to
the facility must be indispensable; there must be no actual or
potential substitute for the facility requested.

In relation to intellectual property rights the Court has
accepted that a refusal to grant licences *may* be an abuse of a
dominant position.[50] In *Magill*[51] the Court applied its refusal to
supply case law to a refusal by TV stations, which owned the
copyright in television listings, to allow a new competitor
Magill, to enter the market to supply a *new* comprehensive TV
guide. The Court viewed the TV stations as holding a monopoly
in a raw material.

The idea of an essential facilities doctrine has been limited in
IMS Health GmbH & Co. OHG v NDC Health GmbH & Co. KG.[52]
IMS had created a brick system for dividing Germany into seg-
ments for the analysis of data for regional sales of pharmaceutical
products. This had become an industry standard. NDC had tried
to create a competing system with no success and applied for a
licence to use the IMS system. IMS refused the application which
would have given a competitor access to its brick system. IMS
sought to use its copyright protection against NDC in the German
courts. An Art.234 EC reference was made to the ECJ. NDC made
a complaint to the Commission. The Commission ordered interim
measures against IMS, using the *Magill* ruling, ordering IMS to
grant NDC a licence. IMS appealed this decision but the CFI and
ECJ suspended the interim measures until after the Art.234 EC
ruling.

In the ruling the ECJ does not refer to a concept of essential
facilities. The Court sets out three cumulative conditions to be fulfilled before a refusal to license a copyright protected product can
be an abuse of a dominant position. There must be a *new* product
involved (*Magill*); access to the copyright protected product must
be indispensable so that the refusal to supply the information will
exclude any, or all, competition on a secondary market; the
refusal to supply must be unjustified. In neither *Oscar Bronner* nor
IMS does the ECJ offer any indication of what amounts to a legitimate justification for refusing to supply. In *Microsoft* the
Commission rejected Microsoft's justification that the refusal to
supply interface information for its software was necessary to
protect innovation.

Abuse Affecting the Structure of a Market

The Court has expanded these examples by applying Art.82 EC to conduct which affects the structure of the market.[53] Later cases have applied Art.82 EC to behaviour which weakens competition on the market. In *Michelin*[54] the Court states:

"The concept of abuse is an objective concept relating to the behaviour of an undertaking in a dominant position which is such as to influence the structure of a market where, as a result of the very presence of the undertaking in question, the degree of competition is weakened and which, through recourse to methods different from those which condition normal competition in products or services on the basis of transactions of commercial operators, has the effect of hindering the maintenance of the degree of competition still existing in the market or the growth of that competition."

The Court signalled that private firms who acquire market power are regarded as having a "special responsibility" which forbids the firm from abusing a dominant position and behaving in ways which may be tolerated by competitors in the same market who do not enjoy such significant market power. This led Amato to comment:

"Market power, just because it is conceptually accepted, is thus loaded with the burdens and limits which, according to the general principles more of public than of private law, bear upon whoever holds power."[55]

Advocate Generally Fenelly used the term "super dominant" for the first time in *Compagnie Maritme Belge*.[56] Over time the Court has suggested that undertakings who are "super-dominant" also have special responsibilities in the way they behave.[57] Super dominance brings with it a special responsibility towards the competitive process and conduct is more likely to be categorised as abuse under Art.82 EC.

Objective Justification of the Behaviour of a Dominant Firm

Article 82 EC forbids the abuse of a dominant position, therefore there is no scope within the wording of the Treaty provision to condone or grant an exemption for abusive behaviour. But the Court and the Commission have developed the concept of "objective justification" to allow for behaviour which is pursued for legitimate commercial reasons. Examples of this justification are seen in the Commission Decision in *Eurofix-Bauco/Hilti*[58] where a producer of nail guns tied the sale of nails to its guns for safety reasons. The Commission has allowed a dominant firm to cut off supplies to a bad debtor in *BBI/Boosey & Hawkes*.[59]

Effect on Trade Between Member States
As with Art.81 EC, the requirement that there must be an effect upon trade between Member States for Art.82 EC to bite is a jurisdictional device demarcating competence between Community law and national law. In *Hugin* the Court quashed the Commission's decision finding an abuse of Art.82 EC because the activities of the firm which relied upon the spare parts was confined to the area of London and there was no inter-state trade. It was also argued that if the firm went out of business it would not upset the competitive structure of the market. But in other cases Art.82 EC has been applied even if there is no alteration to the flow of goods or services between Member States but where the behaviour may alter the structure of competition.[60]

The Commission is now looking at whether Art.82 EC should be modernised in the same way that Art.81 EC has been scrutinised. It is arguable that Art.82 EC has provided enough flexibility to handle the new problems which have emerged such as whether there should be an essential facilities doctrine, issues of collective dominance and super-dominance. Where Art.82 EC is not a useful tool then special rules of regulation have been used in the liberalised sectors and also in the field of merger control. There is some criticism that the Commission has focused too much upon the supply side and neglected the possibilities of abuse in markets where there is a monopsony. Also there are arguments that because Art.82 EC applies *ex post*, more guidance could be given to undertakings to avoid abusing a dominant position.

Mergers
Mergers are an important tool of industrial policy and are more likely to occur when cross-border trade develops. Until the adoption of a Regulation in 1989 there was no systematic approach to mergers in the EU although the Commission had expressed an interest in controlling what were termed "concentrations" since the 1960s. Articles 81 EC and 82 EC were stretched to cover situations where a merger had the potential to disrupt competition,

but it was recognised that a system of *ex ante* regulation of mergers was necessary where there was a Community dimension. At the national level merger control was very under-developed.

Community competence to regulate mergers is contentious since it is arguable that mergers do not constitute anti-competitive behaviour but alter the structure of competition on the market. There was an underlying industrial policy objective in the EU of increasing the scale of national and European firms to enable them to compete in globalised markets. This was seen by encouraging the use of joint ventures. Many of the early cases investigated by the Commission were alleged to have a political motive, rather than an economic analysis of the harm the merger might cause. To allow the Member States to retain some control over national industry policy merger control was divided between Community and national competence.

The Merger Regulation applies to "concentrations". This occurs when two or more independent undertakings merge their activities or where there is a change in control of an undertaking. The approach for determining Community competence to regulate mergers is based upon the turnover of the undertakings. There are two alternative sets of thresholds in Art.1 of Regulation 139/2004.[61] One threshold relates to the "worldwide turnover" and the other relates to the "Community-wide turnover". This is a different approach from the application of Arts 81 and 82 EC which uses the "effect on trade between Member States" as the determinant of Community competence. A Merger Task Force (which has now been disbanded) was created and prior notification of mergers was mandatory with the Commission obliged to take Phase I and Phase II investigations and reach decisions within strict time limits.

The parties to a merger are allowed to raise justifications (or defences), for example that there would be efficiencies in the merger; Art.2(1)(b) of Regulation 139/2004 refers to "the interests of immediate consumers, and the development of technical and economic progress". Another possible defence which has emerged is that of the "failing firm".[62] In the Guidelines on the assessment of horizontal mergers[63] the Commission outlines the policy in this area. The basic requirement is that the deterioration of the competitive structure that follows the merger cannot be said to be caused by the merger. Three criteria must be met. Firstly, the allegedly failing firm would be forced out of the market in the near future because of financial difficulties; secondly, there is no less anti-competitive alternative purchase than the notified merger and finally, in the absence of the merger the assets of the failing firm would inevitably exit the market.

Mergers may be cleared by the Commission subject to "commitments".[64] These are also known as remedies. The parties to a merger may also agree to restrictions directly related and necessary to the implementation of a merger (known as ancillary restraints) Recital 21, Art.6(1)(b) and Art.8(1) and (2) the Commission must consider these restrictions as part of its assessment of the merger.[65]

The Commission was overwhelmed with work and published a number of soft law Notices and Communications to provide guidance on policy. But the Commission was criticised for not taking into account sufficient economic factors in its decisions and a series of high profile defeats in the CFI[66] forced the Commission to re-appraise its practice in relation to mergers.

The Merger Regulation was amended in 2004 as part of the general modernisation package of reforms to competition law which took place with enlargement. The Regulation is supplemented with soft law to provide guidelines on how certain mergers should be handled.[67] Additionally a Chief Competition Economist was appointed and a new internal panel was created to scrutinise the initial investigations of a merger by the Commission staff.

The major change under the new Regulation is the test used to determine if a merger is likely to affect competition in the Internal Market. Under the original Merger Regulation the Commission was able to block a merger if it could show that the merger would create, or strengthen, a dominant position, and that effective competition would be significantly impeded (Kokkoris, 2005; Soames and Maudhuit, 2005). As a result of the case law from Art.82 EC the Commission found it easy to presume that if the merger created or strengthened a dominant position then competition would also be impeded. Under the new Regulation the wording is reversed and requires the Commission only to show that the merger would significantly impede competition; the creation of dominance is only one example of a situation where competition would be impeded.[68]

The change in approach resulted from some controversial decisions taken by the Commission. The Commission clashed with the US over the blocking of a merger between General Electric and GE Honeywell.[69] This was a proposed conglomerate merger which was deemed to be so strong that the massive economic

strength which would be created would undermine rivals and
dominate a range of markets. In the same year the Commission
blocked a conglomerate merger between *Tetra Laval and Sidel*. On
appeal the CFI found that the Commission had committed manifest errors of assessment and quashed the Commission's
Decision; the ECJ upheld the CFI ruling.[70]

A second reason given for the change was that the Commission
argued that the old test failed to capture mergers in oligopolistic
markets. The original test in the Merger Regulation could not
address unilateral effects which emerge from oligolopoly behaviour. But the Commission had used the Merger Regulation to
block mergers which led to the creation of a collective dominant
position. Although the Commission lost appeal of its Decision in
Airtours[71] the CFI confirmed that it was possible to use the old test
of the Merger Regulation to regulate mergers *ex ante* in oligopoly
markets that created a risk of coordinated anticompetitive behaviour. But the Commission had wanted to go further than this and
block mergers that led to tacit collusion through coordinated
effects. As we have seen, it is more difficult to prove tacit collusion under Art.81 EC *ex ante*.

COMPETITION POLICY AND A COMMUNITY INDUSTRIAL POLICY

The Commission has interpreted competition policy widely. By
allowing competition policy to pursue a number of objectives, for
example, the promotion of integration, efficiency, the competitiveness of European industry, and albeit limited in extent, wider
social objectives competition policy has internalised an industrial
policy for the Community. This goes beyond the EC Treaty base
for a Community industrial policy which was first introduced by
the Treaty of European Union 1993. It will be recalled that this
coincided with a greater range of aims and objectives for
European integration, including ideas of social rights and citizenship. Article 3 (1) (m) EC states that the activities of the
Community shall include "the strengthening of the competitiveness of Community industry". Title XVI allows the Commission
to coordinate the Member States' actions in this field (Art.157(2)
EC). The Community and the Member States are to ensure that
the conditions necessary for the competitiveness of the
Community' industry exist. The Council may support action
taken by the Member States to achieve the objectives of the indus-

trial policy (Art.157 (3) EC). But express Community competence in the field of industrial policy is simply not evident in the EC Treaty. Arguably through the competition policy pursued under Arts 81 and 82 EC, the Community, through the policy of the Commission and the European Courts, has found a more interventionist role for an industrial policy of the EU. The close connection between industrial policy and competition policy is recognised explicitly by the Commission in policy documents.[72]

This is reinforced even further in the next Chapter when we turn to look at how competition law and policy has been applied to direct intervention by the State in European markets.

By 2004 the EU had a wide-ranging and sophisticated set of competition tools, and a fair degree of consensus on competition policy for the EU. Enlargement, combined with a dependency upon an almost monopolistic role for the Commission in the policy-making, monitoring and enforcement of competition law, created the necessity to refocus the central role and energy of the Commission on aspects of anticompetitive behaviour which attracted attention at the Community level, especially the pursuit of hard core cartels. As a result of de-centralisation, all the Member States have been obliged to introduce national competition rules which mirror Arts 81 EC and 82 EC.

The control of private power in the market has led to ideas of an economic constitution. Competition policy has imposed a number of restraints not only on the sovereignty of the Member States but also on the behaviour of undertakings. Although the main focus has been upon the anti-competitive *behaviour* of undertakings, Community competition law has proved to be flexible enough to reach into regulating the *structure* of competition in the EU. Particularly in relation to dominant undertakings a special responsibility has been placed upon them not to jeopardise the aims of European integration. This in turn has led to structural adjustments at the national level, including the rationalisation of mergers at the Community level. The effects of the Community competition policy has made an impact upon direct State intervention in the market, changing quite fundamentally the Member States' attitudes towards their role in competitive markets. As a result, competition law and policy has not only complemented the Internal Market but added a new dimension: an industrial policy which encompasses new concepts of social and economic goals for European integration (Sauter, 1997).

THE APPLICATION OF THE COMPETITION RULES TO ECONOMIC ACTIVITIES OF THE STATE

PUBLIC MONOPOLIES AND BODIES GRANTED SPECIAL OR EXCLUSIVE RIGHTS

The Member States used State monopolies to rebuild their war-torn economies, as well as actively encouraging national champions to supply public services such as postal services, utilities (gas, electricity, water), telecommunications and broadcasting. Public monopolies could also perform social functions, as well as raise money for the State (Szyszczak: 2002; 2004b). While public monopolies and undertakings which were given special or exclusive rights were tolerated in the EU they were made subject to the rules on free movement of goods, under what is now Art.31 EC, and the competition chapter of the EC Treaty.

Article 86(1) EC states that the rules of the Internal Market and of competition law shall apply to such undertakings. Public monopolies are bound by the free movement rules of the EC Treaty, including the rules on procurement and the rules in Arts 81 and 82 EC (which are normally perceived to apply to private undertakings), as well as the State Aid provisions.

A central issue in the litigation involving the State is whether there is an "undertaking" pursuing an economic activity. The State will try to argue that such bodies are performing traditional State duties which are not competitive. So, for example, special rules have developed protecting State social security schemes from the competition rules.[1] In other cases the Court has protected the use of State authority. For example, a public *body* was charged with the maintenance and improvement of air navigation safety, collecting route charges levied on users of airspace. The body was considered to be a public authority and was not considered to be an undertaking:

". . . it is in the exercise of that sovereignty that the states ensure . . . the supervision of their airspace and the provision of air navigation control services."[2]

In another case the Court held that anti-pollution supervision:

". . . constitutes a mission of general interest which is part of the essential tasks of the state relating to the environment within the pubic se domain."[3]

In many cases the issues relating to the infringement of the competition rules and public monopolies relate to the abuse of a dominant position addressing *how* public and private dominant firms should behave in competitive markets. The Commission in its *Twentieth Report on Competition Policy* in 1990 had focused upon the pervasive State barriers to market integration:

". . . it is felt that at the present stage of economic integration in the Community the barriers are greatest in markets currently subject to State regulation"[4]

The close scrutiny of public monopolies during the 1990s created an impetus for the Member States to liberalise various sectors as it became clear that Member States could not continue with public monopolies which were inefficient and protectionist. Changes in technology, as well as consumer expectations, created the conditions for the State to shift some of its traditional duties on to private, non-State actors. During the 1990s new hybrid undertakings were conceived, supplying traditional State goods and services under competitive conditions. This led to a shift in the balance between State and market, in harmony with the Internal Market programme, but also created tensions between the vertical (Member State-Community) and horizontal (the Community Institutions *inter se)* division of power in the EU.

Article 86(2) EC provides an exemption from the application of the Internal Market and the competition rules for undertakings which provide "services of general economic interest" if it can be shown that the application of the EC Treaty rules would obstruct the performance, in law or in fact, of the tasks assigned to them. This is a derogation from a fundamental EC Treaty provision and should be interpreted restrictively and is subject the principle of proportionality. It must also be shown that the development of trade must not be affected to such an extent as would be contrary to the interests of the Community.

A central argument for retaining a monopoly to provide services of general economic interest is the necessity for cross-subsidisation. For example, universal postal services are provided efficiently in urban areas but less efficiently in remote or rural areas. Thus a State-provided postal service is able to offset the extra costs of the rural or remote postal services against the profits from the urban service. A commercial competitor may challenge the monopoly by cream-skimming the efficient postal services and not offer the less efficient rural/remote services.

This was the situation in *Corbeau*.[5] A private operator offered a superior postal service and charged less to collect and deliver mail than the State postal service in the Belgian city of Liège. The State postal service viewed this as cream skimming and brought criminal proceedings against Corbeau. The ECJ held that the creation of the State monopoly was a restriction on competition which was incompatible with the Common Market but found that it could be justified because there was a service of general economic interest consisting of the obligation to ensure a basic postal service at similar tariffs and similar conditions throughout Belgium. The Court viewed the use of a monopoly as proportionate since the undertaking providing the service should have the benefit of economically acceptable conditions. This included the use of cross-subsidisation to offset the losses in the unprofitable sectors against profits in the more profitable sectors.

In later cases the Court has taken a generous view of the proportionality principle accepting that the State cannot take the same risks as a private competitor and has not asked the State to show that the service of general economic interest can be provided in a way which does not use a monopoly or is less restrictive of competition.[6] The latter approach would seem necessary in order to satisfy the principle of proportionality. But the increasing liberalisation of markets in Europe has shown that there are other ways of funding and providing services of general economic interest beyond the use of State monopolies. The liberalisation process regulates the provision of such services, which are termed "universal services" (Szyszczak, 2001). This has led to greater challenges and litigation focusing upon the way in which these services are funded and provided in the sectors not liberalised. In the case law of the European Courts, and the practice of the Commission, there are a number of tensions with disagreements as to whether the provision of such services are special and should be subject to non-market principles or whether competition law and policy should be used to open up services of general economic interest to market (competitive) principles.[7]

The use of opportunistic litigation to challenge State monopolies in the 1990s led to the creation of a new Constitutional provision in the EC Treaty at the Amsterdam IGC in 1997. Article 16 EC recognises a positive role for services of general economic interest in:

" . . . the shared values of the Union as well as their role in promoting social and territorial cohesion. . . ".

While the Member States and the Community are charged with ensuring that such services operate on the basis of principles and conditions which enable the services to fulfil their missions Art.16 EC does not provide a legal base to develop the role of services in the future EU. Article 16 EC contains a proviso that it is without prejudice to Arts 73, 86 and 87 EC. This means that the competition law provisions apply and restrict the operation of Art.16 EC. Thus services of general economic interest remain a derogation to the general competition and free market rules, but with a paradoxical duty placed upon the Member States and the Community to promote such services in competitive markets.

Article 36 CCF, which is Art.II–96 (contained within the Title IV Solidarity) of the Constitutional Treaty, recognises, as a fundamental right, "access to services of general economic interest as provided for in national laws and practices, in accordance with the Constitution, in order to promote the social and territorial cohesion of the Union." Only *access* to such services is covered by this provision, but it could be interpreted broadly to cover the terms and conditions and the way such services are provided.

The Constitution does not create a legal base to develop services of general economic interest but states that they are defined within Community law. In the face of increased litigation, especially in the State Aid field, the Commission has adopted a White Paper on Services of General Interest and proposed a package of measures to regulate such services in the EU.[8]

Article 86(3) EC is an unusual provision. It gives the Commission a monopolist position in the monitoring and enforcing Art.86 EC. It also provides a rare legal base for the Commission to use Directives or Decisions addressed to the Member States to ensure that Art.86 EC is observed without involving the Council and the European Parliament. As with Art.232 EC, the Commission cannot be compelled to act.[9]

The Commission has used this legal base to create normative measures. Initially the Commission used this legal base as a preventative legal tool, adopting Directives on Transparency in financial arrangements between Member States and public undertakings.[10] The Commission also used Art.86(3) EC to open up the telecommunications market to liberalisation and this caused controversy. In 1988 the Commission adopted the Telecommunications Terminals Directive[11] on the basis of Art.86(3) EC. It was argued that this legal device imposed new obligations upon the Member States and circumvented the participation of the Member States (and the then limited role of the European Parliament) in the Community legislative procedure. In a legal challenge to the Directive the Court gave a wide interpretation to the preventative functions of Directives and recognised that Art.86(3) EC could be used to specify to *all* of the Member States the obligations that derived from the EC Treaty.[12] This wide-ranging ruling, together with the case law under Art.86(1) EC, provided the incentive for the Member States to consider the liberalisation of public monopolies more closely and to use Art.95 EC (the legal base for Internal Market measures) for further liberalisation measures. In this way they controlled the structured opening up of markets previously insulated from competition.

STATE AID

States may create barriers to integration and free competition within the Internal Market by giving aid and subsidies to national firms. This kind of intervention in markets plays a major role in the industrial policy of the Member States and is often *expected* of the Member States in order to promote social, environmental and regional policies. State aid may be granted to help firms in financial distress; it is expected of the State to save jobs which might be vulnerable in a failing firm. During the oil crisis of the 1970s Member States were obliged to rescue struggling firms and direct intervention of the State in the economy rose dramatically. But this form of retrenchment failed, leading to pressure on public enterprise and public finances.

State Aid creates distortions in the market. Until the 1990s, when the completion of the Internal Market turned greater political attention to the pervasive barriers created by State intervention in markets, the Commission used a diplomatic approach towards the control of State Aid in the Internal Market. By the end of the 1990s a tougher approach was taken towards controlling State Aid at the EU level, firstly by encouraging the reduction of the amounts of State Aid (expressed as a percentage of GDP) and secondly, by encouraging the use of horizontal State Aid. It is felt that the latter is less anti-competitive and promotes European integration.

In the Commission's Ninth Survey on State Aid in the European Union, (COM (2001) 403 final, para.2) the Commission explains why State Aid is a problem for European integration:

"A key element of Competition policy is Community State Aid control, the benefits of which are clear. State aid can frustrate free competition by preventing the most efficient allocation of resources and posing a threat to the unity of the Internal Market. In many cases, the granting of State aid reduces economic welfare and weakens the incentives for firms to improve efficiency. Aid also enables the less efficient to survive at the expense of the more efficient. In addition to creating distortions within the Internal Market, the grant of State aid can affect trade between the EU and third countries thereby encouraging them to adopt retaliatory measures that may be a source of further inefficiency. . ."

The Member States singled out the control of State Aid in the Lisbon Process:

"State aid distorts competition and, whether or not it has an impact on trade between member states, may damage the allocative efficiency of the European economy. In particular, it modifies economic incentives and so may cause the inefficient allocation of scarce private resources to industries receiving aid and away from others. State aid may also encourage rent-seeking behaviour and "capture" of government by industries, and moral hazard in the case of failing industries. Like other government expenditures, the financing of State aid also raises the issue of the marginal cost of public funds, i.e. the loss of efficiency due to taxation.

The consequences of State aid in terms of inefficient functioning of product markets imply that the European Commission's control of State aid needs to be supplemented by an effort of self-discipline on the part of the member states themselves. In view of the cross-border spill-over effects of State aid, this self-discipline can be more rigorous and politically acceptable if the efforts of the Member States are co-ordinated. To this end, since 1999 recommendations on State aid are included in the framework of the Broad Economic Policy Guidelines (BEPG)."[13]

The Stockholm European Council Meeting in 2001 agreed, for the first time, an objective indicator to benchmark Member States' expenditure on State Aid by expressing such expenditure as a percentage of GDP. The enforcement and monitoring of State Aid was enhanced by the introduction of a State Aid Scoreboard and a State Aid Register. The most recent State Aid Score Board of 2005 reveals that not all of the Member States are reluctant to give up the use of State Aid. State Aid continues to be directed at the manufacturing and service sectors, with Germany and France accounting for almost fifty per cent of the State Aid granted.[14]

Articles 87–89 EC address States Aids. These provisions are skeletal in form and have been implemented and modernised by the use of soft law and Block Exemptions. State Aids are, in principle, incompatible with the Internal Market and therefore prohibited unless they are granted an exemption by the Commission in accordance with the procedure under Art.88 EC and the procedural Regulation which was introduced in 1999 and modernised by a Regulation in 2004. The Member States are bound also by the fidelity clause of Art.10 EC.

Exemptions, Justifications and Derogations

Article 87(2) EC grants a number of automatic exemptions from the application of the State Aid rules covering aid for natural disasters, exceptional circumstances, or having a social character granted to individual consumers. The latter must not discriminate according to the origin of the products concerned. Article 87(2) (c) is unusual in that it allows for aid to be granted in certain areas of Germany. This provision is to be phased out in the Constitutional Treaty. The ECJ construed this provision narrowly referring to the economic disadvantages created by the division of Germany in 1948, for example, the loss of markets. Thus Art.87(2) (c) EC has little practical role to play after the reunification of Germany.[15]

Under Art.87(3) EC the Commission may *exempt* certain aid schemes from the competition rules and has produced a range of soft law to provide guidance in this field.

A slightly more complicated exemption from the State Aid rules is the application of Art.86(2) EC where State Aid is given to provide a service of general economic interest. The State Aid rules do not provide for this as an exception but the wording of Art.86(2) EC speaks of the *non-application of the competition rules* to a service of general economic interest and this can justify the reading over of this exception from the rules on state monopolies to the State Aid arena. The Commission is prepared to grant exemptions using Art.86(2) EC. The ECJ in *Altmark*[16] has provided guidelines to establish if funding of services of general economic interest is indeed caught by the State Aid rules. It is not clear if funding, which falls outside of the *Altmark* criteria but within Art.86(2) EC, should be notified and approved by the Commission. Arguably *all* potential State Aid should be cleared, or approved, by the Commission but there are arguments that aid which satisfies Art.86(2) EC is *not* caught by the State Aid rules.

Article 73 EC creates an exception for transport in the field of State aid where finance is used for transport coordination or for the provision of a service of general economic interest.

The production of, and trade in arms, munitions and war material set out in Art.296(2) EC are also subject to special rules under the EC Treaty. Because this provision is part of the general and final provisions of the EC Treaty it affects all the EC Treaty rules, including the provisions relating to competition. Member States are given a wide discretion in matters relating national defence and security. Where State Aid is granted relating to a measure affecting internal security the competition rules do not apply. The Member State does not have to notify the aid to the Commission and the Commission may not use the procedure under Art.88 EC to examine the aid. But the Commission is still under a duty to ensure the measure does not adversely affect the conditions of competition in relation to products which are not intended for specifically military purposes (Art.296(1)9b) EC). If there is a distortion of competition under Art.298(1) EC the Member State and the Commission must examine how the measure can be adjusted to comply with the competition rules. But the Commission is not required to adopt a Decision or address a Decision or Directive to the Member State. If the Commission believes that Art.296 EC cannot be relied upon by the Member State it may used the ordinary State Aid procedures to investigate the aid set out in Art.88(2) EC.

Definition of a State Aid

There is no definition in the EC Treaty as to what is a State Aid. This is deliberate. It allows for flexibility in tackling the wide range of measures States can resort to in order to support domestic firms. Over the years Commission practice, and the rulings of the European Courts, have created a set of criteria which must be satisfied for a measure to be classed as a State Aid. There must be a measure which confers a benefit or an advantage which favours certain undertakings; the benefit or advantage must be granted by, or come from, the instruction of the State and involve State resources; the measure must distort or threaten to distort competition and affects trade between the Member States. In the case law little attention is paid to the last two criteria, but there are differences of opinion between the European Courts and the Commission on the application of a *de minimis* rule. The Commission has published a number of Communications on *de minimis aid* and in 2001 adopted a Regulation[17] In contrast the ECJ has rejected the use of a *de minimis* rule.[18]

Only aid granted by a Member State or through State resources falls within the concept of a State Aid in Art.87(1) EC. In *Neptun*[19] the Court gave this concept a narrow meaning requiring that the measure must be *directly* at the expense of the State. In *Stardust Marine*[20] the question arose as to whether aid granted by public or private bodies created by the State constituted State Aid. The ECJ ruled that even if the State is in a position to control an undertaking, and to exercise a dominant influence over its operations, actual exercise of that control cannot be automatically presumed. The ECJ held that an inquiry should be made in each individual case and set out a series of indicators to be applied. In *Pearle and others*[21] a reference was made asking if charges imposed on its members by a trade association, governed by public law, which represented traders in optical equipment was an illegal State aid. The charge was a compulsory, earmarked levy to finance a collective advertising campaign for opticians. Despite being levied by a public body the charge was not a State aid. The monies used for the advertising campaign came directly from the members of the trade association, not the State.

Private Economy Investor Test

A filter used by the Commission to determine if there is a State Aid is the use of the "private economy investor test".[22] This is used to test if a State measure is a legitimate market investment, or whether the State is subsidising a firm in a way which is likely to disrupt competition. Without such a test commercial activity by the State would be paralysed and the Commission would be inundated with notifications of potential State Aid. The test has been criticised since it is argued that it is a hypothetical test. A private investor would often not be willing to invest in failing firms in the same way that the State feels an obligation to invest for social and political reasons. It is also argued that, subject to the constraints on public expenditure under the Growth and Stability Pact and the Broad Economic Policy Guidelines of the Community and the Member States, the State has a deeper pocket than a normal private investor. As is discussed below, investments in firms are often made merely because the State is willing to a guarantee or underwrite a firm. In this respect the State has a better credit rating than other economic actors. Despite the criticisms, the private investor test continues to be used by the Commission, for example in the Commission Decision in 2004 against State Aid given to Ryan Air in the concessions it obtained to land at Charleroi Airport in Belgium.

Another case which is illustrative of the way the test operates is the case of the German public bank WestLB. Here a complaint was made to the Commission by the federation of private banks in Germany concerning the contribution of certain assets by the Land Nordrhein-Westfalen to WestLB. It was argued that the loans made were a form of State Aid because the rate of return on the investment was only 0.6 per cent after tax, whereas a private investor would have expected a rate of return of 9.3 per cent after tax.

Although the CFI found that the Commission had not given sufficient reasons for its Decision, the CFI did hold that the profitability of the beneficiary is not conclusive but should be taken into account for the purpose of determining whether the public investor behaved in the same way as a market economy investor or whether the beneficiary obtained an economic advantage which it would not have obtained under normal conditions. The Commission ordered the German government to collect 3 billion euro in State Aid, plus interest, which had been given to the German public banks from the 1990s. WestLB was the largest recipient of such aid, totalling some 979 million euro.[23]

The application of the private economy investor test involves complex economic assessment and the European Courts are reluctant to interfere with the Commission's assessment, although in some recent cases the CFI has been prepared to limit the Commission's discretion.[24] A major issue is how to handle the problem of cross-subsidisation in public monopolies supplying a service of general economic interest in what is known as a "reserved sector", alongside their increasing involvement with commercial activity in liberalised markets.[25] Such cases have arisen in the postal sector which is undergoing a structured liberalisation. The former State monopolies have often retained the provision of a service of general economic interest in providing a basic postal service which is protected from competition. But aid or benefits which are allowed to provide the service of general economic interest may also be used to cross-subsidise activities in the commercial sector, making it difficult for competitors to break into these markets which have been opened up to competition.

The CFI in *UFEX* decided that more was required than merely showing that a public undertaking providing a service of general economic interest was paid the full costs for the provision of logistical and commercial assistance provided to its subsidiary which was acting in the commercial competitive sector. Instead the CFI stated that the Commission should have checked that the payment received by the parent company was comparable to that which would be demanded by a private holding company not operating in a reserved sector pursuing a structural policy and guided by long-term prospects.

The ECJ set the CFI judgment aside and referred the case back to the CFI.[26] The ECJ stressed the importance of the service of general economic interest provided by La Poste, pointing out that the huge, and often uneconomic network that La Poste had created to provide a universal postal service could not be assessed by a purely commercial approach and indeed such a network would never be created by a private operator. Since such comparisons would be hypothetical only the available and verifiable elements of the aid should be assessed. This ruling appears to be incompatible with the ruling of *Altmark* but also appears to be in line with the reasoning in *Stardust Marine* of granting greater commercial freedom to public companies.

Problems with Privatisations

With liberalisation came the selling off of State assets: privatisations (Devroe, 1997; Szyszczak 2001). A question arises as to whether the Member States have under-sold assets and whether this can be a form of State Aid. Favourable terms can be offered to investors from the Member State to keep assets within national ownership and can be used to repay political favours. The

Commission would prefer State assets to be sold by an open, transparent and unconditional bidding procedure to avoid any doubts that there may be State Aid involved in privatisations.[27] But the Commission has accepted expert valuations of State assets.[28] A sale to the highest bidder will not always eliminate a suspicion of State Aid, particularly where a substantial amount of public finance is used to enable a sale to take place.[29]

Different Kinds of State Aid

The Commission classifies State Aid into four kinds of categories. Group A aids are grants and tax exemptions; Group B is the type of aid favoured by France, equity participation in the firm; Group C are soft loans and tax deferrals and Group D are guarantees. The last kind of State Aid creates controversy because often no tangible form of aid or subsidy passes from the state to a firm.[30] In the new Member States 41 per cent of the total aid over the period 2000–2003 was in the form of guarantees, whereas guarantees make up only 3 per cent of the identifiable aid in the old Member States.

New Aid

Surprisingly it was not until 1999 that the Commission's practice in relation to the procedures for handling State Aid were codified in a Regulation. It is assumed that State Aid is illegal *per se* unless it can be justified. A new State Aid must be notified to the Commission and approved before it can be put into operation. The Commission has two months in which to act.[31] After two months, if there is no decision, a Member State may notify the Commission that it is proceeding with the aid and the Commission is barred from objecting to the aid.

In the two month period the Commission may initiate a formal investigation. The Commission must, as far as possible, endeavour to take a Decision within 18 months from the opening of the procedure. If no Decision is forthcoming then the Member State may request that a Decision be taken within two months. But if a Member State has supplied insufficient information to the Commission to enable it to determine the compatibility of the State Aid with the Common Market there is a presumption of a negative decision. The Commission enjoys a broad discretion in its decision-making powers but the principle of proportionality plays an important role. The State Aid Register allows for greater transparency in seeing how the Commission develops policy and allows the Member States an insight into what is acceptable aid.

If a Member State fails to notify new aid, or introduces new aid during the Commission's preliminary or formal examination of the proposed aid, the Member State is in breach of Art.88(3) EC. The aid is unlawful, notwithstanding the fact that the Commission may ultimately have come to the conclusion that the aid was lawful. Any recipients of such unlawful State Aid will be under an obligation to repay the aid with interest.[32]

The Commission has exclusive power to find the compatibility of an aid with the Common Market. Over the years the Commission has created a body of soft law processes to develop policy in this area. From 1999 onwards, it has adopted legislation in the form of Block Exemptions creating procedural rules for the regulation of State Aid[33] and allowing certain kinds of aid to be exempt from notification, for example horizontal aid,[34] *de minimis* aid,[35] aid for small and medium size enterprise,[36] employment.[37] There are special sectoral rules applying to agriculture, fisheries, transport shipbuilding and steel.

During the period 2005–2006 a large number of the Commission's existing Regulations, Frameworks and Guidelines come up for renewal. A new programming period for the Structural Funds starts in 2007. Thus the forthcoming period is a time for intensive reflection and appraisal, with an emphasis upon the better co-ordination of policy in the State Aid area.

State Aids and Services of General Interest

Commission Directive 80/723, which was adopted by the Commission using Art.86(3) EC, addressed the need for transparency in State Aid applied to public undertakings. This Directive used a *de minimis* rule but did not usurp the normal Commission powers to control State Aids. This Directive, as amended,[38] aims to enforce transparency by extending the rules on the separation of accounts to any undertaking that enjoys a special or exclusive right under Art.86(1) EC or that is entrusted with a service of general economic interest and receives State Aid in any form whatsoever. Such State Aid is now included in the Commission's surveys of State Aid.

A contentious issue is whether payments or other benefits for services of general economic interest are State Aid or whether they are merely compensatory payments for services provided. The difficulty with a compensation approach is that often it is difficult to assess how much a service of general economic interest would cost because often such services are not provided in competitive markets. In *Ferring*[39] the ECJ held that a tax exemption provided to wholesale distributors of pharmaceutical products was *not* a State Aid since it compensated the pharmaceutical companies for providing a service of general economic interest. The Court demanded a necessary connection between the additional costs incurred by the distributors providing the service and the tax exemption. If the exemption was greater than the costs incurred there was the possibility of trying to justify the advantage or benefit under Art.86(2) EC. This justification/exemption is not written into the rules on State Aid, but can be read across from Art.86 EC in that a Member State is asking for the non-application of the *competition* rules to its activities.

In principle it is hard to see how a Member State can justify payments/benefits in excess of the cost of a service of general economic interest and still satisfy the principle of proportionality contained in the application of Art.86(2) EC. But the Court has accepted that when supplying such services the State is not acting as a normal commercial undertaking and may have to invest in risky undertakings to ensure the delivery of public services.[40]

A difficulty with applying Art.86(2) EC, which has not be answered directly by the European Courts, is whether a Member State must notify new State Aid which is covered by Art.86(2) EC. It is arguable that in order to maintain the integrity and transparency of the State Aid system, and to preserve the central regulatory role of the Commission, the State is still under an obligation to notify new aid which can benefit from an Art.86(2) justification.

In the *Altmark*[41] ruling the ECJ took a prescriptive approach setting out firm criteria to be satisfied in order to find that any aid or benefit was compensation for the provision of a service of general economic interest. The Court adopted a *compensation approach* provided that four conditions were met. First, the recipient undertaking must actually have a clearly defined service of general economic interest to discharge. Second, the parameters on the basis on which compensation is calculated must be established in advance and in an objective and transparent manner in order to avoid conferring an economic advantage which may favour the recipient undertaking over competing undertakings. Third, the compensation must not exceed what is necessary to cover all, or part, of the costs incurred in the discharge of the service of general economic interest, taking into account relevant receipts and a reasonable profit for discharging those obligations. Finally, where there is no public tendering system to choose the provider of the service of general economic interest the level of compensation must be determined by an analysis of the costs which a typical undertaking, well run and adequately provided for to meet the requirements of a service of general economic interest would have incurred in discharging those obligations, taking into account the relevant receipts and a reasonable profit for discharging the obligations.

The last criterion is controversial since the Court seems to be steering the Member States towards a procurement process for providing services of general economic interest. Where there is no procurement process it may be difficult to find a comparator undertaking to benchmark the costs of providing a service of general interest. (Szyszczak: 2004c). Using a procurement process does not necessarily rule out the possibility of illegal State Aid.[42] When a public contract does not correspond with a normal trade agreement illegal State Aid may be present.[43]

The Court applied its *Altmark* criteria in *Enirisorse*.[44] This was an indirect challenge to a claim that there was a service of general economic interest in providing port services in Cagliari, Italy. Enirisorse loaded and unloaded domestic and foreign goods at Cagliari using its own personnel and equipment and not the services of the port authority. It challenged the requests for payment for these services by the Ministry of Finance claiming that the Italian decree under which the port services were created was contrary to Community law. The Court found that none of the four criteria in *Altmark* were met and therefore the financing of the port authority system was a State Aid within the meaning of Art.87(1) EC.

Existing State Aid

Existing aid includes State Aid exempted under Art.87(2) EC. Each year the Member States must submit an annual report on all State Aid schemes. These rules only apply to aid schemes, not individual aid. Existing individual aid cannot be challenged. If an existing aid becomes incompatible with the Common Market the Commission can order its immediate termination, or termination within a reasonable time.[45] If the Member State fails to follow the Commission's Recommendation the Commission must then initiate a formal investigation procedure.

The Court extended the definition of existing aid contrary to the express wording of Regulation 659/1999 by including a system of aid that existed in a certain market which had been closed to competition but had been liberalised.[46] The aid was to be regarded as "existing aid" from the date of liberalisation of the market.

There is an under-used procedure in Art.88(2) EC whereby the Council, acting by unanimity vote, may overrule the Commission's decisions on new and existing aids if this is justified by exceptional circumstances. This procedure was used in 2002 when the Portuguese government asked the Council to approve aid to pig farmers. The Commission had taken a Decision that earlier aid was incompatible with the common market. The Portuguese government wanted to grant new aid which corresponded in amount to the aid which had been declared invalid. The Council adopted a Decision under Art.88(2) EC and this was challenged by the Commission using Art.230 EC, arguing that the Council had exceeded its competence, or in the alternative, that the Council had committed a manifest error of appreciation in concluding that there were "exceptional circumstances" and that the Council's Decision was not adequately and correctly reasoned.[47]

The Special Problem of State Aid in the New Member States.

The enlargement of the EU on May 1, 2004 created new problems for State Aid control. Eight out of the ten accession States have only recently become market economies. There is still a political tendency to look to State intervention in the market as a political and social policy tool. The EU used a system of close monitoring of State Aid in the Accession Reports which took place in the run up to the enlargement in 2004. Under the Europe Agreements, which were the bilateral framework agreements between the EU and each candidate country establishing the legal framework for the adaptation of national legislation to the *acquis communautaire,* each Accession State had to adopt and implement a national State Aid law and a national authority responsible for State Aid.

The Commission approved a series of transitional state aids to address particular problems associated with accession. In particular aid was needed to support the financial sector, coal, steel, agriculture and the new Accession States continue to direct aid towards particular sectors, rather than implementing the Lisbon and Stockholm objectives of directing aid towards horizontal projects. Additionally many Accession States use incentive measures, such as tax breaks, to encourage investment.

Where State Aid was identified as incompatible with the Common Market the Accession States had to adapt or abolish the aid. In order to prevent incompatible State Aid continuing after enlargement a new surveillance mechanism covering all sectors except for transport and agriculture was introduced, known as the "existing aid" mechanism. In transport and agriculture measures could be counted as existing aid provided that they were notified to the Commission by August 31, 2004. These measures enjoy the protection of a sunset clause which allows the new Member States a longer period of time, until April 2007, to ensure the compatibility of the measures with Community law.

During the first phase of this surveillance mechanism in 2002 some 222 measures were approved by the Commission and listed in the Treaty of Accession. During the second phase a new mechanism called the "interim procedure" approved some 278 measures as existing aid. New State Aid measures were notified to the Commission right up until April 30, 2004 and at the time of writing (May 2005) a number of State Aid measures from this period are still being assessed by the Commission.

There was a huge incentive for the new Member States to bring their State Aid into effect before May 1, 2004. Any State Aid granted after that date becomes new aid. The total State Aid granted by the accession states in the four years before May 1, 2004 was some 5.7 billion euros per year. Three Accession States, Poland, Czech Republic and Hungary, accounted for 86 per cent of this aid.

The Treaty of Accession uses the distinctions between "existing aid" and "new aid" which are found in the EC Treaty. The Commission will not necessarily approve aid which was approved by national authorities prior to accession. Existing aid is aid which existed prior to entry into force of the Accession Treaty and has not changed materially in the interim. Such aid also embraces aid which has been authorised, by the Commission or the Council (or is deemed so authorised) or is aid which has been paid prior to the 10 year limitation period set out in Art.15 of Regulation 659/1999. This aid was listed in Annex IV, Chapter 3 to the Accession Treaty.

To be included in Annex 4, the measure had to reviewed, and approved, by the national authority and the Commission did not object to the measure in the framework of the information and consultation mechanisms established by the Europe Agreements. Annex 4 was closed on November 1, 2002. From November 2002 until May 1, 2004 a transitional period was in operation and it is expected that a second list of approved existing aid measures will be adopted. Aid granted prior to December 10, 1994 is deemed to be existing aid *per se.*

The Commission can modify a measure for the future which is deemed to be "existing aid" by using appropriate measures. It cannot order recovery. But there is a presumption that existing aid is legal until the Commission has taken an adverse decision.

Repayment of Illegal State Aid

The Commission must order the recovery of new State Aid which is put into operation before a Commission decision, or State Aid which exists without having been notified to the Commission. A recovery decision can only be avoided if it would infringe a general principle of Community law. It is difficult to apply this defence. The most obvious general principle of Community law which could be infringed is the principle of legitimate expectations. If the Commission makes a mistake, for example, wrongly classifying the aid, or does not follow time limits this situation could give rise to legitimate expectations.

Recovery of the illegal State Aid is through national law.[48] The State Aid must be repaid with interest. No time limit is set for recovery; the Regulation speaks of recovery "without undue delay" While a Member State is under a duty of good faith as a result of the solidarity/fidelity clause of Art.10 EC the monitoring and enforcement of recovery of illegal State Aid does not have any clear cut rules. Usually the Commission asks a Member State in the recovery Decision to inform it within 2 months of the steps taken.

A weakness of the State aid enforcement regime is that the Member State that has acted illegally but it is the *recipient* which is punished. A competitor who has been harmed by an illegal State Aid could bring a *Francovich* action for damages against the State.

AN INDUSTRIAL POLICY FOR THE EU?

The development of an EU industrial policy and the application of the competition rules to Member State, economic activity gradually led to changes in the Member States attitude towards direct

State intervention in the market. The European Courts' use of the procedures of EU law, rather than openly prescribing a particular form of economic policy has shifted the political balance away from Member State power towards the rule of economic law. The Member States' retreat from economic sovereignty has led to the scope for competition to exist in markets previously protected from competition. This can be seen as a process of de-regulation in the same way that the four freedoms, especially the free movement of goods, created de-regulation of trade barriers inhibiting market integration. A major problem in the field of competition, however, is that the Community lacks the competence to re-regulate where intervention in the market is necessary. The EU realised that general competition principles were insufficient to handle the new problems of controlling market power where markets were liberalised. During the 1990s the EU witnessed a degree of experimentation, of using competition *and* regulatory principles to manage the liberalisation of sensitive sectors such as telecommunications, postal services and utilities. Thus new paradigms are emerging for the management of the new economy (Graham and Smith, 2004; Bavasso, 2004). The Community lacks a fully developed industrial policy and also lacks competence for redistributive policies. This explains why the Court has been cautious in areas affecting services of general economic interest. In areas where liberalisation of markets has taken place the legal base of the Internal Market has provided the justification for, and the means to re-regulate markets at the EU level.

8

THE EUROPEAN UNION AND ITS RELATIONS WITH THE OUTSIDE WORLD

INTRODUCTION

In May 2004 the EU became an economic and political union of 25 Member States. Despite this enlargement the EU cannot ignore the wider world. For many internal policies, for example immigration and asylum to operate effectively, the EU requires the co-operation of its neighbours. This necessitates a common EU strategy towards its relations with third countries. The Common Foreign and Security Policy (CFSP), the so-called second pillar of the EU provides the framework for the EU's political relations with third countries. It also provides a Treaty structure for military cooperation between the Member States. The EU's political relations with its neighbours and many developing countries are predominantly based upon a principle of reciprocity. The EU provides economic assistance in return for administrative, political and human rights reforms. For example, in 2003 the EU introduced its Neighbourhood Strategy[1] through which it seeks to develop a partnership with European, North African and Mediterranean States. In return for a commitment from these States to address jointly with the EU problems such as illegal immigration, organised crime and human rights abuses, the EU will provide economic and technical assistance.

The Neighbourhood Strategy has two underlying objectives. Firstly, it seeks to minimise the economic and social disparities between the EU and its neighbours. Secondly, it forms part of a much broader EU objective to develop an ethical foreign policy, by bringing together economic objectives and EU norms on human rights in one strategy. The protection of human rights is not only a foundation for the EU itself, (Art.6 (1) TEU) and an objective of development cooperation, but also an aim of the CFSP (Art.11 TEU). For example in the EC – India Agreement on Scientific and Technical Cooperation[2] there is a clear interaction between commercial objectives and the political objectives of the EU. It can be said that through its external relations policy the EU seeks to export an EU standard of human rights norms.

While a coherent external relations policy remains an important political objective for the EU, it is through the EU's commercial relations with the wider world where integration has proved most successful. This chapter will consider the scope and exclusive nature of the EU's activities in the area of commercial policy and how the Common Commercial Policy (CCP) arrangements govern the import and export of products from the EU. The CCP, which is regulated by the EC Treaty, creates a single coherent economic policy towards third countries in relation to taxes, custom duties and the operation of trade relations. In the latter case this will include a consideration of the EU's participation in the World Trade Organisation (WTO). The chapter will firstly consider the objectives and operation of the CCP and how this compliments the Internal Market. Secondly, it will explore the interaction between the CCP and other political objectives of the EU's external policy under the CFSP. To begin with it is necessary to consider how, why and to what extent the EU has acquired legal competence and capacity, to act on behalf of the Member States in commercial matters.

COMPETENCE AND THE COMMON COMMERCIAL POLICY

Competence is not just restricted to the question of whether the EU has the power to act. It also raises wider, but related, questions of what legal capacity the EU has and what role do the legislative Institutions undertake. It is through the CCP that the EU has its most obvious presence in international relations. Article 281 EC makes it clear that the EC has legal personality and thereby the capacity to make binding agreements on behalf of the EU. The exercise of this legal personality is subject to express or implied powers being granted to act in a particular policy area. In its external relations the EU has a capacity to create contractual relations with third countries over all objectives that are set out in the EC Treaty (de Zwaan, 1999:77). This was confirmed by the ECJ in the judgment of *Costa v ENEL*. The Court stated that:

"By contrast with ordinary international treaties, the EEC Treaty has created its own legal system . . . By creating a Community of unlimited duration, having its own institutions, its own personality, its own legal capacity, and capacity of representation on the international plane and, more particularly, real powers stemming from a limitation of sovereignty or a transfer of powers from the states to the Community, the Member States have limited their sovereign rights, albeit within limited fields and have thus created a body of law which binds both their nationals and themselves."

In the field of commercial policy competence is derived from Arts 131–134 EC. By contrast, the Member States have not granted similar legal personality to the EU in relation to activities under the CFSP. Although under the post Amsterdam Art.24 TEU the Member States have granted the EU some limited treaty-making powers, Dashwood (1999) has argued that these Amsterdam developments have granted the EU *de facto* international legal personality. Article I–6 of the Constitutional Treaty grants, for the first time, explicit legal personality to the EU. This arises as a consequence of the merger of the constituent Treaties of the EU and the abolition of the intergovernmental pillar structure. The precise legal effect of this is unclear and what additional powers this will give the EU.

Article 133 EC grants express competence to develop a "common commercial policy" based on "uniform principles". The provision does not expand upon what the aims and objectives of the common policy should be. The purpose of the CCP is to complement the external aspect of the EU's customs union by providing a single uniform policy in other aspects of international trade, for example, export policy and trade liberalisation.

The CCP is controversial, not only because of the exclusive powers granted by Art.133 EC, but also because of the QMV decision-making procedure it uses. Together with the procedures in Art.300 EC, the EU utilises both autonomous and contractual legislative instruments. Under Art.300 EC the agreements are negotiated by the Commission and concluded by the Council pursuant to the procedures set out in Art.300 (1)–(6) EC. Article 300 (7) EC provides that:

"[a]greements concluded under the conditions set out in this Article shall be binding on the institutions of the Community and on the Member States."

In the context of the CCP autonomous instruments invariably take the form of regulations because of the need for direct implementation by the relevant customs authorities within the Member States. One such example is Regulation 2603/69/EEC[3] which regulates Common Rules for Exports. Additionally, measures which are specifically targeted at a particular product, such as anti-dumping duties or protectionist measures, also come within the scope of Art.133 EC. The introduction of anti-dumping regulations has led to significant litigation before the Court under Art.230 EC. Individuals affected by such measures challenge their validity through judicial review on the basis that these regulations affect their legitimate expectations.[4] The Court has stated that procedural propriety is essential, both in the legislative and enforcement processes, and consequently will declare invalid a measure which does not meet expected standards.

Contractual instruments include treaties or other international agreements. Under the CCP Art.300 EC grants the Commission powers to negotiate the agreement, but the final decision is reserved for the Council. Article 300 EC merely provides the procedural mechanism through which agreements are made and a substantive provision must have a clear legal base to demonstrate external competence, for example Art.133 EC. Through Decision 94/800EC[5] the Council concluded that the WTO Agreement provides a partial framework of the CCP, but it must be noted that the entire WTO Agreement is not within the scope of the CCP. Some aspects of the WTO, such as the Trade Related Aspects of Intellectual Property Rights (TRIPs) agreement (TRIPs), are referred to as mixed agreements because competence is shared with Member States. Shared competence between the EU and Member States has led to tension as to the precise scope of Art.281 EC and how mixed agreements should be enforced.

In *France v Commission* the Court dismissed an action brought by France for annulment of the act which had been used by the Commission to conclude an agreement with the United States. This act created Guidelines intended to improve regulatory competition between the EU and the US and to promote transparency towards third parties in relation to technical rules concerning goods covered by the WTO/TBT agreement. The French government argued that the Commission had concluded a binding international agreement when the conclusion of such an act is normally within the exclusive competence of the Council under Art.300 EC. The Commission argued that the Guidelines were not binding and therefore the Commission had competence to adopt them.

The Court rejected the French government's argument, but also issued a warning to the Commission. The fact that the Guidelines were non-binding was not sufficient to confer competence upon the Commission to adopt them. Account must be taken of the division of powers and the institutional balance established by the Treaty in the field in question:

"... determining the conditions under which a measure may be adopted requires the division of powers and the institutional balance established by the Treaty in the field of the common commercial policy to be duly taken into account, since in this case the measure seeks to reduce the risk of conflict related to the existence of technical barriers to trade in goods."[6]

The Court went to state, at para.42, that the intention of the parties must be the "decisive criterion for the purpose of determining whether or not the Guidelines are binding." The Court reached the conclusion that the Guidelines had no binding force and therefore are not logically concerned by Art.300 EC.

The multilateral agreements of the WTO now encompasses the General Agreement on Tariffs and Trade (GATT), the General Agreement on Trade in Services GATS, and for the first time agreement over certain protection of intellectual property rights through the TRIPs Agreement. The TRIPs Agreement is groundbreaking because it covers several aspects of trade, particularly the granting of patents for, amongst other things, pharmaceutical products. The WTO contributes to the protection of intellectual property and the corresponding commitments made by the Member States have led to some standardisation through EU law of national laws in specific fields. One such example is Directive 98/44 EC[7] which provides legal protection for biotechnological developments.

The impact of TRIPs has been to necessitate a closer coordination of EU intellectual property policy which inevitably results in increased competence for the EU. This has already generated litigation in which the ECJ has examined the scope of TRIPs and its application to intellectual property protection in the EU. More generally, the Commission has published proposals for a European Patent Directive[8], and the necessary changes to allow the ECJ competence to hear cases relating to disputes in intellectual property have already been introduced by the Nice Treaty in Art.229A EC. This is a preparatory Act and creates a legal base to allow the Council, acting unanimously, to adopt provisions to confer jurisdiction on the ECJ in disputes relating to industrial property rights. This provision will apply primarily to disputes between private individuals concerning the future Community Patent.

Decision 94/800 on the WTO signalled the conclusion of many years of negotiation between the EU and its world trading partners. Through this Decision the EU participates in a more liberalised word-trading regime. Though the WTO is a mixed agreement, the ECJ has stated that in those circumstances where competence is transferred to the EU, and the criteria for direct effect are satisfied, these provisions of the WTO will be enforceable within the Member States.[9]

During the 1970s the ECJ sought to develop a clearer concept of the CCP that was based on the needs of a developing Community within a changing international context. The CCP had to react and adapt to changing circumstances of world trade and in particular globalisation. The primary step was to move towards multilateral, rather than bilateral trade negotiations through which the EU had a single commercial policy towards all third countries. For an effective CCP the ECJ identified that the EU must have exclusive competence to act on behalf of all Member States. Exclusive competence is derived from the Treaty and covers both the Common Commercial Policy and the Common Agricultural Policy (CAP), and the signing of Association Agreements. Exclusive competence must be distinguished from concurrent competence to which the principle of subsidiarity applies. In practice the effect of granting exclusive competence to the EU means that Member States lose the right to regulate in that particular policy area. This differs from concurrent competence where the presumption remains that Member States will retain the right to legislate. Member States will only lose this right when the Community has satisfied certain criteria which demonstrate the benefits of action at the supra-national level.

In *Opinion 1/75*[10] the ECJ stated that the objective of the CCP in Art.133 EC arises:

"[i]n the context of the operation of the Common Market. . .with which the particular interests of Member States must endeavour to adapt to each other."

The ECJ viewed the provisions of Art.133 (1)–(4) EC as being incompatible with the exercise of concurrent powers by Member States. The ECJ's justification for this is that without exclusive competence, economic integration and the reciprocity and mutual trust that is required for the EU to function would be undermined. McGoldrick (1997:70) does not consider these arguments as being particularly persuasive and points out that exclusive competence is not the norm in Community decision-making. Furthermore, he argues that the presence of concurrent competence *per se* does not undermine integration. According to McGoldrick, such judgments demonstrate the integrationist interpretation of supremacy which the ECJ has applied.

MIXED AGREEMENTS

A mixed agreement is one to which both the EU and one or more of the Member States is a party because there is shared competence between the Member States and the EU. Mixed agreements are significant from a legal perspective because the Treaty includes a number of policy areas where there is a degree of shared competence and this raises questions of whether regulation falls within the domain of the EU or the Member States.

Even though the Community is granted exclusive competence in the CCP the Court has recognised that in certain circumstances, particularly where Member States are required to contribute financially, that capacity will be shared. In *Opinion 1/78*[11] the ECJ held that the CCP governed an international agreement designed to regulate the world market in natural rubber. Despite this, the ECJ also acknowledged that in this instance there would be shared competence because the agreement required Member States to individually contribute to the financing of natural rubber reserves. The question of financing the surplus rubber was important to the Court's reasoning, though this factor did not detract from the Court's overall expansive view of Art.133 EC and exclusive competence (Koutrakos, 2002:26).

McGoldrick (1997:85) criticises *Opinion 1/78* and argues that on the Court's logic the financing should have come from the Community and not the Member States, thereby making the matter one of exclusive Community competence. For McGoldrick, the Court's conclusions are inconsistent with the reasoning of the Court in *Opinion 1/75*. Eeckhout (2004:18) distinguishes these judgments on the basis that in *Opinion 1/75* the Member States were required to refrain from taking any action, whereas on the facts at issue in *Opinion 1/78* the positive act of expenditure justified the judgment. Despite this academic disagreement regarding the consistency of these two cases, both judicial Opinions are consistent on the crucial point of the importance of exclusive competence to achieve the objectives of the CCP.

An area of dispute, even prior to the EU's signing of the WTO relates to the question of competence for the protection of intellectual property rights. This dispute has become focussed in the light of the TRIPs agreement. According to Dörmer (2000:28) TRIPs represents a new challenge to EU law, in particular that concerning the EU's external relations and the relationship of EU law, international convention law and the legal systems of the individual EU Member States. In *Parfums Christian Dior SA*[12] the ECJ considered how EU law, national law and international conventions operate in the protection of intellectual property rights. This case allowed the ECJ an opportunity to analyse the application of EU law in the light of the WTO Agreements, and explore questions relating to the jurisdiction of the Court and the direct effect of the TRIPs Agreement.

The complexity of the situation relating to mixed agreements such as TRIPs originated with the Court's initial statement in relation to TRIPs, in *Opinion 1/94*.[13] The Commission sought the opinion of the ECJ on the competence of the EU to conclude the Agreement establishing the WTO, and in particular GATS and TRIPs. The ECJ concluded that the Institutions and its Member States were jointly competent to conclude the TRIPs Agreement, as only ceratin aspects of TRIPs, such as trademarks, came within the exclusive competence of the EU. Other aspects of intellectual property, for example the protection of patents, remained within the domain of the Member States.

In *Parfums Christian Dior* the case concerned an action commenced in the Dutch court by Dior, the proprietor of different trademarks for perfumes, against Tuk BV. Dior alleged that Tuk BV had infringed its trademark rights by selling perfumes bearing those marks when they had not been put on the market in the European Economic Area (EEA). The Dutch court considered that the proceedings raised the question of the direct effect of Art.50(6) of TRIPs and made a preliminary reference to the ECJ under Art.234 EC. The Dutch court was seeking guidance on whether Art.50(6) of the TRIPs Agreement is to be interpreted as having direct effect in the sense that the legal consequences set out therein take effect even in the absence of any corresponding provision of national law?

As to the Dutch court's query over its jurisdiction, the ECJ ruled that:

"[w]here the judicial authorities of the Member States are called upon to order provisional measures for the protection of intellectual property rights falling within the scope of TRIPs and a case is brought before the Court of Justice in accordance with the provisions of the Treaty, in particular Article [234] thereof, the Court of Justice has jurisdiction to interpret Article 50 of TRIPs." (para.40)

On the question of direct effect, the Court held that the provisions of TRIPs are:

"[n]ot such as to create rights upon which individuals may rely directly before the courts by virtue of Community law" (para.44).

In its judgment, the ECJ qualified this statement by reference to a field of intellectual property to which TRIPs applies and in respect of which the EU has acquired competence and legislated. One such area is trademarks, through which Regulation 40/94 has established the concept of the Community Trademark. As the EU has exclusive competence in relation to trademarks, national courts are required to apply rules relating to the protection of trademarks as far as possible in light of the wording and purpose of Art.50 of TRIPs. According to Koutrakis (2000:43), the objective of this is to ensure uniformity of application of EU law within the Member States and in such cases references to the ECJ under Art.234 EC are permissible.

Alternatively, in a field of intellectual property in respect of which the EU has *not* yet legislated and which consequently falls within the exclusive competence of the Member States, protective measures adopted by the national courts do *not* fall within the scope of EU law. Accordingly, EU law neither requires nor forbids that the legal order of a Member State should accord to individuals the right to rely directly on the rule laid down by Art.50 of TRIPs with the effect that an Art.234 EC reference is not possible.

COMPLETION OF THE CCP

The expansive interpretation of the CCP expressed by the ECJ in *Opinion 1/75* and *Opinion 1/78* has not been without difficulty. Cremona (1990:283) points out that the removal of internal barriers to trade took place far more quickly than the completion of the

CCP. Furthermore, judicial pronouncements, such as *Opinions 1/75* and *1/78,* raised controversy as to their scope of application, with any increase in competence signalling an inevitable decrease in powers for the Member States. For an effective CCP it was necessary to bridge the gap between internal and external trade. In particular the EU had to find a mechanism through which the protectionist instincts of Member States could be overcome. The CCP can only function if all Member States adopt a uniform view to customs duties from third countries in the same way they have agreed to their abolition for wholly internal trade. The concern for some Member States is illustrated by this simple example. If Member State A operates a quota system with regard to goods imported from a non-EU country, then Member State B, which does not operate such quotas, could import the goods from outside the EU and transport them to Member State A. Member State A could not, under Internal Market principles, prevent the import of these goods which were already in lawful circulation.

This concern is addressed by Art.134 EC which governs so called "indirect imports". Under the Treaty of Rome the import of goods in to the Community allowed Member States to preserve and enforce quotas on imports from third countries and Regulation 288/82 contained a list of approved quotas. Under Art.134 EC and Regulation 288/82 a Member State could control indirect imports, and this effectively provided an exception to the principle of uniformity with regard to imports. The Court approved this action in its judgment in *Dockenwolcke v Procureur de Républic,*[14] but went on to qualify this by stating that only those quotas which did not breach the Treaty, and had been approved by the Community, would be acceptable. As the CCP lies within exclusive competence any deviation required prior approval.

In 1994 the Member States agreed Regulation 3289/94[15] for common rules for imports in to the EU. This Regulation applies to products imported in to the EU and is based upon a principle of free trade. Contained within the Regulation is a list of permitted safeguards which do not originate from the Member States and reflect the list of permitted safeguards agreed by the parties to the WTO, including the EU.

The scope of the CCP was debated by the Member States at the 1996 IGC. Although the Commission wanted an extension to its powers to apply to economic matters more generally, the Member States rejected this. The compromise reached led to the inclusion of a new para.5 in Art.133 EC which allowed for the possible future extension of the CCP to cover international negotiations on intellectual property and services insofar as these were not already covered by the CCP. Cremona (2000:12) criticised the re-drafting of Art.133 (5) EC for failing to provide for a full constitutional procedure that would include each national parliament. Article 133 (5) EC merely requires a unanimous decision of the Council and even excluded the European Parliament. This suggests that internal constraints to procedurally amend the Treaty and extend EU competence are required. The ECJ recognised this through it judgments in relation to the application of TRIPs.

In *Opinion 1/94* the ECJ examined the issue of exclusive and non-exclusive competence within specific areas of the CCP and stated there were limits to EU competence. The Court held that the TRIPs agreement did not fall within the exclusive competence of the EU, either through Art.133 EC or more general Treaty bases such as Arts 95 or 308 EC. On the issue of intellectual property and services, the ECJ stated in *Opinion 1/94* that those areas which were already within the scope of the CCP, such as the protection of trademarks, would continue to be governed by the principles in Art.133 (1)–(4) on the basis of exclusive competence. This was confirmed by the ECJ in *Hermès International v FHT Marketing*.[16] Conversely if the agreement related to intellectual property and services which came within the scope of Art.133 (5) EC, for example, patents, then in such circumstances, the Member States would retain competence, provided that the agreement did not breach EU law.[17] *Opinion 1/94* therefore reinforces the ECJ's cautionary approach to shared competence with regard to the CCP which the ECJ stated in *Opinion 1/75* and where it suggested that amendments to Art.133 EC were required if the EU was to acquire increased competence.

The amendments to Art.133 EC by the Treaty of Nice reflect the views stated by the Court in *Opinion 1/94* and have divided expressly the CCP in to those areas within and those outside the exclusive competence of the EU. Following the reasoning of the judgments in *Hermès* and *Dior* it would appear that if the there is a link between the spheres of competence, for example the protection of the Community Trademark in national courts, then TRIPs would be applicable. Where such a link was lacking, because of an absence of harmonising legislation, such as in disputes covering the protection of patents, TRIPs would not be applicable and the matter could not be referred to the ECJ under Art.234 EC (Koutrakis, 2002:37). For Cremona the judgments in *Hermès* and *Dior* demonstrate the interest of the ECJ to maintain the unity of international representation of the Community. These cases also suggest a need for unity between the EU and the Member States in the determination of the EU's international obligations. This unity is achieved by *not* insisting on an all-embracing exclusivity of EU powers in areas where there is shared competence. According to Cremona (2000:29) the judgments of *Hermès* and *Dior* exhibit judicial self-restraint by not going beyond those areas where the EU has already legislated.

Article III–315 of the Constitutional Treaty simplifies the complicated provisions of Art.133 EC which govern the CCP since Nice. Under Art.I–13 of the Treaty the connection that currently exists between the CCP and exclusivity would be retained and strengthened as it would be extended to apply to the whole CCP. The Constitutional Treaty also states in Art.III–315 that the exercise of exclusive competence will have no effect on the allocation of competences between the EU and the Member States. The primary effect of this will be that action taken externally will *not* extend the EU's internal exclusive competence, thereby leaving Member States to regulate certain external agreements themselves.

With regard to the substance of the CCP, the Constitutional Treaty goes further than the existing Treaty provisions by stating the aims and principles of the CCP and the EU's external relations policy more generally. In Art.III–188 the Constitutional Treaty states that the EU's external policy objectives include "sustainable economic and social development in developing countries, environmental protection and the promotion of multilateral trade". These provisions suggest that the CCP is connected to the EU's other foreign policy objectives and is an integral part of the EU's attempts to create an ethical external relations agenda. The reference to environmental protection is an acknowledgment of the importance that the EU has placed on the international environmental agreements such as the Kyoto Protocol on Climate Change (1997). Similarly, references to sustainable economic and social development highlight that human rights considerations are central to any trade agreements the EU concludes with third countries. The CCP provisions of the Constitutional Treaty would convert the CCP in to a tool which promotes more than just free trade and economic development. These provisions reflect a broader social and human rights agenda of the EU which the EU has been developing incrementally, through policy and case law for over a decade.

The logical conclusion of the transfer of exclusive competence to the EU in the CCP is that as the EU represents all Member

States, it will enter in to agreements on *behalf* of those Member States. The primary issue is what is the status of such agreements in the EU. The principle of supremacy of EU law provides only for the supremacy of EU law and not international agreements. For such agreements to function there is a requirement of mutual trust between the EU and third countries necessitating a mechanism through which they are brought within the scope of the EU law. The position of such international agreements in the EU will now be considered in more detail.

THE STATUS OF INTERNATIONAL AGREEMENTS IN EC LAW

One consequence of exclusive EU competence in the CCP is that it has led to the EU negotiating international agreements with third countries on behalf of the Member States. One such example is the WTO. The primary issue this raises is what legal status is granted to such international agreements within the EU, and in particular how has the ECJ viewed the EU's obligations with regard to these agreements? The WTO, and previously GATT, have raised questions not only in relation to Treaty base issues and competence of the CCP, but also to what extent, if any, do such agreements create enforceable rights within the Member States?

According to the ECJ in *Haegmann*[18] international agreements which are signed by the Community become:

"[a]n integral part of Community law and may, in certain circumstances, have direct effect within the legal systems of the Member States."

The EU contracts with third countries in several ways with the two most common being agreements made directly between the EU and a third country, or an agreement which is made jointly between the EU, the Member States and a third country. Agreements made between the EU and third countries can be in the form of Association Agreements as seen in the pre-accession strategy that led up to the 2004 enlargement. These Association Agreements provided the legal basis for bilateral relations between these countries and the EU. The EU had already established similar Association Agreements with Turkey (1963), Malta (1970) and Cyprus (1972). In the case of Turkey, a Customs Union entered into force in December 1995.

Article 310 EC provides for the conclusion of Association Agreements and other agreements between the EU and third countries. Article 300 EC states that such agreements:

"[s]hall be binding on the institutions of the Community and the Member States."

In *Gloszczuk*[19] the ECJ confirmed that such Association Agreements can have direct effect within the Member States with the consequence that third country nationals may exercise the rights contained within the Agreements (Bogusz, 2002:275). In *Hauptzollamt Mainz v C.A. Kupferberg*,[20] which concerned the pre-accession Association Agreement with Portugal, the ECJ stated that such agreements must have direct effect to ensure uniformity of application within the Member States thereby recognising the relevance of such Association Agreements to the operation of the Internal Market.

DIRECT EFFECT OF INTERNATIONAL AGREEMENTS

The criteria for direct effect have been considered in the context of Community legislation. To give rise to rights which can be enforced in national courts, a measure must first satisfy the criteria laid down by the Court in *Van Gend en Loos*. In particular this requires a measure to be precise and unconditional. With regard to international agreements this can be problematic and the Court has held that an agreement will have direct effect where the objectives of that agreement are the same as those of the EU.[21] In *International Fruit*, the Court considered the status of GATT, which the founding six Member States had signed individually before they agreed the Treaty of Rome. The Court was of the opinion that while the GATT was intended to bind the EEC, the Agreement gave some degree of flexibility to Member States and contained a procedure that could allow them to vary, or even withdraw, from the Agreement. The Court's reasoning reflects a lack of reciprocity and legal certainty, especially in the event of signatories being in dispute. It also acknowledges that agreements such as GATT, and even the WTO, are based upon diplomacy rather than seeking to create legal rights.

By contrast in *Haupzollmat Mainz v Kupferberg* the Court held that certain provisions of a free trade agreement between the EEC and Portugal would have direct effect where they had a uniform impact across the Community. With regard to such agreements the Court has regularly stated that they do not have direct effect, as their primary objective is not to assist in the creation of the single market. For the Court, the defining feature in *Kupferberg* was that Portugal was seeking Community membership. Consequently, the free trade agreement fell within the objective of creating a single market, of which Portugal would eventually become a member.

The position of international agreements in EU law has proved a problematic issue for the Court and the status of GATT in particular has given rise to contentious litigation. Judgments such as *International Fruit* and *Kupferberg*, and the different status the Court awarded to GATT and free trade agreements respectively have been the subject of much criticism. In *Germany v Council (Bananas)*[22] the Court was asked to consider the legality of a Regulation which established the common organization of banana markets in favour of African, Caribbean and Pacific (ACP) growers closely attached to French, Spanish and Portuguese importers. This was to the detriment of third country, mostly US owned, growers which were established in Central America and from where German importers had enjoyed a regime of tariff-free imports. The Regulation, on the one hand, set up a system of assistance to ACP-banana producers, and on the other established quotas and tariffs for third country bananas with a view to restricting their import or making them more costly to consumers. There is no doubt that the Regulation hit German importers particularly hard. They were *de facto* banned or severely restricted from importing third country bananas at the preferential tariffs which had made them particularly popular with German consumers. Prior to this point there had been little or no restrictions on such imports.

Germany challenged the Regulation through Art.230 EC and argued that the Regulation was in breach of the GATT rules. The Court rejected this argument and held that it is not generally open to Member States to challenge Community law by relying on the GATT rules. The Court held[23] that the GATT rules do not have direct effect and that individuals could not rely on them before national courts. The Court did state that this would not be the case where the adoption of measures implementing obligations assumed within the context of the GATT is in issue or where a Community measure refers expressly to specific provisions of GATT. In such cases the Court held that it must review the legality of the Community measure in the light of the GATT rules.

As part of the WTO, a new GATT agreement was signed which included an increased number of binding provisions and the establishment of a quasi-judicial Dispute Settlement Understanding to resolve differences between contracting parties. In such circumstances the ECJ felt that conditions existed, which had not been present previously, under which GATT could bind the EU. The Court stopped short of stating that that it had direct effect. The *Bananas* judgment was controversial and led to significant debate as to whether the arguments hitherto applied by the ECJ to the question of direct effect of GATT should be applied to the new GATT agreement within the WTO. In the light of the improved quasi-judicial system to resolve disputes and the ECJ's acknowledgement in the *Bananas* judgment that GATT *may* prevail over EU law in limited circumstances, would there not now be a more convincing argument to extend direct effect to the WTO agreements generally?

This issue was addressed by the Court in *Portugal v Council*[24]. In this case Portugal challenged a Council Decision, which concluded various agreements on textiles with India and Pakistan, arguing that they breached the WTO agreements including GATT. The ECJ acknowledged the developments in the WTO but concluded that these changes did not suffice to grant direct effect. The Court stated[25]:

"[h]aving regard to their nature and structure, the WTO agreements are not in principle among the rules in the light of which the Court is to review the legality of measures adopted by the Community institutions."

For the ECJ the WTO still lacked certainty and contained a degree of diversity, in particular with regard to application and enforcement of the agreements by the contracting parties. The agreements still operated to a large extent on mutual trust and the quasi-judicial dispute resolution procedure was not sufficiently formal to ensure consistency of application. The underlying assumption of the ECJ's judgment is that WTO law lacks unconditional mandatory force, and an identifiable notion of reciprocity. In *Léon Van Parys NV*[26] the Court points out that the WTO agreements are not in principle among the rules which the Court must take into account when reviewing the legality of measures adopted by the Community Institutions. It is only where the Community has intended to implement a particular obligation assumed in the context of the WTO, or where the Community measure refers expressly to particular provisions of the WTO agreements, that it is for the Court to review the legality of a Community measure in light of the WTO rules.

This judgment follows the Courts reasoning in *Portugal v Council* in which the ECJ did not alter its view which it first expressed in *International Fruit*. WTO law (previously GATT) cannot be relied on to review the legality of acts of the EU. Setting out a two-part reasoning, the Court first denied that the WTO Dispute Settlement Understanding itself obliges the EU to implement rulings by making them directly enforceable. Secondly, it denied the possibility of doing so autonomously. The Court upheld its judgment in the *Bananas* case regarding the limited exceptions to this rule, including the possibility that WTO provisions can serve as a benchmark for reviewing Community acts taken to implement WTO Agreements. As a result of the *Portugal v Council* judgment there remains a degree of dissatisfaction with the status of the WTO in EU law, and with the status of international agreements in EU law more generally. Direct effect is central to ensuring the uniform application of EU law but the principle and the conditions required to satisfy it, do not readily apply to international agreements which are often vague and leave significant discretion in the hands of contracting parties. The ECJ will apply an "interpretative obligation" whereby EU legislative measures will, as far as possible, be interpreted to give effect to WTO rules. By contrast, individual Member States, who have granted the EU competence to negotiate the WTO, remain impotent and cannot use the principles of the WTO to challenge the legality of EU acts.

THE COMMON FOREIGN AND SECURITY POLICY AND THE EXTERNAL RELATIONS OF THE EU

The TEU introduced the pillar structure to the EU. Through the CFSP the EU has sought to become a more prominent entity in international relations. The objective of the CFSP is to galvanise EU action and works on the basis that Member States share similar strategic foreign policy objectives. This political cooperation in foreign affairs compliments the economic cooperation of the CCP. Unlike the CCP, the CFSP has had a chequered history, with Member States lacking agreement on several major foreign policy issues. One identifiable reason for this is that the CCP has a single policy arising from legislative provisions which are enforced by the ECJ. By contrast the CFSP is based upon intergovernmental cooperation that seeks a common policy and which has not always been attainable. The history of the CFSP, for example, the EU's response to the disintegration of the former Yugoslavia in the mid 1990's, or more recently with regard to the war in Iraq demonstrates the lack of consensus that exists. The absence of agreement is not altogether surprising and it must be emphasised that the agreement of the CFSP pillar at Maastricht merely provide the framework for establishing a common policy and did *not* create a common foreign and security policy.

The CFSP is based upon intergovernmental cooperation and not on legislative action which characterises the EC pillar. By Art.12 TEU Member States adopt joint actions, decide on common strategies, adopt joint positions and seek to create a political consensus on foreign and security policy. Article 12 TEU contains a mix of formal legal instruments and informal cooperation which Member States may use in the CFSP. The Council is the primary Institution and is responsible for execution of the CFSP objectives found in Art.11 TEU, which reflects the intergovernmental nature of the cooperation. Unlike the EC Community method of decision-making which encompasses the Council, European Parliament and the Commission and is based upon a clear division of powers and responsibility, the CFSP is dominated by the Council. Furthermore the ECJ has no power of review over the CFSP. Under Art.18 TEU it is the Presidency of the Council that represents the EU in CFSP matters and is assisted by a High Representative for the common foreign and security policy. The latter provides a degree of continuity to policy and negotiations through the six monthly Presidency rotation. The powers of the Council are set out in Art.13 TEU which requires the Council to ensure the unity, consistency and effectiveness of EU action.

Decision-making under the CFSP is defined by Art.23 TEU. All decisions must be taken unanimously. An abstention by a Member State will not prevent the adoption of a decision, but the exercise of a Member States' veto will do so. Eeckhout (2004:411) describes this "constructive abstention" as being unique in EU decision-making and reflects the position that unanimous agreement cannot always be reached. Unlike the Community method of decision-making, the veto has been retained because of the sensitive and political nature of the cooperation. Post Nice, some limited qualified majority voting has been introduced under Art.23 (2) TEU and applies to the agreement of joint actions or common positions or when such agreements are being imple-mented. It will also apply to the appointment of any special EU representatives for the CFSP. The voting rights allocated for use of qualified majority voting are the same as those in Art.205 EC and used in the co-decision process. Given the difficulty of arriving at unanimous agreements one issue considered by the Convention on the Future of Europe was the extension of qualified majority voting to decision-making more generally under the CFSP. Eeckhout points out (2004, p.412) the EU adopted no joint actions or common positions with regard to the war in Iraq because of the requirement for unanimity.

The Commission has a peripheral role in the execution of the CFSP. Article 27 TEU requires it to be "fully associated" with the work of the CFSP and Art.18 TEU requires the Commission to be "fully associated" with the work programme of the Presidency in the CFSP. Of greater value is Art.22 TEU which enables the Commission to refer to the Council any question relating to the CFSP. The Commission has produced Communications outlining strategies for the CFSP, for example in relation to human rights and external relations. In this context the CFSP should be viewed as part of the EU's wider external relations objectives together with the CCP. In the CCP the Commission takes the lead and negotiates on behalf of the Member States, for example, the WTO or bilateral trade agreements. It is in these bilateral trade agree-ments that human rights are mainstreamed through linking trade and/or developmental aid to improved human rights protection. Though peripheral to CFSP decision-making *per se*, it can be argued that the Commission adopts an important role to ensure that wider EU objectives are attained and co-ordinated through both CCP and the CFSP policies.

Under Art.21 TEU the European Parliament is confined to a mere consultative role and has a right to be kept "regularly informed" of progress in the CFSP. Even the consultation is restricted to general questions of policy rather than specific deci-sions, and this reinforces the intergovernmental nature of the cooperation. The Parliament does pay close attention to the CFSP, in particular to human rights issues. It will regularly present to the Council opinions and reports which the Council will invariably incorporate.

In complete contrast to the EC pillar, the ECJ has no jurisdiction over the CFSP. Denza (2002:337) argues that the reasons for this are firstly, that the short-term nature of CFSP, the lack of a legal framework and absence of mutual legal obligations make it difficult to review. Secondly, she argues that the ECJ has considered international relations within the context of the CCP, which has a different objective to the CFSP.

Denza contends that Member States did not want principles of exclusive competence, applied by the ECJ to the CCP, to be applied to the CFSP. It remains to be seen how the ECJ will consider the CFSP in the light of the Constitutional Treaty which incorporates the Charter of Fundamental Rights. Menéndez (2002:485) argues that the Charter should have a positive impact upon the pursuit of a common foreign policy. In the light of the focus of the CFSP on promoting human rights, it would be fair to assume that the ECJ may seek to benchmark the EU's decisions under the CFSP to ensure that they do not breach the fundamental rights principles contained within the Charter.

Article 11 TEU sets out the objectives of the CFSP and includes a commitment to safeguard the values and interests and independence of the EU within the framework of the United Nations Charter. Article 11 TEU also includes the objective to develop and consolidate democracy and respect for fundamental rights and freedoms, suggesting that EU seeks to "export" its values to third countries. This commitment to promoting human rights beyond its borders reflects more generally the EU's increased human rights discourse since the Maastricht Treaty. Article 6 TEU states that:

"The Union is founded on the principles of liberty, democracy, respect for human rights and fundamental freedoms and the rule of law, principles which are common to the Member States."

This policy of promoting democracy and fundamental rights which the EU pursued rigorously following the collapse of the Berlin Wall in 1989 formed an integral aspect of the social, political and economic changes which the countries of Central and Eastern Europe adopted prior to EU Accession in 2004. In the decade leading to Accession the EU signed Association Agreements with all applicant States which contained prominent human rights clauses. Additionally, regular Country Reports produced from 1997 by the Commission evaluated the progress of Accession States towards complying with *acquis communautaire*. These reports considered, not only progress towards economic transformation, but also progress of the Accession States towards improved human rights protection, the combating of corruption and improvement of administrative capacity. Consequently, in 15 years the political and economic systems of these countries were transformed, with economic assistance and ultimately EU membership being conditional on meeting EU norms of human rights. This "carrot and stick" approach to external relations is an integral strategy of the CFSP whereby economic assistance is linked to improved standards of human rights.

Denza (2002:86) has described Art.11 TEU as containing principles rather than operational objectives, with the CFSP being less precise than common policies under the EC Treaty. For Denza (2002:96) this lack of specificity distinguishes the "common" policy of the CFSP from the "single" policy that characterises decisions of the EC. This identifies one reason why progress on the CFSP has remained slow. For example, attempts to create closer military cooperation between the Member States, as provided for by Art.17 TEU, have proved limited. One reason for this is that Member States cannot agree on the objectives of a common policy and how this will co-exist with the responsibilities that many Member States have towards NATO. Furthermore, closer military cooperation creates difficulties for some Member States which feel that this may compromise their status of neutrality. The Nice Treaty strengthened the "security" dimension of the CFSP to form the European Security and Defence Policy (ESDP) and this development has been viewed as creating a military alliance within the EU. This perception of EU military cooperation endangering neutrality can be identified as one reason why Irish citizens voted against the Nice Treaty at the first referendum in April 2001.

The progress towards "common" objectives under the CFSP, where intergovernmental decision-making is characterised by the retention of the veto by Member States, has proved more difficult to achieve than "single" economic policies under the co-decision process of the EC pillar. According to Eeckhout (2004:143), the slow pace of development of the CFSP should not overshadow positive aspects which have taken place since Maastricht. In addition to the very fact that cooperation exists, Eeckhout argues that through Art.11 TEU certain core values of the EU have been constitutionalised. In particular the commitment in Art.11 TEU to "develop and consolidate democracy" and "respect for fundamental rights and freedoms" has, according to Eeckhout, created a "sophisticated human rights policy" which is a core component of the CFSP.

A distinct characteristic of the EU's external relations has been the promotion of human rights. A strong commitment to human rights in Art.6 TEU is a foundation of the EU, so it is not all surprising that the EU seeks to promote human rights through its external policies, for example through the use of development cooperation as provided for by Art.177 (2) EC and Regulation 975/1999. Regulation 975/1999 introduces the European Initiative for Democracy and Human Rights (EIDHR). This Regulation lays down the requirements for the implementation of development cooperation actions. The objective of these actions is to contribute to the development and consolidation of democracy and the rule of law and to that of respecting human rights and fundamental freedoms.

The Commission's action in the field of external relations is guided by compliance with the rights and principles contained in the EU Charter of Fundamental Rights and a European Council Resolution of June 29, 1991. This states that respect for human rights, the rule of law and the existence of political institutions which are effective, accountable and enjoy democratic legitimacy are the basis for equitable development. In 2001 the Commission expanded upon these objectives and published a Communication[27] which considered what role the EU should undertake with regard to promoting human rights beyond its borders. The Communication stated:[28]

"The basis for European Union action is clear. The European Union seeks to uphold the universality and indivisibility of human rights – civil, political, economic, social and cultural. . ."

The Communication identified three areas where the Commission can act effectively in the context of external relations and human rights. Firstly, it suggests that the EU can promote coherent and consistent policies in support of human rights and democratisation. This applies both to coherence between, in particular, the CCP and the CFSP. It also relates to the promotion of consistent and complementary action by the EU and Member States through the promotion and mainstreaming of human rights within development cooperation and other economic assistance.

Secondly the Communication states that by attributing a higher priority on human rights and democratisation in the EU's relations with third countries and taking a more pro-active approach, the EU can take a world lead in promoting fundamental rights. The Commission identifies that by using the opportunities offered by political dialogue, the CCP and external economic assistance, the EU can exert effective pressure particularly in circumstances when broader world opinion, expressed through the United Nations, remains divided. For example, in the case of Zimbabwe the EU has acted to implement economic sanctions despite the absence of a United Nations resolution.[29] This demonstrates that the CFSP objectives operate alongside the CCP and external trade policy of the EC pillar. Thirdly, the Communication suggests that the EU needs to adopt a more strategic approach to the EIDHR and matching aid and technical assistance programmes and projects in the field with EU commitments on human rights and democracy.

To promote human rights and democratisation objectives in external relations, the EU draws on a wide-range of instruments. These derive from the EU's commitment to protect fundamental rights as reaffirmed by the Charter. Some methods constitute traditional diplomacy and foreign policy, such as *demarches* (political acts) and interventions in United Nations fora, and trade sanctions. Others include financial co-operation instruments and bilateral dialogue as complimentary mechanisms. Some are more innovative, and potentially underused, namely Community instruments in policy areas such as the environment, trade, the information society and immigration, which have the scope to include human rights and democratisation objectives. The EU's Neighbourhood Strategy is one such example of this type of co-operation which addresses, *inter alia*, immigration issues with third countries and provides financial support to counteract illegal immigration and social problems. This assistance is provided on the proviso that recipient countries give increased considerations to human rights reforms.

In seeking to define the EU's external relations policy in 2005 it could be suggested that the EU is striving to create an ethical foreign policy. Economic considerations remain central to external relations through the CCP but these economic relations have become progressively influenced by the EU's desire to spread a message of improved human rights protection. Consequently, trade agreements have mainstreamed EU human rights values as seen in the EC-India Agreement. This Agreement demonstrates the interaction between commercial relations and the EU's development policy, and the political objectives of improved human rights protection which the EU has set itself. This would suggest that though still lacking a clear CFSP, the EU has gained confidence in its position on the world stage and will use bilateral trade agreements and the CCP to influence third countries.

EXTERNAL RELATIONS AND THE
CONSTITUTIONAL TREATY

The main institutional innovation is in Art.I–27 of the Constitutional Treaty with the creation of the post of EU Minister of Foreign Affairs, who will be responsible for the representation of the EU on the international scene. This function will merge the present tasks of the High Representative for the CFSP with those of the Commissioner for external relations and seeks to bring together in a more coordinated fashion the policies of the CFSP and external relations. The Minister of Foreign Affairs will be mandated by the Council for the CFSP, while being a full member of the Commission and as such in charge of the Commission's responsibilities in the field of external relations. The Minister will also be responsible for coordinating other aspects of the Union's external action. In addition, under Art.III–197 the Minister will chair the External Relations Council and so replace the current rotating Presidency arrangements. The EU's newly acquired single legal personality in Art.I–7 will also enable it to play a more visible role in world affairs, though the precise scope of this in practice is, at present, unclear.

While the provisions regarding external relations have been rewritten, the distinction between CFSP and the other aspects of EU external action still determines the respective roles of the Institutions and the procedures that apply. Nevertheless, the creation of the post of Union Minister of Foreign Affairs, with the task of developing mutual confidence and a European response of the Member States, strengthens the EU's role in world affairs. Moreover, the possibility of providing for increased cooperation between Member States in the field of defence through Art.III–312 will strengthen the EU's foreign policy.

The developments in relation to CFSP and external relations in the Constitutional Treaty create a unified concept of EU action in international relations. The removal of the pillar structure, the creation of a Minister for Foreign Affairs and the mainstreaming of human rights policy in to trade relations with third countries aims to create a better co-ordinated and more effective voice on the world stage. It is the emphasis on human rights in external relations, for example through the commitment to human rights in external affairs in Art.III–292 which is perhaps most noteworthy and corresponds to a general increase in the EU's protection of fundamental rights for its own citizens. The overarching strategic objective of EU foreign relations policy is to promote democratisation and human rights through the creation of an ethical EU foreign policy. Though this ethical foreign policy remains an aspiration the Constitutional Treaty with its unification of external action provides a comprehensive statement of objectives. These objectives, while pursuing an agenda of economic development recognise the importance of human rights The presence of an enforceable Charter of Fundamental Rights in the Constitutional Treaty should contribute to the realisation of this goal.

FUTURE DIRECTIONS FOR
EUROPEAN INTEGRATION

INTRODUCTION

A key to understanding European Union Law is to understand
the historical evolution of a legal system that has emerged from
an economic trading agreement which introduced the novel idea
of creating supranational Institutions to the present day creation
of a constitutional legal order where a European polity has
emerged. Ambitious aims for economic growth and closer cooperation between the original six Member States of the EEC in 1957
have been realised in 2005 by the creation of a Constitution for the
EU with a set of distinctive symbols normally associated with
statehood: a flag, an anthem, a Europe Day.

The road towards this European polity can be understood by
recognising that the EU is a contested and divided power system.
Vertical power is distributed between the Member States and the
Community/EU; horizontal power is divided between the
Community Institutions which include the power of the Member
States sitting as the Council and the European Council. This simple classification of divided powers is complicated by the introduction of other actors in the political process. Some have been
introduced by formal processes of Treaty change, for example, the
introduction of the social partners in the Treaty of Maastricht 1993
and the creation of new Committees, such as the Committee of the
Regions, the Employment Committee and the Social Protection
Committee. Other actors have emerged through new processes of
governance, especially in the post-Lisbon era of the open method
of coordination. These developments have led to the recognition
that the EU is a multi-level political community, with the various
actors holding different levels, and different kinds, of power.

A second feature of EU Law is the role played by constitutionalism in its development. The European Court of Justice has
played a central role in this evolution of a constitutional legal
order. A significant feature of this process has been the distinctive
supra national nature of the constitution of this "new legal

order". But this in turn has met with criticisms that the EU constitutional order does not match the expectations of a constitutional order normally found in a modern nation State, for example guarantees of human rights protection and democratic legitimacy. Another distinctive feature of the constitutionalism of the EU is the focus by the Court on a material constitution, which until the political processes to create a formal constitution were introduced at Laeken in 2001, was incomplete.

Chapters 1 and 2 show how the process of constitutionalism can be seen as distinct phases. The first phase corresponds to the period where the Court established the supremacy of Community law over national law, the doctrine of direct effect, the doctrine of implied powers and embryonic attempts to establish a human rights underpinning to the process of economic integration. The second stage of constitution building contains a paradoxical element. In response to the Court's expansive view of the Community constitution the Member States responded by tightening their grip on the political process. This was achieved by the retention of unanimity voting through the Luxembourg Accords 1965 and the use of consensus building in the Council. Chapter 3 shows how Art.309 EC allowed the Member States to control the political process and expand the powers of the Community. A final phase of constitution building is focused on the SEA 1987 and the TEU 1993. The SEA created the new concept of an Internal Market and re-introduced majority voting for the development of Community competence. Both Treaties expanded the competence of the Community building upon the consensus building of the second phase. Both Treaties also attempted to introduce a new "social" balance to the aims of economic integration.

This is a significant period. It moved the process of European integration closer to the idea of a polity but created tensions in the spill-over of such policies, especially the creation of economic and monetary union, and the implications for Member States, and individual autonomy. The TEU introduced a political idea of citizenship to balance the economic citizenship rights which had developed under the four economic freedoms discussed in Ch.4. It is during this phase the Court speaks more openly of the EC Treaty as the basic constitutional charter of a Community based upon the rule of law.[1] This phase introduced ideas of subsidiarity and proportionality in the primary EC Treaty but failed to clarify the hierarchy of Community competences, both in the use of Community acts (or powers) and the relationship between the new areas of competence and political, fundamental rights for individuals.

THE TREATY OF MAASTRICHT: A TURNING POINT IN EUROPEAN INTEGRATION

Despite its limitations, the Maastricht Treaty was a significant turning point in the process of EU integration and informs our understanding of the current state of European Union Law and political integration processes. This Treaty marked the introduction of the intergovernmental pillars and genesis of political integration. Subsequent Treaties have refined and added to EU competence under the pillars, particularly in the sphere of the justice and home affairs (JHA) pillar. Today, the comprehensive range of legal provisions that regulate internal aspects of EU policy are referred to as an "area of freedom security and justice". These laws range from provisions within Pillar Three, which coordinate police and judicial co-operation in the fight against organised crime and terrorism, to the incorporation of the Schengen Convention in to the EC Treaty. The Constitutional Treaty reorganises the structure of the EU and abolishes the pillar structure. One practical consequence of this will be the introduction of qualified majority voting as the norm for JHA matters. Additionally, the Charter of Fundamental Rights will provide citizens with protection against arbitrary EU action in regulating the area of freedom, security and justice.

The Treaty of Maastricht was significant for marking a change in emphasis in relation to integration under the EC pillar. The Treaty moved the centre of gravity away from purely economic integration with the inclusion of the new Social Chapter and environmental protection provisions in the EC pillar. Both the Treaty of Rome 1957 and the Single European Act 1987 are categorised by their emphasis on *economic* integration, and in particular the creation of an Internal Market. In Ch.4 we saw how the free movement of goods has consistently been referred to as the "cornerstone" of EU integration; the durability of the *Cassis de Dijon* principle has reinforced this. Mutual recognition and home state control have been extended to apply across *all* four freedoms and are crucial constituents to the efficient operation and regulation of the Internal Market. The durability and centrality of the mutual recognition principle is further underlined through its application to regulating certain aspects of the area of freedom, security and justice.

The Maastricht Treaty formally acknowledged the pivotal role that the citizen has contributed to the process of EU integration. The recognition comes in Arts 17 and 18 EC that established

Citizenship of the Union. These vaguely worded provisions have been applied by the ECJ to expand upon the rights available to EU citizens, most notably to persons who are *not* economically active. The Single European Act created the "market citizen"; the Maastricht Treaty laid the foundations for the creation of the "social citizen" which has been expanded upon by the Court of Justice.

The Maastricht Treaty recognised the importance of the ECHR to EU integration. Article 6 (2) TEU provides that the EU will protect fundamental rights as contained within the ECHR and views them as being part of the general principles of EU law. Article 6 (2) TEU reflects the view which the ECJ first stated in the *Internationale Handelsgesellschaft* judgment. As part of the integration process, the introduction of the citizenship provisions and the acknowledgment of the importance of the ECHR to EU integration collectively increased the scope of rights which individuals enjoy under EU law. The shared characteristic of the citizenship and human rights provisions is that they are *not* dependent upon the pursuit of an economic activity. Article 17 and 18 EC grant EU citizens rights by virtue of their objective status as EU citizens and not because of the existence of a professional or contractual relationship. The significance of Art.6 TEU is that human rights standards of the Member States are recognised as underpinning the process of EU integration; the Charter of Fundamental Rights reinforces this.[2]

During the 2003 IGC, three significant changes were made concerning the arrangements for fundamental rights. First, a special provision was added to the Constitutional Treaty requiring the Court to have due regard to the Official Explanations to the Charter of Fundamental Rights. These Explanations were drawn up during the original Charter drafting process in 2000, and were expanded and modified during the Convention. Their primary purpose is to relate the rights and principles set out in the Charter to existing law, for example, they show which Charter provisions are intended to correspond with those set out in the ECHR. Secondly, a special Declaration has been added to the Constitutional Treaty setting out the texts of the Official Explanations in full. This should contribute to transparency and accessibility regarding the true meaning of the Charter. Finally, the Constitutional Treaty texts now contain two further developments. The text includes a mandate for the EU to accede to the ECHR. It also includes a special Protocol and a Declaration to ensure that accession does not affect the position of the individual Member States in relation to the ECHR. These developments formally address the concerns first raised by the German Federal Constitutional Court in *Internationale Handelsgesellschaft*.

The provisions are designed to guarantee that citizens' basic rights and liberties are fully transparent at EU level, without disturbing the primary responsibilities of the Member States to protect human rights. The Charter does not replace domestic human rights provisions, including the ECHR. In this context, the Charter creates no new powers for the EU, nor does it alter any of the EU's existing powers. Furthermore, it will apply to Member States only when they are implementing EU law.

SECURITISATION AND EU INTEGRATION

A feature of EU integration since Maastricht has been the pursuance of a common "internal" policy for the EU. This compliments the EU's external affairs policy and in particular shares the fundamental rights objectives which have become central to EU external relations. The focus of the EU's external policy is to promote economic development in neighbouring states and the developing world through favourable trade agreements and bilateral economic assistance programmes. The EU sees this "at source" economic assistance as preferable to economic migrants entering the EU. The EU's search for a common immigration and asylum policy reinforces this objective and seeks to create a hard border through which it deters non-EU nationals who are economic migrants. The Treaty of Amsterdam changed the nature of cooperation in the field of justice and home affairs by defining the area of freedom, security and justice. The aim of these developments was to establish the free movement of EU citizens and non-EU nationals legally present in the EU, while simultaneously guaranteeing security through the introduction of measures to combat organised crime and terrorism.

Since the Amsterdam Treaty some aspects of JHA co-operation have been brought within the scope of the EC Treaty, for example, Title IV covering "visas, asylum, immigration and other policies related to the free movement of persons". This covers measures concerning external border controls, asylum, immigration and judicial cooperation in civil matters. The effect of this was to bring these areas under the EC pillar where they can be the subject of Directives, Regulations, Decisions, Recommendations and Opinions. Furthermore, since the Treaty of Nice the Member

States decided that most of those areas would no longer require unanimity but would be subject to the co-decision procedure. One exception is police and judicial co-operation between Member States which continues to fall under the reshaped third pillar.

The area of freedom, security and justice includes the Schengen Agreements which were integrated in to the framework of the EU by the Amsterdam Treaty. The Schengen Agreements are formally within the scope of the EC Pillar. The United Kingdom, Ireland and Denmark indicated in various protocols to the Amsterdam Treaty that they do not wish to participate fully in all the measures relating to the area of freedom, security and justice, but with the proviso of "opting in" where appropriate. The strategy of the EU since Maastricht can be defined in the following manner; free movement of persons and securitisation are inter-linked. The objective is to facilitate the free movement of citizens within the EU while simultaneously maintaining the integrity of the EU's borders and tackling criminal activity.

The Tampere Summit in 1999,[3] which was devoted to the creation of an area of freedom, security and justice, considered that the objective was as important as the establishment of the single market. The aims are to develop an open and secure EU, fully committed to the obligations of the International Refugee Conventions and other relevant human rights instruments, and to improve European citizens' access to justice throughout the Union. The Charter of Fundamental Rights is an integral part of this process and it is no coincidence that the Tampere European Council established the body to draw up the Charter first mentioned in the Presidency Conclusions of the Cologne European Council in June 1999.[4]

The process of EU integration has been incremental with both the Treaties of Amsterdam and Nice refining and expanding upon the Maastricht arrangements. The Constitutional Treaty continues this trend. Some developments have greater significance such as the abolition of the intergovernmental pillars and the merger of the two main Treaties. The Constitutional Treaty brings together the police and judicial co-operation provisions of the TEU and the immigration, asylum and judicial cooperation provisions of the EC Treaty under a single Treaty and Institutional structure. One effect is that this will extend qualified majority voting and closer supervision by the ECJ of decision-making which is currently within the scope of the third pillar. Furthermore, decisions will be subject to review and compatibility with the Charter of Fundamental Rights.

These developments are a natural progression from the conclusions of the Tampere European Council, 1999, which decided that the principle of mutual recognition should become the cornerstone of judicial cooperation in both civil and criminal matters within the Union. Enhanced mutual recognition in these fields intends to facilitate cooperation between authorities while simultaneously improving the judicial protection of individual rights. Mutual recognition, a principle hitherto associated with economic integration, has been a assigned a central role in the creation of an area of freedom security and justice. Article III–270 (1) of the Constitutional Treaty states that mutual recognition is the basis of judicial co-operation in this field but the provision does not exclude the approximation of Member States' laws and regulations in certain areas. This reflects current practice and builds upon the conclusions of the Tampere European Council. Article III–270 (1) provides for QMV and co-decision to be the norms for decision-making.

Since the Amsterdam Treaty there has been harmonisation of some procedural aspects of criminal law. Member States, such as the UK, have been cautious about pursuing this form of integration and the Constitutional Treaty includes the option of an "emergency brake" provision. The consequence of this is that a Member State in Council, which cannot accept a criminal procedure harmonising measure, can "pull the brake". This suspends discussion in the Council and automatically refers it to the European Council where decisions are made by unanimity. If it is still impossible to agree, then the enhanced co-operation provisions in Art.I–44 can be applied. Under the Constitutional Treaty this will require the consent of one third of the Member States who wish to pursue the proposal.

The ECJ has already acknowledged the existence of mutual recognition of judgments in the context of the Schengen Agreements. In Joined Cases C–187/01 and C–385/01 *Criminal proceedings against Hüseyn Gözütok and Klaus Brügge*[5] the ECJ applied the *ne bis in idem* principle enshrined in Art.54 of the Convention implementing the Schengen Agreements. In *Gözütok and Brügge*, the ECJ considered the situation where the Public Prosecutor of a Member State discontinues criminal proceedings brought in that State, without the involvement of a court. The ECJ held that once the accused has agreed to a settlement with one prosecutor, this precludes other Member States from prosecuting the same accused for the same facts. By contrast, in *Miraglia*,[6] the Court took the view that the rules do not apply where a criminal investigation is ended as a result of the commencement of another investigation in another Member State.

The *Gözütok and Brügge* judgment reflects the trend towards recognising the creation of the EU as a genuine judicial space (Harding, 2000). The judgment has human rights implications relating to the principle of legal certainty which is protected by both the ECHR (Art.7) and the Charter of Fundamental Rights (Arts II–47 and II–50). The European legal space is therefore one which has the protection of fundamental rights as it core value. Furthermore, the judgment confirms that EU policies relating to free movement of persons serve two purposes. One aim is to facilitate the pursuit of offenders across borders. The second is to guarantee citizens' rights in judicial proceedings across the EU and ensure the principle of legal certainty applies within the European legal space. Without this, rights of free movement would be infringed. In *Gözütok and Brügge* the ECJ recognised a necessary implication of the principle is that the Member States have mutual trust in their criminal justice systems. This requires a Member State to recognise the criminal law in force in the other Member States in circumstances when the outcome would be different if its national laws are applied.

INSTITUTIONAL STRUCTURES AND THE CONSTITUTIONAL TREATY

The main changes proposed by the Constitutional Treaty to the composition and structure of the EU Institutions has been considered in Chapter 1. Enlargement has required streamlining of the Institutions, particularly the Commission. From a strategic perspective the most important change in the EU's institutional arrangements is the creation of a President of the European Council under Art.I–21. The President will be elected by the members of the European Council for a mandate of two and a half years, renewable once. The President will chair the European Council, drive forward its work and provide some much needed continuity to EU policy making.

To compliment this change, Art.I–22 provides for the replacement of the existing six-monthly rotating Presidency by a "Team Presidency" system. Under it, a team of three Member States holding the Presidency for 18 months will chair all Councils apart from the Foreign Affairs Council, which the European Union Foreign Minister will chair. In principle, one Member State will preside over all the Councils for 6 months, supported by others in the Team, though the Member States concerned may agree alternative arrangements amongst themselves. The details of rotation will be set out in a separate Council Decision. The aim of the Team Presidency is to provide a longer-term, more stable decision-making structure and provide greater coherence and consistency in the work of various sectoral Councils.

Strategically this is important for several reasons. Firstly, this organisation will provide continuity and consistency in EU policy making. Secondly, the election of the President of the Council, though not by EU citizens, could improve the legitimacy of EU policy-making. Thirdly, citizens may identify more closely with the EU if they can identify with a single figurehead. The institutional reform proposed by the Constitutional Treaty and the improved democracy within the EU are intended for the consumption of EU citizens. The Laeken Declaration identified the need to reconnect with the citizen and the Convention identified the role to be played by national parliaments to secure this.

The Laeken Declaration recognised the over-intrusive nature and volume of EU legislation as one reason for citizen disaffection with the process and outcomes of European integration. Though subsidiarity is an essential element of EU law making, the principle has failed to adequately address the concerns of many EU citizens that EU legislation is over-intrusive. The Constitutional Treaty links the issue of citizen disaffection with the application of the subsidiarity principle and considers national parliaments as institutions which can contribute to bridging this democracy gap.

The Constitutional Treaty includes a mechanism, the objective of which is to ensure that subsidiarity is enforced, and grants powers to national parliaments to review legislation for its compatibility with subsidiarity. Under this mechanism, national parliaments will gain the power to send back any legislative proposal for review, if one-third of national parliaments concur that it infringes the principle of subsidiarity. The subsidiarity mechanism is set out in the Protocols 1 and 2 of the Constitutional Treaty on the Application of the Principles of Subsidiarity and Proportionality.

The importance of these Protocols is twofold. Firstly, it will be very difficult to ignore the strongly held views of one-third of the national parliaments. EU citizens associate most closely with their national legislatures. Consequently amendment, or even withdrawal, by the Commission of a proposal which national parliaments have rejected on behalf of their electorate, would be a positive step for EU democracy. In practice any proposal meeting such opposition would be very unlikely to prosper. This is primarily because if a third of national parliaments were against any proposal, it is likely that their governments would follow suit. Consequently it would be difficult to put together the qualified majority required in the Council.

Secondly, it gives the national parliaments a direct say in the EU's law-making procedures for the first time. At present, there is no obligation on Member States, or the Commission, even to inform national parliaments about draft EU laws, still less to let them have any power. Under the new mechanism, all national parliaments must be notified independently, and given six weeks to respond. This development can be interpreted as national parliaments being brought within the European legal space through acquiring a formal role in the decision-making process. This development also recognises that the foundations of EU citizenship, laid by the Maastricht Treaty can only be fully realised with the assistance of nation-state political and legal institutions. Despite the process of EU integration, EU citizens continue to identify most closely with national institutions which provide the primary form of political representation. The Constitutional Treaty, by providing these participatory powers to national parliaments is seeking proxy assistance and legitimacy for further integration.

A CITIZENS' EUROPE

The individual is central to the future progress of EU integration. On one level, institutional reform, democratisation, increased accountability and a higher profile for national parliaments are all developments intended to reconnect the EU with the citizen. The Laeken Declaration identified re-engagement with the citizen as central to remedying the democratic deficit. The Convention pursued the theme of a citizens' Europe and the Constitutional Treaty reflects this.

The prominence given to human rights through the Charter and the social and employment protection which EU law grants to citizens is evidence of how the individual has become central to the process EU integration. This is reinforced by the European Court of Justice giving prominence to the concept of Citizenship, discussed in Chapter 4. The Citizenship provisions included at Maastricht were intended to express a new type of direct relationship between the polity and individuals at the European level. This is a relationship where the individuals are no longer considered exclusively in their economic roles as factors of production. The introduction of EU citizenship is the first link in a series of developments through which the citizen is identified as central to remedying the EU's democratic deficit. The Social Chapter, the Charter of Fundamental Rights and the Constitutional Treaty have subsequently followed this line of thought. The ECJ has, through its case law, also contributed to the broader understanding of EU Citizenship.

Maduro (1998:68) argues that the EU's democratic deficit arose because of two parallel developments, namely constitutionalisation and Europeanisation. The Member States have been addressing this deficit since the Single European Act. Constitutionalisation refers to the idea by which Community law has established itself as an independent legal order. This process has mainly proceeded through the judgments of the ECJ, for example in relation to fundamental rights and direct effect. As an end result, EU law has detached itself from the control of the Member States, the parties to the founding Treaties. Consequently, the Treaties have been transformed into constitutional documents representing a new legal order. The process of constitutionalisation has also changed the relationship of the individual *vis-a vis* EU law. Individuals are no longer connected to the EU's legal and institutional structure merely through the mediation of the Member States, but also directly through Treaty rights. The consequence is that EU law confers rights on citizens which are enforceable in national courts.

The requirement of a direct relationship of legitimacy has been accentuated by the parallel move towards Europeanisation. The competences of the EU have gradually expanded through Treaty revisions and through the extensive interpretations given by the ECJ. The scope of contemporary EU law and EU activities has extended beyond the original economic objectives envisaged in 1957. Articles 17 and 18 EC, together with their expansive interpretation by the ECJ in judgments such as *Martínez Sala* and *Grzelczyk*, are evidence of that.

As for the future, the EU's political goals stated within the Constitutional Treaty emphasise the empowerment of the individual. The achievement of EU integration is not measured exclusively by the success of economic integration. The level of individual participation in EU affairs and the impact that EU rights and policies have on the lives of ordinary citizens are equally important considerations. The EU citizen cannot be considered as merely someone who emanates from one of twenty-five Member States and is exercising economic rights. Market access is no longer the overriding criteria. The EU citizen of the twenty-first century is not just a "citizen-worker" or "economic citizen" but also a "social citizen" who is in possession of a distinct set of rights which are provided by the Treaties.

The Constitutional Treaty takes the process of constitutionalisation and Europeanisation further. This is illustrated by the abolition of the pillar structure of the EU and extension of jurisdiction of the ECJ to the field of Justice and Home Affairs. The scope of majoritarian decisions is also enlarged. Although the Constitutional Treaty is intended to remedy the democratic deficit, it also contributes to the main background factor of this deficit, by *deepening* the process of Europeanisation.

Taken together, constitutionalisation and Europeanisation have led to the reinforcement of the democratic deficit at the European level. This deficit manifests itself most obviously in citizen apathy, seen for example, in the low turnout in the elections of the European Parliament. The proposed referenda on the Constitutional Treaty in many Member States will indicate comprehensively how citizens view the process of integration and particularly whether the Treaty provides the framework to bring them closer to the EU. The introduction of EU Citizenship was a response to the legitimacy deficit resulting from the processes of constitutionalisation and Europeanisation. Is the concept of EU Citizenship sufficient to bridge this gap?

Citizenship is an aspect of the process of constitutionalisation and intends to form a direct link between individuals and the EU. On its own Citizenship does not accurately reflect the relationship which individuals have with EU law. The concept of the social citizen in the EU necessitates the individual being granted additional protection in the form of rights. The most important post-Maastricht development with regards to EU Citizenship was the introduction of Art.13 EC in the Treaty of Amsterdam 1997 and the creation of the Charter of Fundamental Rights which is included in Part I of the Constitutional Treaty.

The Preamble to the Charter explicitly refers to EU Citizenship. The EU is declared to:

"... place the individual at the heart of its activities, by establishing the citizenship of the Union and by creating an area of freedom, security and justice".

Most of the rights provided for are universal human rights. Additionally, the Charter also includes a Chapter entitled *Citizens' Rights*, although some of the rights laid down in this Chapter are attributed to "every person". These include Art.41 which provides a right to good administration and Arts 42 and 43 which contain a right of access to documents and the right to refer to the Ombudsman of the Union.

The Charter demonstrates the strengthening of EU citizenship. The Chapter containing Citizens Rights reinforces the concept of the social citizen. It includes provisions which mirror the provisions of the Citizenship Title of the EC Treaty and also Art.255 EC in relation to Transparency and access to documents. Furthermore Chapter II (*Freedoms*) contains provisions relating to political participation such as freedom of assembly and association. Article 12 (2) reinforces the political dimension of EU Citizenship by stating that political parties at the EU level "contribute to expressing the political will of the citizens of the Union". Collectively, these various provisions, which provide rights to EU citizens or which encourage their participation in EU affairs, suggest that EU Citizenship is constituted of a combination of rights which are political, social and economic (Barber, 2002). In this sense the Charter guarantees for the EU citizen civil liberties in relation to political rights and participation in EU affairs.

EU Citizenship should not be considered as the development of a competing or parallel citizenship to that of nationality. It is more accurate to describe the relationship as complimentary; EU Citizenship is wholly dependent on national citizenship. In the definition of its personal scope through nationality of the Member States in Art.17 (1) EC, EU Citizenship is parasitic on national citizenship. The Treaty of Amsterdam explicitly provides that EU Citizenship shall compliment, and not replace, national citizenship. On this basis, the relationship between EU Citizenship and national citizenship is not based upon one of equality. EU Citizenship is dependent upon national citizenship, but national citizenship exists independently of any EU provisions. EU citizens are granted social, political and economic rights through domestic constitutions in conjunction with documents such as the ECHR, the importance of which EU law has acknowledged.

The strongest argument rebutting the view that EU citizenship has enveloped national citizenship is that abstract documents containing vaguely worded rights do not create a single European identity. Though the rights in the EU Treaties and also the ECHR have contributed to the creation of a European legal space, this has not been matched by the creation of a single European cultural, social or political identity. The Charter of Fundamental Rights has symbolic value and expresses in its Preamble that it reiterates the values contained in Art.6 (1) TEU which were first included in the Maastricht Treaty. Yet the expression that the EU is founded on the principles of "human dignity, freedom, equality, democracy and the rule of law" does not form a unified political, social or even legal culture. The provisions of Art.6 (1) TEU are not controversial and the overwhelming majority of EU citizens would subscribe to them without reservation. While these objectives may be universally are accepted, they do not provide the cement of a single EU identity.

EU Citizenship, as a legal, political and social objective, is still developing and the Constitutional Treaty has consolidated developments to date. Free movement of persons is one way in which cultural barriers have been broken down. The concept of a "worker" under Art.39 EC is a Community concept and has facilitated free movement. Directive 2004/38 EC, the Citizenship Directive, will improve matters further. Movement by citizens has, on the whole, been restricted to professional categories such as lawyers or to students. In this context, EU citizenship will continue to develop slowly and remains linked for the most part to the pursuit of some kind of economic activity. Citizenship is, according to Weiler (1999:343), linked to cultural identity and in this sense the EU lacks a distinct cultural identity. The Treaty provides citizens with rights and Weiler (1999:346) considers this as forming a "social contract" between EU citizens and not just between the Member States. Yet the development of EU Citizenship remains restricted by national considerations and particularly the social and political cultures which prevail in the Member States and with which citizens identify most readily. It is difficult to see how one coherent view of EU citizenship can develop, within a cultural, social or political context, in an EU of twenty-five Member States.

Despite the limited contribution of EU Citizenship to the creation of a shared political and social identity, its impact upon legal integration in the EU should not be underestimated. The issue that remains is whether EU Citizenship, in its current form, can provide greater legitimacy to the EU? Can the objectives of Laeken be achieved and the EU reconnect with its citizens? The answer may lie, at least in part, with the ratification process of the Constitutional Treaty. The use of referenda in many Member States[7] may provide more than a symbolic opportunity to provide greater substance to EU citizenship. The debates, which arise out of the ratification process, could provide citizens with an opportunity to involve themselves directly in EU affairs in a way which Laeken envisaged. These public discussions could be part of the process of identifying what, if any, is the shared cultural, political and social identity of the EU and whether the Constitutional Treaty embodies it.

Yet if Weiler's analysis is correct and that citizenship is *indeed* linked to cultural identity, the prospects for ratification of the Constitutional Treaty remain in the balance. If not ratified by all Member States the Constitutional Treaty will fall, but the EU will continue, presumably on the basis of the Nice Treaty 2000. While the politicians may view rejection as unsatisfactory, and a core of Member States may wish to continue with closer integration, this will not automatically address the concerns of EU citizens, or meet the objectives of the Laeken Declaration. The key feature of EU integration, which distinguishes it from other attempts to unify Europe, is that it is based upon political and legal consent. In practice this means the consent of the citizen. A citizen's Europe requires individuals to have tangible social, economic, political and human rights, but it also requires that citizens feel part of the political process that provides them with these rights.

ENDNOTES

CHAPTER 1

1 *Opinion 1/94 (Competence of the Community to Conclude International Agreements Concerning Services and the Protection of Intellectual Property)* [1994] ECR I–5267.
2 See Case C–85/96 *Martínez Sala v Freistaat Bayern* [1998] ECR I–2691.
3 COM(2003) 104 final. Communication from the Commission to the Council and the European Parliament Wider Europe – Neighbourhood: A New Framework for Relations With Our Eastern and Southern Neighbours.
4 COM (2004) 373 final.
5 Laeken European Council December 15, 2001.
6 Named after the then Dutch Foreign Minister Paul Henri Spaak.
7 COM (85) 220.
8 Case 120/78 *Cassis de Dijon* [1979] ECR 649.
9 COM(2001) 428 *European Governance – A White Paper*.
10 Presidency Conclusions Cologne European Council 3–4 June 1999.
11 C–173/99 *BECTU* [2001] ECR I–4881
12 Case 25/62 *Van Gend en Loos v Nederlanse Administratie der Belastingen* [1963] ECR 1.
13 Lisbon Presidency Conclusions June 2000.
14 COM(2005) final. Second Implementation Report of the Internal Market Strategy 2003–2006.
15 See for example Case 6/64 *Costa v ENEL* [1964] ECR 585 and Joined Cases C–6 & 9/90 *Francovich and Bonifaci v Italian State* [1991] ECR I–5357.
16 See for example Cases 286/82 & 26/83 *Luisi and Carbone v Minister del Toro* [1984] ECR 377.
17 Case C–376/98 *Germany v Council (Tobacco advertising)* [2000] ECR I–8419.
18 Case 149/77 *Defrenne v Sabena* [1978] ECR 1365.
19 Supra M.8 Case C–415/93 *Union Royal Belges de Sociétés de Football Association v Jean-Marc Bosman* [1995] ECR I 4921.

20 See Case C–84/94 *United Kingdom v Council* (*Working Time Directive*) [1996] ECR I–5755.
21 Case C–300/89 *Commission v Council* (*Titanium Dioxide*) [1991] ECR I–2867.
22 Case C–70/88 *European Parliament v Council* (*Chernobyl*) [1990] ECR I–2041.
23 Case C–21/94 *European Parliament v Council* (*Road Taxes*) [1995] ECR I–1827.
24 Case C–295/90 *European Parliament v Council* (*Students Rights of Residence*) [1992] ECR-I 4193.
25 Case 322/88 *Grimaldi v Fondes des Maladies Professionnelles* [1989] ECR 4407.
26 Case 39/72 *Commission v Italy* [1973] ECR 101.
27 C–213/89 *R v Secretary State of Transport ex parte Factortame Ltd* [1990] ECR I–2433.
28 Joined Cases C–6 and 9/90 *Francovich v Italian State* [1991] ECR I–5357.
29 Case 41/74 *Van Duyn v Home Office* [1974] ECR 1337.
30 Case 148/78 *Ministero del Publico v Ratti* [1979] ECR 1629.
31 Case 138/79 *Roquette Frères v Council* [1980] ECR 3333.
32 See for example the *Chernobyl* 22 and *Students Rights of Residence*, Supra M. 24, Supra M. 22 judgments.
33 See M22 above.
34 See Case 25/62 *Plaumann v Commission* [1963] ECR 95 and Case C–50/00 *Unión de Pequeños Agricultores v Council* [2002] ECR 1–6677.
35 Committee of Independent Experts: *Fraud and Mismanagement in the Commission* para.9.4.25.
36 See Case C–45/91 *Commission v Greece* [2000] ECR I–5047.
37 Case 25/70 *Einfuhr-und- Vorratsstelle für Getreide und Futternittel v Köster* [1970] ECR 1161.
38 Case 302/87 *European Parliament v Council* (*Comitology*) [1988] ECR 5615.
39 Case T–174/95 *Svenska Journalistförbundet v Council* [1998] ECR II–2289.

CHAPTER 2

1 Case 53/81 *Levin v Staatssecretaris van Justitie* [1982] ECR 1035.
2 Case 27/76 *United Brands v Commission* [1978] ECR 207.
3 Case 168/91 *Konstantinidis v Stadt Altensieg, Standesamt, & Landramsamt Colw, Ordnungsamt* [1993] ECR I–1191.

4 Case 222/84 *Johnson v Chief Constable RUC* [1986] ECR 1651.
5 See for example Case C–387/97 *Commission v Greece* [2000] ECR I–5047.
6 Case 340/02 *Commission v France* Opinion of Advocate General Geelhoed 18 November 2004.
7 Case 789/79 *Calpak SpA v Commission* [1980] ECR 1949.
8 Case 25/62 *Plaumann v Commission* [1963] ECR 95.
9 Case C–309/89 *Cordoniu v Commission* [1994] ECR-I 1853.
10 Case C–358/89 *Extramet Industrie SA v Council* [1991] ECR I–2501.
11 Case 4/73 *Nold v Commission* [1974] ECR 491.
12 Case 11/82 *PiriakI-Patraiki v Commission* [1985] ECR 207.
13 See Case C–321/95 *Stichting Greenpeace v Commission* [1998] ECR I–1651; Case C–50/00 *Unión de Pequeños Agricultores v Council* [2002] ECR 1–6677.
14 At para.101.
15 At para.39.
16 Case 263/02 *Commission v Jégo-Quéré* judgment of April 1, 2004, not yet reported.
17 Case 13/83 *European Parliament v Council* (Transport) [1985] ECR 1513.
18 Case 104/79 *Foglia v Novello* (1) [1980] ECR 745.
19 Case C–206/01 *Arsenal Football Club v Reed* [2002] ECR I–273.
20 Case 283/81 *CILFIT* [1982] ECR 3415.
21 *R v International Stock Exchange of the UK and the Republic of Ireland, ex p Else and ors* [1993] 1 ALL ER 420.
22 Case 28–30/62 *Da Costa en Schaake v Nederlandse Belastingadministratie* [1963] ECR 31.
23 Case C–224/01 *Köbler v Republik Österreich* [2003] ECR I–239.
24 C–15/96 *Schöning-Kougebetopoulou v Freie und Hansestadt Hamburg* [1998] ECR I–4730.
25 See for Case C–66/95R *v Secretary of State for Social Security ex parte Sutton* [1997] ECR I–2163.
26 Para.74.
27 Para.37.
28 Case 5/71 *Zuckerfabrik Schöppenstedt v Council* [1971] ECR 975.
29 Case 83/76 *Bayerische HNL v Council and Commission* [1978] ECR 1209.
30 Joined Cases C–104/89 and C–37/90 *Mulder and Others v Council and Commission* [1992] ECR I–3061.
31 See for example Case 11/70 *Internationale Handelsgesellschaft* [1970] ECR 1125 and Case 92/78 *Simmenthal SpA v Ministero dello Finance* [1979] ECR 777.

32 *Opinion 2/94 Accession by the Community to the European Convention for the Protection of Human Rights and Fundamental Freedoms* [1996] ECR I–1759.
33 Para.14.
34 Case 345/82 *Wünsche Handelsgeselschaft v Germany* [1984] ECR 1995.
35 [1994] 1 CMLR 57.
36 Case 43/75 *Defrenne v Sabena (No.2)* [1976] ECR 455.
37 Case 149/77 *Defrenne v Sabena (No.3)* [1978] ECR 1365.
38 See Case 4/73 *Nold v Commission* [1974] ECR 491.
39 Case C–221/89 *R v Secretary of State for Transport ex parte Factortame* [1991] ECR I–3905.
40 Joined Cases C–6 and 9/90 *Francovich v Italian State* [1991] ECR I–5357.
41 Case C–271/91 *Marshall v Southampton Health Authority No 2* [1993] ECR I–4367.
42 See for example *Thoburn v Sunderland County Council (The Metric Martyrs Case)* [2002] 3 WLR 247.
43 Case 6/64 [1964] ECR 585.
44 Para.21.
45 Case 80/86 *Kolpinghuis Nijmegen BV (Criminal Proceedings)* [1986] ECR 3969.
46 Case C–188/89 [1990] ECR I–3313.
47 Case 152/84, *Marshall v Southampton Area Health Authority (No 1)* [1986] ECR 723.
48 Advocate General Lenz in Case C–91/92 *Facini Dori* [1994] ECR I–1325 and Advocate General Jacobs in Case C–316/93 *Vannetveld* [1994] ECR I–763.
49 See for example *Defrenne (No.2)* M36 and [1995] ECR I–4921. Case C–415/93 *Bosman*.
50 [1992] ICR 538.
51 Case 14/83 [1984] ECR 1891.
52 Para.26.
53 Case C–106/89 *Marleasing SA v La Comercial Internacional de Alimentacion SA* C–106/88 [1990] ECR I–4135.
54 Case C–168/95 [1996] ECR I–4705.
55 [1988] AC 618.
56 For example, *Pickstone v Freemens* plc [1988] AC 66 and *Litster v Forth Dry Dock Ltd* [1990] 1 AC 546.
57 [1992] All ER 43.
58 C–334/92 *Wagner Miret v Fondo de Garantia Salarial* [1993] ECR I–6911.
59 Para.28.

60 Para.27.
61 Para.42.
62 Joined Cases C–46/93 and C–48/93 [1996] ECR I–1029.
63 Case 178/84 *Commission v Germany (Beer Purity)* [1987] ECR 1227.
64 Para.51.
65 *Factortame (V)* [1999] 3 WLR 1062
66 Case C–283/93 [1996] ECR-5063.
67 Case C–392/93 [1996] ECR I–1631.
68 Joined Cases C–178–/94 *Dillenkofer v Germany* [1996] ECR I–4845.
69 Case C–5/94 *Hedley Lomas* [1996] ECR I–2553.
70 See M23, *Köbler*, para.53.
71 Case C–453/99 [2001] ECR I–6297.
72 Para.19.

CHAPTER 3

1 Opinion 2/94 [1994] ECR I–1759.
2 Case C–376/98 *Germany v Parliament and Commission* [2000] ECR I–8419.
3 Case 91/79 *Commission v Italy* [1980] ECR I–1099, para.8.
4 Close, 1978.
5 Curtin, 1993.
6 OJ 1988 L 178/5.
7 Council Regulation 1466/97, OJ L209/1; Council Regulation 1467/97, OJ L 209/6; Resolution 97/C 236/01, OJ 1997 C 236/1.
8 Case C–27/04 *Commission v Council* judgment of July 13, 2004.
9 Council Directive 2000/43/EC, OJ 2000 L180/22; Council Directive 2000/78/EC, OJ 2000 L303/16; Council Decision of 27 November, 2000, OJ L 303/23.
10 Weatherill, 2005.
11 Case 120/78 Rewe_Zentrale AG v Bundesmonopolverwaltung für Branntwein [1979] ECR 649.
12 Joined Cases C–19/01, C–50/01 and C–94/01 *INPS v Alberto Barsotti et al* [2004], paras 34 and 25.
13 Case C–101/01 [2003] ECR I–2005 [2003] ECR I–12971.
14 Case 60/86 *Commission v UK (Dim Dip Headlights)* [1988] ECR 3921; Case C–2/90 *Commission v Belgium* [1992] ECR I–4431.
15 above n.10.
16 A common position on the Commission's proposal to replace the mutual recognition Directives with one consolidated text (COM(2004) 317) was reached on December 21, 2004.

17 Case 815/79 *Criminal Proceedings Against Gaetano Cremonini and Maria Luisa Vrankovich* [1980] ECR 3583, para.13.
18 Decision 3052/95/EC, OJ 1995 L321/1.
19 Directive 98/34/EC, OJ 1998 L204/37.
20 Council Directive 94/45/EC, OJ 1994 L 254/64.
21 Council Regulation No. 2157/2001; Council Directive 2001/86, OJ 2002 L294/22; EP and Council Directive 2002/14 OJ 2002 L80/29.
22 See Special Issue on Law and New Approaches to Governance in Europe (2002) 8.1. *European Law Journal*.
23 Case C–376/98 *Germany v Parliament and Council (Tobacco Advertising)* [2000] ECR I–8419.
24 EC Commission, *Communication from the Commission Regarding the Cassis de Dijon judgment*, OJ 1980 L 256/2; White Paper, *Completing the Single Market*, COM(85) 310.
25 Commission, *Communication on an Open Method of Co-ordination for the Community Immigration Policy*, COM (2001) 387 final; Bogusz, 2004.
26 Lenschow, 2002.
27 Radaelli, 2003.
28 Case C–491/01 *ex parte BAT* [2002] ECR I–11453; *cf.* Case 211/01 *Commission v Council* [2003] ECR I–8913.
29 Case 300/89 *Commission v Council* [1991] ECR I–2867.
30 Case C–155/91 *Commission v Council* [1993] ECR I–939.
31 Case C–269/97 *Commission and Parliament v Council* [2000] ECR I–2257.
32 Case C–233/94 *Germany v Parliament and the Council* [1997] ECR I–2405.
33 Case 84/94 *UK v Council* [1996] ECR I–5755; Case C–377/98 *Netherlands v Parliament and Council* [1997] ECR I–2405.
34 Case C–491/01 [2002] ECR I–11453.
35 Case C–376/98 *Germany v European Parliament and Council (Tobacco Advertising)* [2000] ECR I– para 83.
36 *ibid.*
37 Case C–5/02 *Rinke* [2003] ECR I–12575.
38 OJ 1994 L237/4.
39 Case C–319/97 *Criminal Proceeedings Against Kortas* [1999] ECR I–3143.
40 OJ 1991 L85/34.
41 Case C–3/00 *Commission v Denmark* [2003] ECR I–2643, para.65.
42 above n.36.
43 Case C–3/00 *Commission v Denmark* [2003] ECR I–2643, para.65.

CHAPTER 4

1 Article I–3(2) of the Constitution: "The Union shall offer its citizens an area of freedom, security and justice without internal frontiers, and an internal market where competition is free and undistorted.".

2 Case 152/82 *Forcheri v Belgium* [1983] ECR 2323, para.11.

3 Case C–228/98 *Dounias v Minister for Economic Affairs* [2000] ECR I–577, para.64.

4 Article II–111 of the Constitution.

5 Article I–2: "The Union is founded on the values of respect for human dignity, freedom, democracy, equality, the rule of law and respect for human rights, including the rights of persons belonging to minorities. These values are common to the Member States in a society in which pluralism, non-discrimination, tolerance, justice, solidarity and equality between men and women prevail.".

6 Case C–280/93 *Germany v Council* [1994] ECR I–4973, para.78; Case C–200/96 *Metronome* [1998] ECR I–1953, para.21.

7 Case C–4/73 *Nold* [1974] ECR 491; Case C–84/95 *Bosphorus* [1996] ECR I–3953.

8 Case C–60/00 *Mary Carpenter* [2002] ECR I–6279.

9 Case 120/78 *Rewe Zentrale v Bundesmonopolverwaltung für Branntwein* [1979] ECR 3961("Cassis de Dijon"); Case 178/84 *Commission v Germany* [1987] ECR 1227 (Beer Purity); Case 205/84 *Commission v Germany* [1986] ECR 3755 (Insurance Services).

10 Case 302/86 *Commission v Denmark* [1988] ECR 4607; Case –2/90 *Commission v Belgium (Walloon Waste)*[1992] ECR I–4431; Case C–379/98 *PreussenElektra AG v Schleswag AG* [2001] ECR I–2099.

11 Case C–154/89 *Commission v France* [1991] ECR I–659 (Tourist Guides). See Craufurd-Smith, 2004.

12 Case 155/80 *Oebel* [1981] ECR I 1993; Case C–448/98 *Criminal Proceedings Against Guiot and Climatec SA* [2000] ECR I–10663; Joined Cases C–369 & 376/96 *Criminal Proceedings Against Arblade and Arblade & Fils SARL and Leloup and Sofrage SARL* [1999] ECR I–8453.

13 Case C–368/95 *Vereinigte Familiapress* [1997] ECR I–3689.

14 Case C–112/00 [2003] ECR I–5659.

15 Baquero Cruz, 2002 ; Van den Bogaert, 2002.

16 Cases 177 & 17882 *van de Haar Vlaamse* [1984] ECR 1787; Case 311/85 *Vlaamse Reisbureaus* [1987] ECR 3801; Case 65/86 *Bayer v Süllhofer* [1988] ECR 5249.

17 Case 58/80 *Dansk Supermarked* [1981] ECR 181, para.17.
18 Case C–159/00 *Sapod Audic* [2002] ECR I–5031, para.74.
19 Joined Cases C–266 & 267/87 *Royal Pharmaceutical Society* [1989] ECR 1295; Case C–325/00 *Commission v Germany* [2002] ECR I–9977.
20 Case C–415/93 *Union Royale Belge de Societé de Football Association v Bosman* [1995] ECR I–4921.
21 Case C–281/98 *Roman Angonese v Cassa di Risparmio di Bolzano* [2000] ECR I–4139
22 Council Regulation 2913/92, OJ 1992 L302/1.
23 Council Regulation 384/96, OJ 1996 L56/1.
24 Council Regulation 2026/97, OJ 1997 L288/1.
25 Case 7/68 *Commission v Italy (Art Treasures)* [1968] ECR 423.
26 Case 26/62 [1963] ECR 1.
27 Case 18/87 [1988] ECR 5427.
28 Case 193/85 *Co-frutta* [1987] ECR 2085.
29 Case 57/65 *Lütticke v Hauptzollamt Saarlouis* [1966] ECR 205.
30 Case 112/84 *Humblot* [1985] ECR 1367.
31 Case 45/75 *REWE v HZA Landau* [1976] ECR 181.
32 Case 106/84 *Commission v Denmark* [1986] ECR 833.
33 Case 170/78 *Commission v United Kingdom* [1983] ECR 2265.
34 Case 68/79 *Hans Just I/S* [1980] ECR 501.
35 Directive 83/189/EEC, now amended by Directive 98/34/EC, OJ 1998 L204/37.
36 Case C–194/94 [1996] ECR I–2201.
37 Case C–443/98 *Unilever* [2000] ECR I–7535, para.45.
38 Case 8/74 *Procureur du Roi v Dassonville* [1974] ECR 837, para.5.
39 Case 120/78 *Rewe Zentrale v Bundesmonopolverwaltung für Branntwein* [1979] ECR 649.
40 EC Commission, *Communication from the Commission Regarding the Cassis de Dijon judgment*, OJ 1980 C 256/2; White Paper, *Completing the Single Market*, COM (85) 310.
41 Case 261/81 *Rau* [1982] ECR 3961. See generally, Ellis, 1999.
42 Other examples include: Case 407/85 *Drei Glocken GmbH v USL Cenro-Sud and Provincia Autonoma di Bolzano* [1988] ECR 4233; Case 286/86 *Ministère Public v Deserbais* [1988] ECR 4907; Case 182/84 *Criminal Proceedings against Miro BV* [1985] ECR 3731.
43 Case 249/81 *Commission v Ireland* [1982] ECR 4005.
44 Joined Cases C–267 & 268/91 [1993] ECR I–6097.
45 Reich, 1994.
46 Case C–412/93 [1995] ECR I–182.

47 Case C–190/98 *Volker Graf* [2000] ECR I–493, paras 18–19.
48 Oliver and Roth, 2004.
49 Case C–309/02, judgment of December 14, 2004.
50 Case C–463/01 judgment of December 14, 2004.
51 Cases C–34–36/95 *De Agostini* [1997] ECR I–3843; Case C–405/98 *Konsumentombudsmannen (KO) and Gourmet International Products AB (GIP)* [2001] ECR I–1795; Case C–416/00 *Morellato* [2003] ECR I–9343. See Kurzer, 2001; Craufurd-Smith, 2004.
52 Case 15/79 *Groenveld* [1979] ECR 3409; Case 155/80 *Oebel* [1981] ECR 1993.
53 Case C–376/98 *Germany v Commission (Tobacco Advertising)* [2001] ECR I–8419.
54 Case 98/86 *Criminal Proceedings against Mathot* [1987] ECR 809.
55 Case C–363/93 *Lancry* [1994] ECR I–3957; Cases C–485–6/93 *Simitzi v Kos* [1995] ECR I–2665.
56 Case C–321/94 *Pistre* [1997] ECR I–2343.
57 Case C–448/98 *Guimont* [2000] ECR I–10663, para.23.
58 Case C–281/98 *Roman Angonese v Cassa di Risparmio di Bolzano* [2000] ECR I–4139.
59 Case C–6/01 *Anomar v Portugal,* [2003] ECR I–8621.
60 Joined Cases C–515 & 527–540/99 *Reisch v Salzburg* 2002] ECR I–2157; Case C–300/01 *Salzmann* [2003] ECR I–4899.
61 Case C–1/96 *R v MAFF ex parte Compassion in World Farming* [1988] ECR I–1251.
62 Case 7/61 *Commission v Italy* [1961] ECR 317.
63 Case C–385/99 *Müller-Fauré VG v Onderlinge and van Riet v Onderlinge* [2003] ECR I–4509.
64 Cases C–34–36/95 *Konsumentombudsmannen v De Agostini* [1997] ECR I–3843; Case C–120/95 *Decker v Caisse de maladie des employés privés* [1998] ECR I–1831; Case C–379/98 *Preussen Elektra AG v Schleswag AG* [2001] ECR 2099; Case C–472/99 *Clean Car Autoservice v Stadt Wien and Republik Österreich* [2001] ECR I–9687. Barnard, 2001.
65 Case C–224/97 *Ciola Vorarlberg* [1999] ECR I–2517.
66 OJ 1995 L 321/1.
67 OJ 1998 L 337/8. See Case C–265/95 *Commission v France* [1997] ECR I–6959.
68 Case C–363/89 *Roux v Belgium* [1991] ECR I–273.
69 Council Directive 90/364 (General Right of Residence), OJ 1990 L 180/26; Council Directive 90/365 (Residence for ex-employees and the self-employed) OJ 1990 L 180/28; Council

Directive 93/96 (Right of Residence for Students), OJ 1993 L 317/59.

70 Case C–184/99 *Gryzelczyk* [2001] ECR I–6193; Case C–224/98 *D'Hoop* [2002] ECR I–6191; Joined Cases C413/99 *Baumbast and R v Secretary of State for the Home Department* [2002] ECR I–7091; Case C–200/02 *Chen* judgment of October 19, 2004; Case C–224/02 *Pusa* [2004] ECR I–5763.

71 See for example, AG Jacobs' Opinion in Case C–168/91 *Konstantinidis* [1993] ECR I–1191.

72 Case C–86/96 *Martínez Sala* [1998] ECR I–2691; Joined Cases C413/99 *Baumbast and R v Secretary of State for the Home Department* [2002] ECR I–7091; Case C–200/02 *Chen* judgment of October 19, 2004.

73 Case C–200/02 *Chen* judgment of October 19 2004; Case C–456/02 *Trojani* judgment of September 7, 2004; Case C–209/03 *Bidar* judgment of March 15, 2005.

74 Case C–224/98 *D'Hoop* [2002] ECR I–6191, para.30.

75 OJ 2004 L 158/77.

76 Case C–459/99 *MRAX v Belgium* [2002] ECR I–6591, Joined Cases C–413/99 *Baumbast and R v Secretary of State for the Home Department* [2002] ECR I–7091; Case C–60/00 *Mary Carpenter* [2002] ECR I–6279.

77 Commission, *Communication on immigration, integration and employment* COM(2003) 336 final.

78 Joined Cases 281, 283–285/85 *Germany, France, Netherlands, Denmark, United Kingdom v Commission* [1987] ECR 3203.

79 In Case C–51/03 *Georgescu* order of March 31, 2004 (a reference from a first instance criminal court was rejected).

80 Council Directive 2003/86/EC, OJ 2003 L251/12.

81 Council Directive 2003/109/EC, OJ 2004 L16/44.

82 Case C–109/01 [2003] ECR I–9607.

83 Case 167/73 *Commission v France* 1974] ECR 359; Case 41/74, *Van Duyn v Home Office* [1974] ECR 1337.

84 Case C–415/93 *Union Royale Belge de Societé de Football Association v Bosman* [1995] ECR I–4921; Case C–281/98 *Roman Angonese v Cassa di Risparmio di Bolzano* [2000] ECR I–4139; Case 36/74 *Walrave and Koch v AUCI* [1974] ECR 1405; Case C–472/99 *Clean Car Autoservice v Stadt Wien and Republik Österreich* [2001] ECR I–9687.

85 Cf. Case C–386/02 *Baldinger*, judgment of September 16, 2004 with Case C–400/02 *Merida* judgment of September 16.

86 Case C–369/90 *Micheleti v Delagación del Gobierno en Cantabria* [1992] ECR I–4239.

87 Case 75/63 *Unger v Bestuur der Bedrijfsvereniging voor Detail handel en Ambachten* [1964] ECR 177; Case 53/81 *Levin v Staatssecretaris van Justitie* [1982] ECR 1035; paras 11–12.

88 Case 66/85 [1986] ECR 2121, paras 16–17.

89 Case C–265/03 *Simutenkov*, judgment of April 12, 2005.

90 Case C–415/93 *Union Royale Belge de Societé de Football Association v Bosman* [1995] ECR I–4921; *Simutenkov, ibid.*

91 Case C–224/02, judgment of April 29, 2004.

92 Case C–292/89 *R v IAT, ex parte Antonissen* [1991] ECR I–745.

93 Case C–138/02, judgment of March 23, 2004.

94 Case C–313/02 *Nicole Wippel v Peek & Cloppenburg GmbH & Co KG*, Opinion of AG Kokott of May 18, 2004

95 Case C 175/78 *R v Saunders* [1979] ECR 1129.

96 Case C–370/90 *R v IAT and Surinder Singh ex parte Secretary of State for the Home Department* [1992] ECR I–4265. cf the Court's reliance upon the *exercise* of free movement rights in C–109/01 *Akrich*, judgment of September 23, 2003 and Case C–200/02 *Chen* judgment of October 19, 2004.

97 Case C–257/00 *Givane v Secretary of State for the Home Department* [2003] ECR I–345.

98 Case C–10/90 *Masgio v Bundesknappschaft* [1991] ECR I–1119 paras 18–19; Case C–415/93 *Bosman* [1995] ECR I–4921, para.104).

99 Case 13/76 *Donà* [1976] ECR 1333; Case C–415/93 *Union Royale Belge de Societé de Football Association v Bosman* [1995] ECR I–4921.

100 Case 222/86 [1987] ECR 4097.

101 Para.129. See also Case C–438/00 *Kolpak* [2003] ECR I–4135; Case C–176/96 *Lehtonen* [2000] ECR I–2681.

102 Case C–68/89 *Commission v Netherlands*[1991] ECR I–2637.

103 Case C–378/97 *Wijsenbeek* [1999] ECR I–6207.

104 Council Regulation 539/2001, OJ 2001 L81/1

105 Case C–459/99 *MRAX v Belgium* [2002] ECR I–6591.

106 Case C–109/01, judgment of September 23, 2003.

107 Case 118/75 *Watson and Belmann* [1976] ECR 1185.

108 Case 131/85 [1986] ECR 1573.

109 Joined Cases C413/99 *Baumbast and R v Secretary of State for the Home Department* [2002] ECR I–7091.

110 Case C–17/92 *FDC* [1993] ECR I–2239; Case C–388/01 *Commission v Italy* [2003] ECR I–721.

111 Case 41/74 *Van Duyn v Home Office* [1974] ECR 1337; Case C–348/96 *Criminal Proceeedings against Calfa* [1999] ECR I–11; Case C–114/97 *Commission v Spain* [1998] ECR I–671.

112 Commission Communication of May 11, 1999, *Implementing the framework for financial markets: action plan* COM (1999) 232 final.

113 COM (2004) 2 ; SEC 2004, 21.

114 Case C–76/90 *Säger* [1991] ECR I–4221; Joined Cases C–369 & 376/96 *Arblade*; [1999] ECR I–8453; Case C–58/98 *Corsten* [2000] ECR I– 7919.

115 Case C–60/00 [2002] ECR I–6279.

116 Case 263/86 *Belgium v Humbel* [1988] ECR 5365; Case C–159/90 *SPUC v Grogan* [1991] ECR I–4685.

117 C–157/99 *Geraets-Smits and Peerbooms* [2001] ECR I–5473; Case C–385/99 *Müller-Fauré* [2003] ECR I–4509).

118 Case C–55/94 [1995] ECR I–4165.

119 Joined Cases 286/82 and 26/83 *Luisi and Carbone v Ministero del Tesoro* [1984] ECR 377.

120 Case C–243/01 *Piergiorgio Gambelli* [2003] ECR I–13031.

121 Case C–355/98 [2000] ECR I–1221.

122 Case C–113/89 [1990] ECR I–1417.

123 Case C–43/93 [1994] ECR I–3803.

124 But see Joined Cases C–165/98 *Criminal Proceedings against Andre Mazzoleni and Inter Surveillance Assistance SARL* [2001] ECR I–2189; Case 493/99 *Commission v Germany* [2001] ECR I–8163.

125 OJ 1998 L18/1.

126 Case 33/74 *van Binsbergen* [1974] ECR 1299; Case C–288/89 *Gouda* [1991] ECR I–4007; Case C–17/92 *FDC* [1993] ECR I–2239.

127 Case 205/84 *Commission v Germany* [1986] ECR 3755.

128 Case 186/87 *Cowan* [1989] ECR 195; Case 63/86 *Commission v Italy* [1988] ECR 29; Case C–484/93 *Svensson* [1995] ECR I–3955; Case C–45/93 *Commission v Spain* [1994] ECR I–911.

129 Case C–17/00 *De Coster* [2001] ECR I–9445.

130 Case C–76/90 *Säger* [1991] ECR I–4221; Case C–384/93 *Alpine Investments v Minister van Financiën* [1995] ECR I–1141, Case C–275/92 *Schindler* [1994] ECR I–1039.

131 Case C–165/98 *Mazzoleni* [2001] ECR I–2189, para.22

132 Joined Cases C–430 &431/99 *Sea-Land Service Inc* [2002] ECR I–5235.

133 Case C–55/98 *Skatteministeriet* [1999] ECR I–7641.

134 Case C–272/94 *Guiot* [1996] ECR I–1905.

135 Joined Cases C–369 & 376/96 *Arblade* [1999] ECR I–8453; Case C–180/89 *Commission v Italy* [1991] ECR I–709 ("Tourist Guide" cases).

136 Case C–67/98 *Zenatti* [1999] ECR I–7289, but cf C–124/97 *Laara* [199] ECR I–6067; Case C–6/01 *Anomar* [2003] ECR I–8621; Case C–243/01 *Gambelli* [2003] ECR I–13031; Case C–42/02 *Diana Elisabeth Lindman*, 2003.

137 Case C–36/02 judgment of October 14, 2004.

138 Case C–148/91 *Vereniging Veronica Omroep Organisatie v Commissariaat voor de media* [1993] ECR I–487.

139 Case C–56/96 *VT4 Ltd v Vlaamse Gemeenschap* [1997] ECR I–3143.

140 Case C–158/96 *Kohll* [1998] ECR I–1931; Case C–120/95 *Decker* [1998] ECR I–1831; Case C–368/98 *Vanbraekel* [2001] ECR I–5363.

141 Case C–157/99 *Geraets-Smits and Peerbooms* [2001] ECR I–5473; Case C–385/99 *Müuller-Fauré* 2003] ECR I–4509. See Davies, 2002; Hatzopoulos, 2002.

142 Directive 2004/18, OJ 2004 L134/1, and Directive 2004/17, OJ 2004 L134/114. Details of the public procurement programme can be found at http://europa.eu.int/scadplus/leg/en/s11000.htmpp

143 Case C–221/89 *R v Secretary of State for Transport, ex parte Factortame* [1991] ECR I–3905, para.20.

144 Case C–55/94 *Gebhard v Consiglio dell'Ordine degli Avvocati e Procuratori di Milano* [1995] ECR I–4165 para.25.

145 Case 182/83 *Fearon v Irish Land Commission* [1985] ECR 3677; Case 251/98 *Baars v Inspecteur der Belastingdientst Particulieren/Ondernemingen Gorinchem* [2000] ECR I–2728; Case C–212/97 *Centros v Erhvervs-og Selskabsstyylrelsen* [1999] ECR I–1459.

146 Case C–221/89 *Factortame II* [1991] ECR I–3905.

147 Case C–268/99 *Jany v Staatssecretaris van Justitie* [2001] ECR I–8615.

148 Case C–257/99 *R v S/S for the Home Department, ex parte Barkoci and Malik* [2001] ECR I–6557, para.50.

149 Council Directive 75/34/EEC OJ 1975 L14/10.

150 OJ 1973 L172/14.

151 Case C–363/89 *Roux v Belgium* [1991] ECR I–273.

152 Case 107/83 [1984] ECR 2971.

153 Case 292/86 *Güllung* [1988] ECR 111.

154 Case 2/74 *Reyners v Belgian State* [1974] ECR 631.

155 Case C–55/94 [1995] ECR I–4165.

156 Case C–190/98 *Graf v Filzmozer GmbH* [2000] ECR I–493, para.25.

157 Case C–439/99 *Commission v Italy* [2002] ECR I–305.

158 Case C–424/97 *Haim II* [2000] ECR I–5123.
159 Case C–309/99 *Wouters* [2002] ECR I–1577.
160 OJ 1989 L 19/16.
161 OJ 1992 L209/25.
162 Case 71/76 [1977] ECR I 765.
163 Case C–340/89 [1991] ECR I–2357, para.15.
164 Case C–104/91 *Borrell* [1992] ECR I–3003; Case 222/86 *UNECTEF v Heylens* [1987] ECR 4097.
165 See also Case C–108/96 *Mac Quen* [2001] ECR I–837; Case C–313/01 *Morgenkesser* [2003] ECR I).
166 Case 197/84 *Steinhauser v City of Biarritz* [1985] ECR 1819.
167 Case 63/86 *Commission v Italy* [1988] ECR 29.
168 Case C–80/94 *Wielockx* [1995] ECR I–2493; Case C–107/94 *Asscher* [1996] ECR I–3089.
169 Case C–53/95 *Inasti v Kemmler* [1996] ECR I–703.
170 Case 81/87 [1988] ECR 5483.
171 Case C–200/98 *X AB and Y AB v Riksskatteverket* [1999] ECR I–8261.
172 Case 212/97 [1999] ECR I–1459.
173 Case C–167/01 [2003] ECR I–10155.
174 Case C–208/00 [2002] ECR I–9919.
175 Case C–101/94 *Commission v Italy* [1996] ECR I–2691.
176 Case C–213/89 *R v Secretary of State for Transport ex parte Factortame Ltd* (I) [1990] ECR I–2433; *R v Secretary of State for Transport ex parte Factortame Ltd* (II) [1991] ECR I–3905.
177 Case 3/88 *Commission v Italy* [1989] ECR 4035.
178 Case C–153/02 *Neri* [2003] ECR I–13555.
179 Case 270/83 *Commission v France* [1986] ECR 273; Case C–250/95 *Futura Participations SA* [1997] ECR I–2471; Case 311/97 *Royal Bank of Scotland plc v Elliniko Dimosio (RBS)* [1999] ECR I–2651; Case C–330/91 *ex parte Commerzbank* [1993] ECR I–4017.
180 Case C–446/03, Opinion of 7 April 2005.
181 Case 203/80 *Casati* [1981] ECR 2595, para.19.
182 OJ 1988 L178/5.
183 Case C–222/97 *Manfred Trummer and Peter Mayer* [1999] ECR I–1661.
184 Case C–7/78 *R v Thompson* [1987] ECR 2247, para.22.
185 Cases 286/82 and 26/83 *Luisi and Carbone v Minisero del Tesoro* [1984] ECR 377.
186 Case 308/86 *Ministère Public v Lambert* [1988] ECR 4369, para.10.

187 Case C–302/97 *Klaus Konle v Republik Österreich* [1999] ECR I–3099; Case C–423/98 *Albore* [2000] ECR I–5965.

188 Case C–463/00 *Commission v Spain* [2003] ECR I–4581; Case C–367/98 *Commission v Portugal* [2002] ECR I–4731; Case C–98/01 *Commission v UK* [2003] ECR I–4641 Szyszczak, 2002).

189 *ibid.*

190 Case C–279/93 *Schumacker* [1995] ECR I–225; Case C–204/90 *Bachmann v Belgium* [1992] ECR I–249.

191 Case C–319/02 judgment of September 7, 2004.

192 Case C–204/90 *Bachmann* [1992] ECR I–249; Case C–300/90 *Commission v Belgium* [1992] ECR I–305. See Wathelet, 2001.

CHAPTER 5

1 Case C–198/01 *CIF v Autorità Garante della Concorrenza e del Mercato* [2003] ECR I–8055, para.47.

2 Case 6/72 *Europemballage Corpn. and Continental Can Co Inc v Commission* [1973] ECR 215.

3 Gerber, 1998.

4 Case 229/83 [1985] ECR 1.

5 Case 123/83 *BNIC v Clair* [1985] ECR 391.

6 Case 231/83 *Cullet v Leclerc* [1985] ECR 305.

7 Case C–185/91 *Reiff* [1993] ECR I–5801; Case C–2/91 *Meng* [1993] ECR I–5751; Case C–245/91 *OHRA* [1993] ECR 5851.

8 above n.1.

9 Joined Cases T–228/99 and T–233/99 *WestLB v Commission* [2003] ECR II–445; Case C–209/00 *Commission v Germany* [2002] ECR I–11695.

10 Cases C–264, 306, 354 & 355/01 *AOK* [2004] ECR I–2493; Case T–319/99 *FENIN v Commission* [2003] ECR II–357.

11 European Commission, Communication on Services of General Interest in Europe, COM (2000) 580 final, p. 3; Report to the Laeken European Council on Services of General Interest COM (2001) 598 final; Non-Paper Services of General Economic Interest and State Aid, 12 November 2002 *http:// europa.eu.int/comm/competition/state_aid/others/1759_sieg_en.pdf;* Report From the Commission on the state of play in the work on the Guidelines For State Aid and Services of General Economic Interest, *http://europa.eu.int/comm/competition/ state_aid/others/sieg_en.pdf;* Green Paper on Services of

General Interest, COM (2003) 270 final; White Paper on Services of General Interest COM (2004) 374 final. These documents may be downloaded from *http://europa.eu.int/comm/ competition/state_aid/others/*

12 Case 139/79 [1980] ECR 3393.

13 Case 240/83 [1985] ECR 531.

14 Case C–126/97 *Eco Swiss China Time Ltd v Benetton International NV* [1999] ECR I–3055, para 36.

15 Case C–453/99 *Courage v Crehan* [2001] ECR I–6297, paras 19–20.

16 Maduro, 1998.

17 Szyszczak, 2004.

18 above n.6.

19 Case C–376/98 *Germany v Parliment and Council* [2000] ECR I–8419.

20 Case C–41/90 *Höfner v Macrotron* [1991] ECR I–2010.

21 Case C– 280/00 *Altmark* [2003] ECR I–7747.

22 Case C–141/02P *Commission v T-Mobile Austria GmbH formerly max.mobil Telekommunikation Service* judgment of February 22, 2005.

23 OJ 2004 L1/1.

CHAPTER 6

1 Case C–41/90 [1991] ECR I–1979.

2 Case 30/87 [1988] ECR I–2479.

3 Cases C–264/01, C–354/01, C–355/01 judgment of March 16, 2004.

4 Case C–73/95P [1996] ECR I–5457.

5 Case 85/76 *Hoffman La-Roche & Co AG v Commission* [1979] ECR 461; Case T–51/89 *Tetra Pak Rausing SA v Commission (Tetra Pak I)* [1990] ECR II–309.

6 Case T–41/96 [2000] ECR II–3383; Case C–2/01 & C–3/01P, judgment of January 6, 2004.

7 *National Sulphuric Acid Association*, OJ 1980 L 260/24.

8 *Visa International-Multilateral Interchange Fee*, OJ 2002 L 318/17.

9 Case 45/85 *VDS v Commission* [1987] ECR 405.

10 Case C–303/ 99 *Wouters v Algemene Raad van de Nederlandse Order van Advocaten* [2002] ECR I–1577.

11 Cases 6 & &/73 *Istituto Chemioterapico Italiano SpA and Commercial Solvents Corp v Commission* [1974] ECR 223, paras 64 and 65.

12 Cases 40–48, 50, and 54–56/73 [1975] ECR 1663.

13 Case C–199/92P [1995] ECR I–4287.

14 Cases 56 & 58/64 [1966] ECR 299.

15 Case 23/67 *Brasserie de Haecht SA (No. 1) v Wilkin* [1967] ECR 407.

16 Communication from the Commission, *Guidelines on the application of Article 81(3) of the Treaty*, O J 2004 C 101/97.

17 Case 8/74 *Procureur du Roi v Dassonville* [1974] ECR 837.

18 Cases 56 & 58/64 *Etablissements Consten SA & Grundig-Verkaufs-GmnH v Commission* [1966] ECR 299, 341.

19 Commission Notice, *Guidelines on the effect on trade concept contained in Arts 81 and 82 of the Treaty*, O J 2004 C 101/ 81.

20 Case 5/69 *Völk v Vervaecke* [1969] ECR 295.

21 *Commission Notice on Agreements of Minor Importance Which Do Not Appreciably Restrict Competition Under Art.81(1) of the Treaty establishing the European Community (de minimis)*, OJ 2001 C 368/11.

22 *Commission Notice Guidelines on the effect on trade concept contained in Arts 81 and 82 of the Treaty*, OJ 2004 C101/86.

23 See Case T–112/99 *Métropole Télévision (M6) v Commission* [2001] ECR II–2459.

24 OJ 2004 C 101/1.

25 Case 6/72 *Europemballage Corp and Continental Can Co Inc v Commission* [1973] ECR 215; Cases 6 &7/73 *Istituto Chemioterapico Italiano Spa and Commercial Solvents Corp v Commission* [1974] ECR 223.

26 Cases T–68, 77 & 78/89 *Società Italiano Vetro SpA v Commission ("Flat Glass")* [1992] ECR II–1403.

27 Cases C–395 & 396/96P *Compagnie Maritime Belge Transports SA v Commission* [2000] ECR II–1365

28 Case T–102/96 *Gencor v Commission* [1999] ECR II–753, para.276.

29 Case 6/72 *Europemballage Corp and Continental Can Co Inc v Commission* [1973] ECR 215.

30 Case 27/76 *United Brands Co and United Brands Continental BV v Commission* [1978] ECR 207.

31 Case 85/76 *Hoffmann-La Roche & Co AG v Commission* [1979] ECR 461.

32 *Commission Notice on the Definition of the Relevant Market for the purposes of Community Competition Law*, OJ 1997 C372/5, para.43.

33 Case T–203/01 [2003] ECR II–1.

34 Para.371.

35 Case C179/90 *Merci convenzionali Porto di Genova SpA v Siderugica Gabrielii SpA* [1991] ECR I–5889; Case 66/86 *Ahmed Saeed Flugreisen and Silver Line Reisburo GmbH v Zentrale zur Bekampfung unlauteren Wettbewerbs eV* [1989] ECR 803.

36 *Commission Notice on the Definition of the Relevant Market for the Purposes of Community Competition Law*, OJ 1977 C 372/5.

37 Case 85/76 *Hoffmann-La Roche & Co AG v Commission* [1979] ECR 461.

38 Case C–62/86 *AKZO Chemie BV v Commission* [1991] ECR I–3359.

39 Case T–203/01 *Michelin v Commission* [2003] ECR 11–4071; Case T–219/99 *British Airways v Commission* December 17, 2003.

40 Joined Cases 40–48/73, 50, 54–56/73, 111/73, 113/73 & 114/73 *Coöperatieve Vereniging "Suiker Unie" UA and others v Commission (European Sugar Cartel) [1975] ECR 1663;* Case 85/76 *Hoffmann-La Roche & Co AG v Commission* [1979] ECR 461.

41 Case T–65/98 [2003] ECR II–4653.

42 Case T–30/89 [1991] ECR II–1439.

43 Case 22/78 [1979] ECR 1869. The Commission did not show that trade between the Member States was affected.

44 Commission Press Release IP/97/868.

45 Commission Decision March 24, 2004 COMP/C–3/37.792. Kühn and Caffarra (2005).

46 Cases 6/73, 7/73 *Istituto Chemioterapico Italiano* SpA and Commercial Solvents *Corp v Commission* [1974] ECR 223.

47 *British Midland/AerLingus*, OJ 1993 L96/34; *Sealink/B&I Holyhead Interim Measures* [1992] 5 CMLR 255; *Sea Containers Ltd/Stena Sealink* [1994] OJ 1995 L15/8; Cases T–374–375, 384 & 388/94 *European Night Services v Commission* [1998] ECR II–3141.

48 For example, in the area of telecommunications, now called "electronic communications", European Parliament and Council Directive (EC) 2002/19 on access to, and interconnection of, electronic communications networks and associated facilities, OJ 2002 L108/7.

49 Case C–7/97 [1998] ECR I–7791.

50 Case 238/87 *AB Volvo v Erik Veng* [1988] ECR 6211; Case 53/87 *CICCRA Maxicar v Renault* [1988] ECR 6039.

51 Cases C–241/91 P *RTE &ITP v Commission* [1995] ECR I–743.

52 Case C–418/01 judgment of April 29, 2004.

53 *Continental Can*, above n.30.

54 Case 322/81 [1983] ECR 3461.

55 Amato, 1997:66.

56 Cases C–395 & 396/96P [2000] ECR I–1365, para.137.

57 Case C–333/94 P *Tetra Pak International SA v Commission* [1996] ECR I–5951; Case T–228/97 *Irish Sugar plc v Commission* [1999] ECR II–2969; *Football World Cup* 1998 OJ 2000 L 5/55.

58 OJ 1988 L65/19.

59 OJ 1988 L286/36.

60 Cases 6 & &/73 *Istituto Chemioterapico Italiano SpA and Commercial Solvents Corp v Commission* [1974] ECR 223.

61 Council Regulation (EC) No 139/2004 of January 20, 2004 on the control of concentrations between undertakings (the EC Merger Regulation), OJ 2004 L 24/1.

62 Joined Cases C–68/94 and C–30/95 *French Republic and SCPA v Commission (Kali and Salz)* [1998] ECR I–1375.

63 *Guidelines on the assessment of horizontal mergers under the Council Regulation on the control of concentrations between undertakings,* OJ 2004 C31/5, paras 89–91.

64 Article 6(2); 8(2) and Recital 30 Regulation 139/2004. Commission also published a Notice on Remedies.

65 Case T–251/00 *Lagardère SCA and Canal+ SA v Commission* [2002] ECR II–4825.

66 Case T–342/99 *Airtours plc v Commission* [2002] ECR II–2585; Case T–310/01 *Schneider Electric v Commission* [2002] ECR II–4071; Case T–80/02 *Tetra Laval v Commission* [2002] ECR II–4519.

67 For example, *Guidelines on the assessment of horizontal mergers under the Council Regulation on the control of concentrations between undertakings,* OJ 2004 C31/5.

68 Article 2(3).

69 *General Electric/ Honeywell* OJ 2004 L 48/01; on appeal Case T–209/01 & 210/01.

70 Case T–5/02 *Tetra Laval BV v Commission* [2002] ECR II–4519; Cases C–12/03P, C–13/0P judgment of 15 February 2005.

71 Case T–342/99 *Airtours plc v Commission* [2002] ECR II–2585.

72 EC Commission, *Fostering Structural Change: An Industrial Policy for an Enlarged Europe,* COM (2004) 274 final.

CHAPTER 7

1 Joined Cases C–159/91 and C–160/91 *Poucet and Pistre* [1993] ECR I–666; Case C–218/00 *Battistello* [2002] ECR I–691.

2 Case C–364/92 *SAT v Eurocontrol* [1994] ECR I–43, para.20.

3 Case C–343/95 *Diego Cali v Servizi ecologici porto di Genova SpA* [1997] ECR I–1547 para.23.

4 Case C–41/90 *Höfner v Macrotron* [1991] ECR I–1979.
5 Case C–320/91 *Corbeau* [1993] ECR I–2533.
6 Case C–159/94 *French Gas and Electricity Monopolies* [1997] ECR I–5815; Case C–158/94 *Italian Electricity Monopoly* [1997] ECR I–5789; Case C–157/94 *Dutch Electricity Monopoly* [1997] ECR I–5699. Soriano, 2003.
7 C–280/00 *Altmark Trans GmbH and Regierungspraesidium Magdeburg v Nahverkehrsgesellschaft Altmark GmbH* [2003] ECR I–7747; Joined Cases C–83/01 P, C–93/01 P and C–94/01P *Chronopost SA, La Poste v Commission* [2003] ECR I–6993.
8 *White Paper on Services of General Interest*, COM (2004) 374 final.
9 Case C–141/02P *Commission v T-Mobile Austria GmbH formerly max.mobil Telekommunikation Service* judgment of February 22, 2005.
10 Commission Directive 80/723, OJ 1980 L195/35; amended by Commission Directive 85/413, OJ 1985 L229/20; Commission Directive 93/84, OJ 1984 L54/16, Commission Directive 2000/52/EC, OJ L 2000 193/75.
11 Commission Directive (EEC) 88/301, OJ 1988 L131/73.
12 Case C–202/88 *Telecommunications Terminal Equipment* [1991] ECR I–1223.
13 Lisbon European Council, March 2000 SN 100/1/100 point 17.
14 The Score Board can be found at: *http://europa.eu.int/comm/competition/state_aid/scoreboard/*
15 Case C–301/96 *Germany v Commission* [2003] ECR I–9919; Case C–277/00 *Germany v Commission* [2004] ECR I–3925.
16 Case C–280/00 *Altmark* [2003] ECR I–7747.
17 Commission Regulation (EC) 69/2001 of January 12, 2001 on the application of Arts 87 and 88 of the EC Treaty to *de minimis aid*, OJ 2001 L10/30.
18 Case C–280/00 *Altmark* [2003] ECR I–I–7747.
19 Joined Cases C–72 and C–73/91 *Sloman Neptun Schiffahrts AG v Seebetriebsrat Bodo Ziesemer der Sloman Neptun Schiffahrts AG* [1993] ECR I–887.
20 Case C–482/99 *France v Commission* [2002] ECR I–4397.
21 Case C–345/02 *Pearle and others* judgment of July 15, 2004.
22 Case C–142/87 *Belgium v Commission* [1990] ECR I–959.
23 Joined Cases T–228/99 and T–233/99 *WestLB v Commission* [2003] ECR II–445 Case C–209/00 *Commission v Germany* [2002] ECR I–11695.
24 Case T–11/95 *BP Chemicals v Commission* [1998] ECR II–3235.
25 Case C–39/94 *SFEI and others* [1996] ECR I–3547; Case T–613/97 *UFEX v Commission* [2000] ECR II–4055.

26 Joined Cases C–83/01 P, C–93/01 P and C–94/01P *Chronopost SA, La Poste v Commission* [2003] ECR I–6993.

27 1991 XXI Report on Competition Policy, para.248.

28 *Koninklijke Schelde Groep*, OJ 2003 L14/56, para.79.

29 Opinion of AG Jacobs Joined Cases C–278/92, C–279/92 and C–280/92 *Spain v Commission* [1994] ECR I–4103, para.30.

30 Friend, 2004; Nicolaides, 2005.

31 Case 120/73 *Lorenz v Germany* [1973] ECR 1471; Arts 4(5)–(6) of Regulation 659/1999).

32 Case C–39/94 *SFI v La Poste* [1996] ECR I–3547.

33 Council Regulation (EC) 659/1999, OJ 1999 L 83/1, now modernised by Commission Regulation (EC) No. 794/2004, OJ 2004 L140/1.

34 Council Regulation 994/98, OJ 1998 L 142/1.

35 Commission Regulation (EC) No 69/2001 OJ 2001 L10/30.

36 Commission Regulation (EC) No 70/2001, OJ 2001 10/33.

37 Commission Regulation (EC) No 2204/2002, OJ 2002 L.

38 Commission Directive 80/723, OJ 1980 L195/35; amended by Commission Directive 85/413, OJ 1985 L229/20; Commission Directive 93/84, OJ 1984 L54/16, Commission Directive 2000/52/EC, OJ 2000 L 193/75.

39 Case C–53/00 *Ferring v ACOSS* [2001] ECR 9067.

40 Joined Cases C–157/94 *Commission v Netherlands* [1997] ECR I–5699; Case 158/94 *Commission v Italy* [1997] ECR I–5789; Case 159/94 *Commission v France* [1997] ECR I–5815; Case C–160/94 *Commission v Spain* [1997] ECR I–5851.

41 Case C– 280/00 *Altmark* [2003] ECR I–7747.

42 Bartosch, 2002.

43 Joined Cases T–116/01 and T–118/01 *P&O European Ferries (Vizcaya) SA and Diputación Foral de Vicaya v Commission* [2003] ECR II–2957; on appeal to the ECJ).

44 Cases C–34–38/01 judgment of November 27, 2003.

45 Joined Cases C–182/03 and C–217/03 *R Belgium and Forum 187 ASBL v Commission* [2003] ECR I–6887, para.124.

46 Joined Cases T–298/97, 312/97, 313/97, 315/97, 600–607/97, 1/98, 3–6/98, 23/98 *Alzetto Mauro and Others v Commission* [2000] ECR II–2319.

47 Case C–110/02 *Commission v Council* judgment of June 29, 2004.

48 Case C–404/00 *Commission v Spain* [2003] ECR I–6695, para.22. Art.14(3).

CHAPTER 8

1 COM(2003) 104 final *Communication from the Commission to the Council and the European Parliament Wider Europe – Neighbourhood: A New Framework for Relations With Our Eastern and Southern Neighbours.*
2 OJ 2001 C 304, 16.
3 OJ 1969 L 324, 34.
4 See Joined Cases 113 & 118/77 *Japanese Ball Bearings* [1979] ECR I–1185.
5 OJ 1994 L 336, 1.
6 Case C–233/02 *Commission v France* [2004] ECR I–2759, para.40.
7 OJ 1998 L213, 1.
8 COM(2000) 412 final.
9 Case 181/73 *Haegmann* [1974] ECR 449.
10 Opinion 1/75 (*OECD Local Cost Standard*) [1975] ECR 1355 1363.
11 Opinion 1/78 (*Natural Rubber Agreement*) [1979] ECR 2871.
12 Joined Cases C–390 & 392/98 *Parfums Christian Dior SA v Tuk Consultancy BV* [2000] ECR I–11307.
13 *Opinion 1/94 (Competence of the Community to Conclude International Agreements Concerning Services and the Protection of Intellectual Property)* [1994] ECR I–5267.
14 Case 41/76 *Dockenwolcke v Procureur de République* [1976] ECR 1921.
15 OJ 1994 L 349, 85.
16 See Case C–53/96 *Hermès International v FHT Marketing* [1998] ECR I–3603.
17 See for example *Parfums Christian Dior* (above no.12).
18 Note 9 above. See also Case C–239/03 *Commission v France* judgment of October 7, 2004.
19 Joined Cases C–63/99, C–257/99 and C–235/99 *The Queen v Secretary of State for the Home Department ex parte Wieslaw Gloszczuk and Elzbieta Gloszczuk; The Queen v Secretary of State for the Home Department ex parte Julius Barkoci and Marcel Malik; The Queen v Secretary of State for the Home Department ex parte Eleonora Ivanova Kondova* [2001] ECR I–6369.
20 Case 104/81 [1982] ECR 3641.
21 Cases 21–24/72 *International Fruit* [1972] ECR 1219.
22 Case C–280/93 *Germany v Council (Bananas)* [1994] ECR I–4737.
23 Paragraphs 103 to 112.
24 Case C–149/96 *Portugal v Council* [1999] ECR I–8395.
25 Para.47.

26 Case C–377/02 *Léon Van Parys NV v Belgisch Interventie- en Restitutiebureau*, judgment of March 14, 2005.

27 COM (2001) 252 final, *Communication From the Commission to the Council and the European Parliament the European Union's Role in Promoting Human Rights and Democratisation in Third Countries*.

28 At p.3.

29 Common Position 2002/145/CFSP OJ L 2002 50/1.

CHAPTER 9

1 Case 294/83 *Parti Ecologiste "Les Verts" v European Parliament* [1986] ECR 1339, para.23.

2 See the Opinion of Advocate General Geelhoed in Case C–209/03 *Bidar* November 11, 2005.

3 Tampere European Council, Presidency Conclusion, 15 and 16 October 1999, Annex 1.

4 Cologne European Council, Presidency Conclusions, 3 and 4 June 1999, paras 44–45.

5 Joined Cases C–187/01 *Hüseyin Gözütok* and C–385/01 *Klaus Brügge* (2003) ECR I–1345.

6 Case C–469/03, *Filomeno Mario Miraglia*, judgment of March 10, 2005.

7 By May 1, 2005 six Member States had ratified the Constitutional Treaty. These are Greece, Hungary, Italy, Lithuania, Slovenia and Spain. Of these only Spain has held a referendum with parliamentary ratification taking place in all other Member States. Of the remaining Member States only Denmark, France, Ireland, Portugal and the UK have formally stated that they will hold referenda. On May 29, 2005 France held a referendum where the vote was against the Constitutional Treaty. On June 1, 2005 The Netherlands also voted against the Treaty.

BIBLIOGRAPHY

Amato, G. (1997) *Antitrust and the Bounds of Power* (Oxford: Hart).

Areeda, P. (1999) "Essential Facilities: An Epithet in Need of Limiting Principles" 58 *Antitrust Law Journal* 841.

Armstrong, K. (2002) "Mutual Recognition" in C. Barnard and J. Scott (eds), *The Law of the Single Market: Unpacking the Premises* (Oxford: Hart).

Arnull, A. (1999) *The European Union and its Court of Justice* (Oxford: OUP).

Arnull, A. (2001) "Private Applicants Since *Cordoniu*" 38 *Common Market Law Review* 1.

Arnull, A. (2004) "Editorial" 29 *European Law Review* 288.

Arnull, A., Dashwood, A., Ross, M., Wyatt, D. (2000) *Wyatt and Dashwood's European Union Law* (London: Sweet and Maxwell).

Baquero Cruz, J. (2002) *Between Competition and Free Movement* (Oxford: Hart).

Barber, N.W. (2002) "Citizenship, Nationalism and the European Union" 27 *European Law Review* 241.

Barnard, C. (2001) "Fitting the Pieces into the Goods and Services Jigsaw?" 26 *European Law Review* 35.

Bartosch, A."The Relationship Between Public Procurement and State Aid Surveillance – the Toughest Standard Applies?" (2002) 39 *Common Market Law Review* 551.

Bavasso, A. (2004) "Electronic Communications: A New Paradigm For European Regulation" 41 *Common Market Law Review* 87.

Bishop, W. (1981) "Price Discrimination under Article 86: Political Economy in the European Court" 66 *Modern Law Review* 282.

Bogusz, B. *et al.* (eds) *Irregular Migration and Human Rights* (The Hague: Brill/Kluwer).

Bogusz, B. (2004) "Modes of Governance for an EU Immigration Policy – What Role for the Open Method of Co-ordination" in B. Bogusz *et al.* (eds.) *Irregular Migration and Human Rights* (The Hague: Brill/Kluwer).

Bogusz, B. (2002) "Regulating the Right of Establishment For Accession State Nationals: Reinforcing the Buffer Zone or

Improving Labour Market Flexibility?" (2002) *European Law Review* 272.

Chalmers, D. (1998) *European Union Law (Volume 1) Law and EU Government* (Dartmouth: Ashgate)

Close, G. (1978) "Harmonisation of Laws: Use or Abuse of the Powers Under the EEC Treaty?" 3 *European Law Review* 461.

Competition Law Forum Article 82 Review Group, (2005) 1 *European Competition Law Journal*.

Coppell, J. and O'Neill A., (1992) "The European Court of Justice: Taking Rights Seriously" 29 *Common Market Law Review* 669.

Craig, P. (1993) "Francovich, Remedies and the Scope of Damages Liability" 109 *Law Quarterly Review* 595.

Craig, P. (1991) "United Kingdom Sovereignty after Factortame" 11 *Yearbook of European Law* 221.

Craig, P. (1997) "Directives, Direct Effect, Indirect Effect and the Construction of National Legislation" 22 *European Law Review* 519.

Craig, P. (1999) "The Nature of the Community: Integration, Democracy and Legitimacy" in P. Craig and G. De Búrca (eds) *The Evolution of EU Law* (Oxford: OUP).

Craig, P. (2002) "The Evolution of the Single Market" in C. Barnard and J. Scott (eds) *The Law of the Single European Market* (Oxford: Hart) 1.

Craig, P. and De Búrca, G. (2003) *EU Law Text, Cases and Materials* (Oxford: OUP)

Craufurd-Smith, R. (2004a) "Community Intervention in the Cultural Field: Continuity or Change?" in Craufurd-Smith, R. (ed.) *Culture and European Union Law* (Oxford: OUP).

Craufurd-Smith, R. (ed.) (2004b) *Culture and European Union Law* (Oxford: OUP).

Cremona, M. (1990) "The Completion of the Internal Market and the Incomplete Commercial Policy of the European Community" 15 *European Law Review* 283.

Cremona, M. (2000) "EC External Commercial Policy after Amsterdam: Authority and Interpretation within Interconnected Legal Orders" in J. Weiler (ed.) *Towards a Common Law of International Trade? The EU, the WTO and the NAFTA* (Oxford: OUP).

Curtin, D. (1993) "The Constitutional Structure of the Union: A Europe of Bits and Pieces" 30 *Common Market Law Review* 17.

Curtin, D. and Meijers, J. (1995) "The Principle of Open Government in Schengen and the European Union: Democratic Retrogression" 32 *Common Market Law Review* 391.

Cygan, A. (2000) "Defining a Sufficiently Serious Breach of Community Law – the House of Lords Casts its Nets in to the Waters" 25 *European Law Review* 117.

Cygan, A. (2003) "Protecting the Interests of Civil Society in Community Decision-Making – The Limits of Article 230 EC" 52 *International Comparative Law Quarterly* 995

Cygan, A. (2004) "European Union Immigration Policy after Enlargement – Building the New Europe or the New Iron Curtain?" in B.Bogusz *et al.* (eds), *Irregular Migration and Human Rights: Theoretical, European and International Perspectives* (The Hague: Brill/Kluwer)

Dashwood, A. (1999) "External Relations of the Amsterdam Treaty" in D. O'Keeffe and P. Twomey (eds) *Legal Issue of the Amsterdam Treaty* (Oxford: Hart Publishing).

Davies, G. (2004) "Community Law and National Health Systems in the Light of Muller-Fauré" 67 *Modern Law Review* 97.

de Zwaan, J.W. (1999) "The Legal Personality of the European Communities" *Netherlands Yearbook of International Law* 75.

Deakin, S. (1999) "Two Types of Regulatory Competition: Competitive Federalism versus Reflexive Harmonisation. A Law and Economics Perspective on Centros" 2 *Cambridge Yearbook of European Legal Studies* 231.

Dehousse, R. (1998) "European Institutional Architecture After Amsterdam: Parliamentary System Or Regulatory Structure?" 35 *Common Market Law Review* 595.

Denza, E. (2002) *The Intergovernmental Policies of the EU* (Oxford: OUP).

Devroe, W. (1997) "Privatizations and Community Law: Neutrality versus Policy" 34 *Common Market Law Review* 267.

Doherty, B. (2001) "Just What Are Essential Facilities?" 38 *Common Market Law Review* 397.

Dörmer, S. (2000) "Dispute Settlement and New Developments Within the Framework of TRIPs – An Interim Review" 31 *International Review of Industrial Property and Copyright Law* 1.

Douglas-Scott, S. (2002) *Constitutional Law of the European Union* (London: Longman).

Edwards, V. (1999) *EC Company Law* (Oxford: OUP).

Eeckhout, P. (2004) *External Relations of the European Union, Legal and Constitutional Foundations* (Oxford: OUP).

Egan, M. (2001) *Constructing a European Market* (Oxford: OUP)

Ehlermann, C-D.(1992) "The Contribution of EC Competition Policy to the Single Market" 29 *Common Market Law Review* 257.

Ellis, E. (ed) (1999) *The Principle of Proportionalilty in the Laws of Europe* (Oxford: OUP).

Friend, M. (2004) "State Guarantees as State Aid: Some Practical Difficulties" in A. Biondi *et al.* (eds), *The Law of State Aid in the European Union*, (Oxford: OUP).

Gerber, D. (1998) *Law and Competition in Twentieth Century Europe: Protecting Prometheus* (Oxford: Clarendon Press).

Graham, C. and Smith, F. (eds.) (2004) *Competition Law and the New Economy* (Oxford: Hart).

Gravells, N. (1991) "Effective Protection of Community Law Rights: Temporary Disapplication of an Act of Parliament" *Public Law* 180.

Hahn, H. (1998) "The Stability and Growth Pact for European and Monetary Union: Compliance with Deficit Limit as a Constant Legal Duty" 35 *Common Market Law Review* 77.

Harding, C. (2000) "The Identity of European Law: Mapping Out the European Legal Space" 6 *European Law Journal* 128.

Harlow, C. (1996) "Francovich and the Problem of the Disobedient State" 2 *European Law Journal* 199.

Harlow, C. (2002) "Public Law and Popular Justice" 65 *Modern Law Review* 1.

Harm, S. (2002) "Delegation of Regulatory Powers to Private Parties under EC Competition Law: Towards a Procedural Public Interest Test" 39 *Common Market Law Review* 31.

Hartley, T. (1998) *Foundations of European Community Law* (Oxford: OUP).

Hartley, T. (2001) "The Constitutional Foundation of the European Union" 117 *Law Quarterly Review* 225

HL 106 (2002–3) *The Future of Europe: Constitutional Treaty – Articles 33–37 (The Democratic Life of the Union)* (London: HMSO).

Joerges, C. and Vos E. (eds.), (1999) *EU Committees: Social Regulation, Law and Politics* (Oxford: Hart).

Joerges, C. (1999) "Bureaucratic Nightmare, Technocratic Regime and the Dream of Good Transnational Governance" in C. Joerges and E. Vos (eds.), *EU Committees: Social Regulation, Law and Politics* (Oxford: Hart).

Kokkoris, I. (2005) "SLC v Dominance" 26 *European Competition Law Review* 37.

Koutrakos, P. (2002) "The Interpretation of Mixed Agreements under the Preliminary Reference Procedure" 7 *European Foreign Affairs Review* 25.

Kühn, K-U. and Caffara, C. (2005) "Economic Theories of Bundling and their Policy Implications in Abuse Cases An

Assessment in the Light of the Microsoft Case" 1 *European Competition Law Journal*.

Kurzer, P. (2001) *Markets and Moral Regulation, Cultural Change in the European Union* (Cambridge: CUP).

Langrish, S. (1998) "The Treaty of Amsterdam: Selected Highlights" 23 *European Law Review* 3

Lasok, D. and Bridge, J. (1991) *Law and Institutions of the European Community* (London: Butterworths).

Lenaerts, K. (2003) "Interlocking Legal Orders in the European Union and Comparative Law" 52 *International Comparative Law Quarterly* 873.

Lenschow, A. (2002) "New Regulatory Approaches in "Greening" EU Policies" 8.1. *European Law Journal* 19.

Lenz, M, Sif Tynes, D, Young, L. (2000) "Horizontal What? Back to Basics" 25 *European Law Review* 509.

Maduro, Poiares, M. (1998) *We the Court: The European Court of Justice and the Economic Constitution* (Oxford: Hart).

Maduro, Poiares, M. (2000) "The Scope of European Remedies: The Case of Purely Internal Situations and Reverse Discrimination"" in C. Kilpatrick, *et al.* (eds), *The Future of Remedies in Europe* (Oxford: Hart).

McGee, A and Weatherill, S. (1990) "The Evolution of the Single Market – Harmonisation or Liberalisation" 53 *Modern Law Review* 578.

McGoldrick, D. (1997) *International Relations Law of the European Union* (London: Longman).

Menéndez, A.J. (2002) "Chartering Europe: Legal Status and Policy Implications of the Charter of Fundamental Rights of the European Union" 40 *Journal of Common Market Studies* 471.

Millns, S. and Aziz, M. (2005) (eds.), *Values in the Constitution of Europe* (Dartmouth: Ashgate).

Monnet, J. (1978) *Memoirs* (New York: Doubleday & Company Inc).

Monti, G. (2002) "Article 81 EC and Public Policy" 39 *Common Market Law Review* 1057.

Mortelmans, K. (2001) "Towards Convergence in the Application of the Rules on Free Movement and On Competition" 38 *Common Market Law Review* 613.

Nichol, J. (1984) "The Luxembourg Compromise" 23 *Journal of Common Market Studies* 35.

Nicolaides, P. (2005) "Markets and Words: the Distortive Effect of Government Pronouncements" *European Competition Law Review* 119.

O'Neill, A. (1994) *Decisions of the European Court of Justice and their National Implications* (London: Butterworths).

Odudo, O, (2001) "Interpreting Article 81(1): object as subjective intention" 26 *European Law Review* 60.

Oliver, P. and Roth, W-H. (2004) "The Internal Market and the Four Freedoms" 41 *Common Market Law Review* 407.

Peers, S. (2002) "Free Movement of Capital: Learning Lessons or Slipping on Spilt Milk?" in C.Barnard and J. Scott. (eds.) *The Law of the Single European Market: Unpacking the Premises* (Oxford: Hart).

Pescatore, P. (1983) "The Doctrine of 'Direct Effect: An Infant Disease of Community Law" 8 *European Law Review* 155

Pescatore, P. (1987) "Some Critical Remarks on the Single European Act" 24 *Common Market Law Review* 9.

Radaelli, C. (2003) "The Code of Conduct Against Harmful Tax Competition: Open Method of Co-ordination in Disguise?" 81.3. *Public Administration* 513.

Rasmussen, H. (1988) "Between Self-Restraint and Activism: a Judicial Policy for the European Court" 13 *European Law Review* 28

Reich, N. (1994) "The 'November Revolution' of the European Court of Justice: *Keck, Meng and Audi* revisited" 31 *Common Market Law Review* 459.

Reich, N. (2005) "The 'courage' doctrine: or discouraging compensation for antitrust injuries?" 42 *Common Market Law Review* 35

Ross, M. (1993) "Beyond *Francovich*" 56 *Modern Law Review* 55.

Sauter, W. (1997) *Competition Law and Industrial Policy in the EU* (Oxford: Clarendon Press).

Scharpf, F.W. (1999) *Governing in Europe: Effective and Democratic?* (Oxford: OUP).

Schmitter, P. (2000) *How to Democratize the European Union . . . and Why Bother?* (Maryland: Lantham).

Senden, L. (2004) *Soft Law in European Community Law* (Oxford: Hart).

Shackleton, M. (2000) "The Politics of Co-decision" 38 *Journal of Common Market Studies* 325

Shapiro, M (1999) "The European Court of Justice" in P. Craig and G. De Búrca (eds.) *The Evolution of EU Law* (Oxford: OUP).

Shuibhne, Nic, N. (2002) "Free Movement of Persons and the Wholly Internal Rule: Time to Move On?" 39 *Common Market Law Review* 731.

Shuibhne, Nic, N. (ed.) (2005) *Regulating the Internal Market* (Cheltenham: Edward Elgar).

Snell, J. (2002) *Goods and Services in EC Law. A Study of the Relationship Between the Freedoms* (Oxford: OUP)

Snell, J. (2004) "And Then There Were Two: Products and Citizens in Community Law" in T. Tridimas and P. Nebbia (eds), *European Union Law for the Twenty-First Century: Volume II* (Oxford: Hart Publishing).

Snell, J. (2005) "Economic Aims as Justification for Restrictions on Free Movement" in A. Schrauwen (ed.), *Rule of Reason; Rethinking another Classic of EC Legal Doctrine* (Groningen: Europa Law Publishing).

Snyder, F. (1999) "EMU Revisited: Are We Making a Constitution? What Constitution Are We Making?" in P. Craig and G. De Búrca (eds) *The Evolution of EU Law* (Oxford: OUP).

Soames, T. and Maudhuit, S. (2005) "Changes in Merger Control: Part 1 and II" 26 *European Competition Law Review* 57 and 75.

Soriano, L. (2003) "How Proportionate Should Anti-Competitive State Intervention Be?" 28 *European Law Review* 112.

Steiner, J. (1992) "Drawing the Line: Uses and Abuses of Article 30" 29 *Common Market Law Review* 749.

Szyszczak, E. (2000) *EC Labour Law* (Harrow: Longman)

Szyszczak, E. (1994) "Social Policy: A Happy Ending or a Reworking of the Fairy Tale?" in D. O'Keeffe and P. Twomey (eds) *Legal Issues of the Maastricht Treaty* (Oxford: Hart).

Szyszczak, E. (1996) "Making Europe More Relevant to its Citizens: Effective Judicial Process" 21 *European Law Review* 351.

Szyszczak, E. (2000a) "A Fundamental Right To Trade?" in K.Economides *et al.* (eds) *Fundamental Values* (Oxford: Hart).

Szyszczak, E. (2000b) "The Evolving European Employment Strategy" in J. Shaw (ed) *Social Law and Policy in an Evolving European Union* (Oxford: Hart).

Szyszczak, E. (2001) "The New Paradigm for Social Policy: A Virtuous Circle?" *Common Market Law Review* 1125–1170.

Szyszczak, E. (2002) "Golden Shares and Market Governance" 29.3 *Legal Issues of Economic Integration* 35.

Szyszczak, E. (2003) "Social Policy in the Post-Nice Era" in A. Arnull and D. Wincott, (eds), *Accountability and Legitimacy in the European Union* (Oxford: OUP).

Szyszczak, E. (2004a) "Regularising Regular Migration in the EU" in *Irregular Migration and Human Rights* B.Bogusz *et al.* (eds), (The Hague: Kluwer, Brill).

Szyszczak, E. (2004b) "State Intervention in the Market" in T. Tridimas and P. Nebbia (eds.), *EU Law for the 21st Century: Rethinking the New Legal Order. Volume 2* (Oxford, Hart).

Szyszczak, E. (2004c) "Financing Services of General Economic Interest: 67(6) *Modern Law Review* 982.

Szyszczak, E. (2005) "The Regulation of Competition" in N. Nic. Shuibhne (ed.), *The Regulation of the Internal Market* (Cheltenham: Edward Elgar).

Temple Lang, J. (1997) "The Duties of National Courts under Community Constitutional Law" 22 *European Law Review* 3.

Tomkins, A. (1999) "Responsibility and Resignation in the European Commission" 62 *Modern Law Review* 744.

Trepte, P. (2004) *Regulating Procurement* (Oxford: OUP).

Tridimas, T. (1994) "Horizontal effect of directives: a missed opportunity?" 19 *European Law Review* 621.

Tridimas, T. (1996) "The Court of Justice and Judicial Activism" 21 *European Law Review* 187.

Tridimas, T. (2003) "Knocking on Heaven's Door: Fragmentation, Efficiency and Defiance in the Preliminary Rulings Procedure" 40 *Common Market Law Review* 9.

Usher, J. (2003) "Direct and Individual Concern – an Effective Remedy or a Conventional Solution?" 29 *European Law Review* 300.

Usher, J. (2005) "Monetary Movements and the Internal Market" in Nic Shuibhne, N. (ed) *Regulating the Internal Market* (Cheltenham: Edward Elgar).

Van den Bogaert, S. (2002) "Horizontality" in C. Barnard and J. Scott (eds), *The Law of the Single Market* (Oxford: Hart).

Van der Mei, A. P (2002) "Cross-border Access to Health Care Within the European Union: Some Reflections on Geraets-Smit and Peerbooms and Vanbraekel" 9 *Maastricht Journal* 189.

Van Gerven, W. (1996) "Bridging the Unbridgeable: Community and National Tort Laws After Francovich and Brasserie" 45 *International Comparative Law Quarterly* 507.

Wade, W. (1996) "Sovereignty – Revolution or Evolution" 112 *Law Quarterly Review,* 568.

Wathelet, M. (2001) "The Influence of Free Movement of Persons, Services and Capital on National Direct Taxation" 20 *Yearbook of European Law* 1.

Weatherill, S. (1995) "Playing Safe: the United Kingdom's Implementation of the New Approach Directive" in T. Daintith, (ed.) *Implementing EC Law in the UK: Structures for Indirect Rule* (Chichester: Wiley).

Weatherill, S. (2000) "New Strategies for Managing the EC's Internal Market" 53 *Current Legal Problems* 595.

Weatherill, S. (2002) "Pre-emption, Harmonisation and the Distribution of Competence to Regulate the Internal Market" in C. Barnard and J. Scott (eds), *The Law of the Single Market: Unpacking the Premises* (Oxford: Hart)

Weatherill, S. (2004) "Why Harmonise?" in T. Tridimas and P. Nebbia (eds.) *Challenges for EU Law in the 21st Century. Volume I* (Oxford: Hart).

Weatherill, S. (2005) "Better Competence Monitoring" 30 *European Law Review* 23.

Weatherill, S. (2005) *EC Consumer Law and Policy* (Edward Elgar: Cheltenham).

Weiler, J. (1999) *The Constitution of Europe* (Cambridge: CUP).

Westlake, M. (1998) "The European Parliament's Emerging Powers of Appointment" 36 *Journal of Common Market Studies* 434.

White, R. (2004) *Workers, Establishment, and Services in the European Union* (Oxford: OUP).

Wils, W. (2003) "Should Private Antitrust Enforcement Be Encouraged in Europe?" 26(3) *World Competition* 473.

Winter, J. (1972) "Direct Effect and Direct Applicability: Two Distinct and Different Concepts in Community law" 9 *Common Market Law Review* 42.

Wouters, J. (2000) "European Company Law: *Quo Vadis?*" 37 *Common Market Law Review* 257.

ALPHABETICAL TABLE OF CASES

CHRONOLOGICAL TABLE OF CASES

TABLE OF CASES BEFORE UK COURTS

INDEX